eBay Time

eBay's clocks are set to military time in the Pacific Time Zone.

For quick time zone conversion, try

www.timezoneconverter.com

or look at the table on our Web site, which has a printable conversion chart of eBay times:

www.collierad.com/CooleBayTools

Know Your Auction Terms

- **Reserve price:** The minimum price a seller is willing to accept for an item up for auction. Setting a reserve is optional and only the seller knows the reserve price. If the bidding doesn't exceed the reserve, the seller has the option to keep the item. eBay charges a small fee for this option.

- **Minimum bid:** The lowest acceptable bid for an item, set by the seller. This amount must be determined by the seller and is not kept secret. Minimum bid amounts are often different from reserve prices.

- **Dutch auction:** An auction that allows a seller to put multiple, identical items up for sale instead of holding multiple, separate auctions. The seller must sell all items at the *lowest winning price.* You can bid on one, some, or all of the items.

- **Proxy bid:** You can decide the most you're willing to pay for an item and allow eBay's bidding program to place bids for you while you go on with your life. The proxy bidder ups the ante incrementally to beat out your competition until you're outbid or until you win the auction.

Tips for Sellers

Before you put an item up for auction, follow these tips:

- Find out as much as you can about the item's value, history, and condition.

- Check out your eBay competition. If there are a ton of other auctions for the same time for the same kind of item, and the bidding is competitive, wait until the competition is fierce for a couple of select items.

- Set your auction to end during peak eBay hours, around 8 p.m. Pacific Time.

- Make sure your item isn't prohibited or considered questionable by eBay. If you're not sure, read eBay's guidelines and check your local laws.

- Add a digital image to spruce your auction up, and make sure your title and description highlight the item's assets — don't gloss over its flaws. Being direct, informative, and to the point shows potential buyers that you're honest and easy to work with.

...For Dummies®: Bestselling Book Series for Beginners

eBay™ For Dummies®

Cheat Sheet

Tips for Buyers

Before you bid on an item in an auction, follow these tips:

- ✔ Research the item before you bid, and search completed auctions to see what price similar items have sold for in the past. Don't overbid!

- ✔ Check the seller's feedback. No matter how high the feedback rating is, be sure the latest feedback isn't negative and that the majority of the feedback is transaction-related.

- ✔ Bid in odd increments. Bidders often bid in round numbers (like 25-cent increments). If you bid in 27-cent increments you can win by just 2 cents!

- ✔ Have fun, and be prepared to pay for whatever you bid on. *Remember:* In many states, placing a bid is a binding contract.

Feedback Stuff You Need to Know

Take a breather before you leave negative feedback. eBay won't remove feedback if you change your mind or overreact to a situation.

If someone gives you positive feedback, respond. If you receive negative feedback and feel your side of the transaction is worth telling, give your reply in a neutral tone.

When checking an eBay user's feedback, check to see if the majority of the feedback is transaction-related. If you see a lot of wonderful feedback, but no transaction numbers, beware.

IDG BOOKS WORLDWIDE

...For Dummies®: Bestselling Book Series for Beginners

by Roland Woerner, Stephanie Becker, and Marsha Collier

IDG Books Worldwide, Inc.
An International Data Group Company

Foster City, CA ◆ Chicago, IL ◆ Indianapolis, IN ◆ New York, NY

eBay® For Dummies®

Published by
IDG Books Worldwide, Inc.
An International Data Group Company
919 E. Hillsdale Blvd.
Suite 400
Foster City, CA 94404
www.idgbooks.com (IDG Books Worldwide Web site)
www.dummies.com (Dummies Press Web site)

Library of Congress Catalog Card No.: 99-64902

ISBN: 0-7645-0610-2

Printed in the United States of America

10 9 8 7 6 5 4 3 2 1

1B/SS/QZ/ZZ/IN

Distributed in the United States by IDG Books Worldwide, Inc.

Distributed by CDG Books Canada Inc. for Canada; by Transworld Publishers Limited in the United Kingdom; by IDG Norge Books for Norway; by IDG Sweden Books for Sweden; by IDG Books Australia Publishing Corporation Pty. Ltd. for Australia and New Zealand; by TransQuest Publishers Pte Ltd. for Singapore, Malaysia, Thailand, Indonesia, and Hong Kong; by Gotop Information Inc. for Taiwan; by ICG Muse, Inc. for Japan; by Intersoft for South Africa; by Eyrolles for France; by International Thomson Publishing for Germany, Austria and Switzerland; by Distribuidora Cuspide for Argentina; by LR International for Brazil; by Galileo Libros for Chile; by Ediciones ZETA S.C.R. Ltda. for Peru; by WS Computer Publishing Corporation, Inc., for the Philippines; by Contemporanea de Ediciones for Venezuela; by Express Computer Distributors for the Caribbean and West Indies; by Micronesia Media Distributor, Inc. for Micronesia; by Chips Computadoras S.A. de C.V. for Mexico; by Editorial Norma de Panama S.A. for Panama; by American Bookshops for Finland.

For general information on IDG Books Worldwide's books in the U.S., please call our Consumer Customer Service department at 800-762-2974. For reseller information, including discounts and premium sales, please call our Reseller Customer Service department at 800-434-3422.

For information on where to purchase IDG Books Worldwide's books outside the U.S., please contact our International Sales department at 317-596-5530 or fax 317-596-5692.

For consumer information on foreign language translations, please contact our Customer Service department at 1-800-434-3422, fax 317-596-5692, or e-mail rights@idgbooks.com.

For information on licensing foreign or domestic rights, please phone +1-650-655-3109.

For sales inquiries and special prices for bulk quantities, please contact our Sales department at 650-655-3200 or write to the address above.

For information on using IDG Books Worldwide's books in the classroom or for ordering examination copies, please contact our Educational Sales department at 800-434-2086 or fax 317-596-5499.

For press review copies, author interviews, or other publicity information, please contact our Public Relations department at 650-655-3000 or fax 650-655-3299.

For authorization to photocopy items for corporate, personal, or educational use, please contact Copyright Clearance Center, 222 Rosewood Drive, Danvers, MA 01923, or fax 978-750-4470.

About the Authors

Roland Woerner is an Emmy Award-nominated producer and writer for NBC's *The Today Show*. In addition to his news duties, he enjoys writing and producing segments exploring the world of technology and pop culture. In his spare time he enjoys going on adventures with his daughters, flying airplanes, driving boats, and collecting lunchboxes and T.V. memorabilia.

Stephanie Becker is an Emmy Award-nominated television producer for NBC News. Her essays as Gadget Gal have appeared both in *Gadget Guru Guide Magazine* and on the Web. She is an avid cyclist and has several unique collections, including refigerator magnets, momentos from catastrophes around the world, and dust bunnies.

Marsha Collier is a multi-tasking professional who uses all aspects of graphics in her advertising business, The Collier Company. In her spare time, she's mastered the art of eBay and has over 600 positive feedback comments. Using her ability to spot trends, she continues to buy and sell on eBay, while also winning awards for her achievements in advertising and for her work in the community.

ABOUT IDG BOOKS WORLDWIDE

Welcome to the world of IDG Books Worldwide.

IDG Books Worldwide, Inc., is a subsidiary of International Data Group, the world's largest publisher of computer-related information and the leading global provider of information services on information technology. IDG was founded more than 30 years ago by Patrick J. McGovern and now employs more than 9,000 people worldwide. IDG publishes more than 290 computer publications in over 75 countries. More than 90 million people read one or more IDG publications each month.

Launched in 1990, IDG Books Worldwide is today the #1 publisher of best-selling computer books in the United States. We are proud to have received eight awards from the Computer Press Association in recognition of editorial excellence and three from Computer Currents' First Annual Readers' Choice Awards. Our best-selling ...*For Dummies*® series has more than 50 million copies in print with translations in 31 languages. IDG Books Worldwide, through a joint venture with IDG's Hi-Tech Beijing, became the first U.S. publisher to publish a computer book in the People's Republic of China. In record time, IDG Books Worldwide has become the first choice for millions of readers around the world who want to learn how to better manage their businesses.

Our mission is simple: Every one of our books is designed to bring extra value and skill-building instructions to the reader. Our books are written by experts who understand and care about our readers. The knowledge base of our editorial staff comes from years of experience in publishing, education, and journalism — experience we use to produce books to carry us into the new millennium. In short, we care about books, so we attract the best people. We devote special attention to details such as audience, interior design, use of icons, and illustrations. And because we use an efficient process of authoring, editing, and desktop publishing our books electronically, we can spend more time ensuring superior content and less time on the technicalities of making books.

You can count on our commitment to deliver high-quality books at competitive prices on topics you want to read about. At IDG Books Worldwide, we continue in the IDG tradition of delivering quality for more than 30 years. You'll find no better book on a subject than one from IDG Books Worldwide.

John Kilcullen
Chairman and CEO
IDG Books Worldwide, Inc.

Steven Berkowitz
President and Publisher
IDG Books Worldwide, Inc.

Eighth Annual
Computer Press
Awards ≥1992

Ninth Annual
Computer Press
Awards ≥1993

Tenth Annual
Computer Press
Awards ≥1994

Eleventh Annual
Computer Press
Awards ≥1995

IDG is the world's leading IT media, research and exposition company. Founded in 1964, IDG had 1997 revenues of $2.05 billion and has more than 9,000 employees worldwide. IDG offers the widest range of media options that reach IT buyers in 75 countries representing 95% of worldwide IT spending. IDG's diverse product and services portfolio spans six key areas including print publishing, online publishing, expositions and conferences, market research, education and training, and global marketing services. More than 90 million people read one or more of IDG's 290 magazines and newspapers, including IDG's leading global brands — Computerworld, PC World, Network World, Macworld and the Channel World family of publications. IDG Books Worldwide is one of the fastest-growing computer book publishers in the world, with more than 700 titles in 36 languages. The "...For Dummies®" series alone has more than 50 million copies in print. IDG offers online users the largest network of technology-specific Web sites around the world through IDG.net (http://www.idg.net), which comprises more than 225 targeted Web sites in 55 countries worldwide. International Data Corporation (IDC) is the world's largest provider of information technology data, analysis and consulting, with research centers in over 41 countries and more than 400 research analysts worldwide. IDG World Expo is a leading producer of more than 168 globally branded conferences and expositions in 35 countries including E3 (Electronic Entertainment Expo), Macworld Expo, ComNet, Windows World Expo, ICE (Internet Commerce Expo), Agenda, DEMO, and Spotlight. IDG's training subsidiary, ExecuTrain, is the world's largest computer training company, with more than 230 locations worldwide and 785 training courses. IDG Marketing Services helps industry-leading IT companies build international brand recognition by developing global integrated marketing programs via IDG's print, online and exposition products worldwide. Further information about the company can be found at www.idg.com. 1/24/99

Dedication

Roland dedicates this book to his loving daughters, Allie and Katie. Now that *eBay For Dummies* is written, they can have their daddy back!

Stephanie dedicates this book to her Mom, who taught her to bargain, and to her Dad, who taught her to type with all ten fingers. She loves them both.

Marsha dedicates this book to her eBay buddy and daughter, Susan, her husband, Beryl Lockhart, for his love and encouragement, and her mother Claire Berg, who is always there when things get too frustrating.

Authors' Acknowledgments

Roland would like to thank the gentlemen of Nashville: Attorney and Agent extraordinaire John Lentz, and NBC's Gadget Guru Andy Pargh, for their constant support, inspiration, and friendship over the years. They made this book possible. He'd also like to thank his family: Debbie, Herman, Marianne Mohr, Robert, Anne, Stephanie, Christopher, Renate and John Cazalet, who listened and nodded as he talked incessantly about the writing of this book. Sincere thanks to his "sounding boards": Sandy Teller (New York's finest PR maven), Allen J. Bernstein (the man who put the "wow" on the menu at Morton's of Chicago Steakhouse), Glenn Evans (Food4Less rules, check out the avocados!), Glenn Cryan (fellow Parrotthead and flying buff) and Denis de Pierro (the finest aviation TV producer in the country). And finally, to Katie Couric, Matt Lauer, Al Roker, Jeff Zucker, and Ric Romo of the *NBC Today Show*, thanks for the most amazing day job one could ever dream of.

Stephanie would like to thank our Agent John Lentz for his calming influence and never-ending support. She would like to thank her sisters Gwendolyn and Melanie, and her friends Amy Sohnen, Tammy Haddad, Suzan and Al Fein, Lisa and Dave Ellis, Sheila and Jeff Greene, and Sandy and Lenny Berger for putting up with her at Defcon 5 on the cranky meter. And thanks to Rosalyn Cosentino for letting me do a three month Houdini. Heartfelt thanks to all my gentle readers, particularly Martha Caskey, Kathy Riggins (now I can come over for dinner), and Heather Allan (thanks for my Nightly snooze). Stephanie would like to thank the folks at the *NBC Today Show* for some truly extraordinary experiences, Katie Couric, Matt Lauer, and most especially her boss Jeff Zucker, who continues to pretend he's listening to her rant and rave when actually, he's humming a Ricky Martin tune in his head. But her deepest thanks go to Roland for giving her the opportunity to complain on a daily basis about something entirely new and different . . . and of course for his unflappable friendship.

Marsha would like to thank her assistant, Joni Lusk, for picking up whatever fell through the cracks while she was working on this book (and of course listening to babble about eBay). She thanks her clients, especially Louise Marquez, for putting up with her sliding into deadlines at the last minute due to doing double-duty with this book. A special thank you to David Goldman, who was always ready with words of encouragement. Thank you to John Lentz for doing what he does best, and a sincere thank you to Roland Woerner ("Would 'ya like to write a book on eBay?") and Stephanie Becker, who's been the ying to my yang throughout this project . . . you've both been great and you're both awesome professionals. Last but not least, a very special thanks to all the eBay users out there who shared their thoughts and insights for this book.

All three authors particularly thank our editors at IDG Books Worldwide, Inc., Nicole Haims, Barry Childs-Helton, and Sherri Morningstar for helping us take a wacky idea and actually turn it into a book so that others can have as much fun on eBay as we do.

Publisher's Acknowledgments

We're proud of this book; please register your comments through our IDG Books Worldwide Online Registration Form located at http://my2cents.dummies.com.

Some of the people who helped bring this book to market include the following:

Acquisitions, Editorial, and Media Development

Project Editor: Nicole Haims

Acquisitions Editors: Joyce Pepple, Sherri Morningstar

Copy Editors: Barry Childs-Helton, Ted Cains, Pam Wilson-Wykes

Technical Editor: Dave Melone

Associate Permissions Editor: Carmen Krikorian

Media Development Coordinator: Megan Roney

Editorial Manager: Rev Mengle

Media Development Manager: Heather Heath Dismore

Editorial Assistants: Jamila Pree, Beth Parlon

Production

Project Coordinator: Maridee Ennis

Layout and Graphics: Amy M. Adrian, Brian Drumm, Angela F. Hunckler, Kate Jenkins, Barry Offringa, Tracy Oliver, Jill Piscitelli, Anna Rohrer, Brent Savage, Janet Seib, Jacque Schneider, Michael A. Sullivan, Brian Torwelle, Maggie Ubertini, Mary Jo Weis, Dan Whetstine

Proofreaders: Melissa Martin, Nancy Price, Marianne Santy, Rebecca Senninger, Toni Settle

Indexer: Sharon Hilgenberg

Special Help: Kel Oliver, Joe Bednarek, Jerelind Charles, Darren Meiss

Special Thanks to eBay Inc.: especially Buffy Poon, Patti Kirk, George Koster, and Jay Monahan

---

General and Administrative

IDG Books Worldwide, Inc.: John Kilcullen, CEO; Steven Berkowitz, President and Publisher

IDG Books Technology Publishing Group: Richard Swadley, Senior Vice President and Publisher; Walter Bruce III, Vice President and Associate Publisher; Steven Sayre, Associate Publisher; Joseph Wikert, Associate Publisher; Mary Bednarek, Branded Product Development Director; Mary Corder, Editorial Director

IDG Books Consumer Publishing Group: Roland Elgey, Senior Vice President and Publisher; Kathleen A. Welton, Vice President and Publisher; Kevin Thornton, Acquisitions Manager; Kristin A. Cocks, Editorial Director

IDG Books Internet Publishing Group: Brenda McLaughlin, Senior Vice President and Publisher; Diane Graves Steele, Vice President and Associate Publisher; Sofia Marchant, Online Marketing Manager

IDG Books Production for Dummies Press: Michael R. Britton, Vice President of Production; Debbie Stailey, Associate Director of Production; Cindy L. Phipps, Manager of Project Coordination, Production Proofreading, and Indexing; Tony Augsburger, Manager of Prepress, Reprints, and Systems; Laura Carpenter, Production Control Manager; Shelley Lea, Supervisor of Graphics and Design; Debbie J. Gates, Production Systems Specialist; Robert Springer, Supervisor of Proofreading; Kathie Schutte, Production Supervisor

Dummies Packaging and Book Design: Patty Page, Manager, Promotions Marketing

◆

The publisher would like to give special thanks to Patrick J. McGovern, without whom this book would not have been possible.

◆

Contents at a Glance

Cartoons at a Glance

By Rich Tennant

The 5th Wave — By Rich Tennant

"My gosh, Barbara, if you don't think it's worth going a couple of weeks without dinner so we can afford to bid on that small Mediterranean island we saw on eBay, just say so!"

page 81

The 5th Wave — By Rich Tennant

"Oh sure, it'll float alright, but I want to check your feedback rating before you place a bid."

page 319

The 5th Wave — By Rich Tennant

"Nah—he's not that smart. He can't set up his My eBay page to track his auctions and he drools all over the keyboard."

page 7

The 5th Wave — By Rich Tennant

"Frankly, I'm not sure this is the way to enhance your eBay auction item page."

page 149

The 5th Wave — By Rich Tennant

"What troubles me is that he spends all his time on eBay's Beanie Babies chat board."

page 269

Fax: 978-546-7747 • **E-mail:** the5wave@tiac.net

Table of Contents

Part IV: Oy Vay, More eBay!: Special Features 269

Chapter 13: Privacy: To Protect and Serve 271

Chapter 14: eBay's SafeHarbor Program 285

Introduction

Welcome to *eBay For Dummies!* This book is designed to help you understand everything you need to know about buying and selling on eBay, the most successful online auction Web site on the Internet. We give you all the tools you need to get moving on eBay whether you're new to the Internet or a Webaholic. We show you how to turn your everyday household clutter into cold, hard cash — and how to look for items that you can sell at a profit on eBay. If you're a collector (or you'd like to be), we show you how to figure out how much you should spend, how to make smart bids, and how to win the auction. How much money you earn (or spend) depends entirely on how *often* and how *smartly* you conduct your eBay transactions. You decide how often you want to run auctions and place bids; we're here to help you out on the *smart* part.

A Web site as complex as eBay has many nooks and crannies that may be confusing to the first-time user. Think of this book as a detailed roadmap that can help you navigate eBay, getting just as much or as little as you want from it. Unlike an actual roadmap, you won't get frustrated folding it back to its original shape. Just close the book and come back any time you need a question answered.

After figuring out the nuts and bolts of eBay, you can start buying and selling. We have a ton of terrific buying and selling strategies that help you get the most out of your auctions. With this book and a little elbow grease, you can join the ranks of millions of people who have used their home computers to make friends, become part of the eBay community, and have a lot of fun while making a profit.

Caution: Information highway roadwork next 3 miles

You'd think that with millions of people accessing the eBay Web site every day, those Silicon Valley guys would have enough to keep them busy. (As if!) But hey, everybody's sprucing up for the new millennium, and eBay wants to make the site *even more* new and exciting — and that means switching things around to see if you notice. For example, you may see a *link* (an image or group of words that takes you to a different part of the site after you click on it) on the Home page that's here today and gone tomorrow, replaced with something else. Don't have a cow — the *main navigation bar* is like your own personal breadcrumb trail that never changes — it can get you into eBay, around the block, and out of the woods with nearly no hassles.

About This Book

Remember those open-book tests that were sprung on you in high school? Well, sometimes you may feel like eBay is pop-quizzing you while you're online. Think of *eBay For Dummies* as your open-book-test resource with all the answers. You don't have to memorize anything; just keep this book handy to help you get over the confusing parts.

With that in mind, we divided this book up into pertinent sections to help you find your answers fast. We show you how to

- ✔ Get online and register on eBay.

- ✔ Navigate eBay to do just about anything you can think of — search for items for sale, set up auctions, monitor your transactions, and join the chat room circuit.

- ✔ Bid on and win eBay auctions.

- ✔ Choose an item to sell, pick the right time for your auction, market it so a ton of bidders see it, and make a profit with eBay.

- ✔ Communicate well and close deals without problems, whether you're a buyer or a seller.

- ✔ Become a part of a really unique community of people who like to collect, buy, and sell items of just about every type.

Do not adjust your eyes. To protect the privacy of eBay users, screen shots in this book blur User IDs.

Foolish Assumptions

You may have picked up this book because you've heard that people are making big bucks trading on eBay and you want to find out what's going on. Or you heard about the bargains and wacky stuff you can find in the world's largest garage sale. If either of these assumptions is true, then this is the right book for you.

Other foolish assumptions we've made about you:

- ✔ You have or would like to have access to a computer, a modem, and the Internet so that you can do business on eBay.

- ✔ You have an interest in collecting stuff, selling stuff, and buying stuff, and you want to find out more about doing that stuff online.

- ✔ You want tips and strategies that can save you money when you bid and make you money when you sell. (You too? We can relate. Talk about all things to all people . . . !)

✔ You're concerned about maintaining your privacy and staying away from people who try to ruin everyone's good time with negligent, sometimes-illegal, activity.

If you think the expression *surfing the Web* has something to do with spiders and boogie boards, then this book can get you started, but you may want to browse through *The Internet For Dummies,* 6th Edition, by John Levine for a crash course in Internet confidence. The book comes from IDG Books Worldwide, just like the book you're reading now. From time to time (and by astounding coincidence) we mention other titles in the ...*For Dummies* series that you may find helpful.

How This Book Is Organized

This book has five parts. The parts stand on their own, which means that you can read Chapter 5 after you read Chapter 9 or skip Chapter 3 altogether. It's all up to you. We do think that you should at least dip into Chapter 1 and Chapter 2 to get an overview on what eBay is all about and how you can register.

If you are already conducting transactions on eBay, you certainly can jump ahead to get good tips on advanced strategies to enhance your auctions. Don't wait for permission from us — just go for it. We won't argue with you that jazzy auctions equal higher profits!

Part I: Forget the Mall: Getting a Feel for eBay

We tell you what eBay is and how you use it in this part. We take you through the registration process, help you organize your eBay transactions and interactions using the My eBay page, and get you comfortable navigating the site from the Home page.

Part II: Are You Buying What They're Selling?

If you're pretty sure you want to start making bids on items, this part gives you the lowdown on searching, grading an item's value, researching, bidding, and winning auctions.

That old cliché, "let the buyer beware," became a cliché because even today (maybe especially today) it's sound advice. Use our friendly, fat-free tips to help you decide when to bid and when to take a pass.

Part III: Are You Selling What They're Buying?

This part gets you up to speed on how to sell your items on eBay. Think of it as an eBay graduate course in marketing. Here you find important information on how to conduct your auction, what to do after you sell an item, how to ship the item, and how to keep track of all the money you're making. Even Uncle Sam gets to chime in on his favorite topic: Taxes. Know the rules so you won't get that queasy feeling if your friendly local tax office invites you over for a snack and a little audit.

We give you some insider information on how to spot a trend before the rest of the world catches on, as well as how to acquire items cheaply that others may spend a bundle on. We also show you how to jazz up your auctions by adding pictures and how to use basic HTML to link your auctions to your own Home page. (If you don't have a Home page, don't freak out — links are optional.) You can make your digital images look like high art with our tips, hints, and strategies.

Part IV: Oy Vay, More eBay!: Special Features

Check this part out to find out how to handle privacy issues relating to eBay and how you can resolve buying and selling issues with the help of SafeHarbor, eBay's problem-solving clearinghouse. Also included here are ways of having fun with the eBay community and using charity auctions to bid on great items for a good cause.

Part V: The Part of Tens

In keeping with a long tradition, this part is a compendium of short chapters that gives you ready references and useful facts. We share more great tips for buying and selling, as well as a description of our favorite software programs that help lighten your auction load.

BTW (by the way), we also added a glossary of eBay terms and acronyms in the Appendix, which lists some more common chat room lingo that you may find on eBay. You can talk the talk even as you're learning to walk the eBay walk. Lots of luck remembering them all, but that's what glossaries are for!

Icons Used in This Book

Time is money on eBay. When you see this shortcut or time-saver come your way, read the information and think about all the moola you just saved.

Think of this icon as a Post-It note for your brain. If you forget one of the pearls of wisdom revealed to you here, you can go back and reread it. If you *still* can't remember something here, go ahead, dog-ear the page — we won't tell.

Don't feel our pain. We've done things wrong on eBay before and want to save you from our mistakes, so we put these warnings out there bright and bold so that you don't have to have a bad experience. Don't skip these warnings unless you're enthusiastic about masochism.

When you see this icon, you know you're in for the real deal. We created this icon especially for you to give you war stories (and success stories) from eBay veterans (*learn from their experience* is our motto!) that can help you strategize, make money, and spare you from the perils of a poorly written auction item description. You can skip over these icons if you want to, but we think you may get burned if you do.

What Now?

Like everything else in the world, eBay is constantly evolving. At this point, you're armed with everything you need to know to join the eBay community and begin conducting transactions. If you hit some rough waters, just look up the problem in the table of contents or index in this book. We either help you solve it or let you know where you can go on eBay for some expert advice.

While eBay makes its complex Web site as easy to navigate as possible, you may still need to refer back to this book for help. Don't feel bad if you have to keep reviewing topics before you feel completely comfortable trading on eBay.

After all, Albert Einstein once said, "Don't commit to memory something you can look up." (We forgot when he said that . . . .)

Feedback, Please

Communication makes the world go round, and we'd love to hear from you. Check out our Web site at the address below or e-mail us at `dummies@collierad.com`.

`www.collierad.com/coolebaytools`

Part I

Forget the Mall: Getting a Feel for eBay

"Nah—he's not that smart. He can't set up his My eBay page to track his auctions and he drools all over the keyboard."

In this part . . .

*e*Bay may feel kind of big and scary, especially if you're new to the Internet. What you need is someone to point out the most useful tools you need to get around, find out how eBay works, and start preparing to do your own transactions.

In this part, you can get the information you want about how eBay works and what it offers its members; you also find out what kind of equipment you should have so that you can log on and start bidding and holding auctions of your own. You can find out how to become a registered eBay user, maneuver the eBay Home page, and customize your own private My eBay page. You can also find out about the all-important Feedback Profile that follows every eBay user around like a shadow.

Chapter 1

Why eBay Is Better Than Your Local Antique Shop

Take a look around your house. Nice toaster. Great-looking TV. Spiffy microwave. Not to mention all the other cool stuff you own. The fact of the matter is, all these household appliances and collectibles are fabulous to own, but when was the last time your toaster actually turned a profit? When you connect to eBay, your PC or Mac magically turns into a money machine. Just plug in to eBay and marvel at all the collectibles that are just a few mouse clicks away from being bought and sold.

In this chapter we tell you what eBay is, how it works, and how to get your computer connected to it. eBay is the perfect alternative to spending hours wandering through antique shops or swap meets looking for the perfect doodad. Not only can you buy and sell stuff in the privacy of your own home, you can meet people who share the interests that you enjoy. The folks who use the eBay site are a friendly bunch — soon you'll be buying, selling, swapping stories, and trading advice with the best of them.

Before you can get to eBay, you need to access the Internet. To access the Internet, you need a computer (either PC or Mac) with a modem, or you can get Web TV. We know where to find new and used ones, and we give you pointers on how to set up a system on the cheap. If you're not quite ready to take the high-tech plunge, we can show you exactly how to start operating on eBay (and earning money) without owning a single cyber-thing.

eBay's humble beginnings

It all started with a Pez. You know, those little plastic dispensers with funny heads that flip up and present you with a rectangular piece of candy. To help out his girlfriend (who is an avid Pez collector), a Silicon Valley software engineer named Pierre Omidyar created a Web site so she could chat and trade with other people online. The site was so successful that he expanded it to include other kinds of collectibles.

He began charging a small fee to list items, just so he could break even. Legend has it that one day $10,000 in fees arrived in Pierre's mailbox; he quit his day job. eBay was born on Labor Day 1995. The name eBay is taken from *electronic* and *bay* for the Bay Area of San Francisco, where Pierre is from. (We can't wait to see *that* bit of trivia turn up on *Jeopardy!*)

What Is eBay and How Does It Work?

The Internet is spawning all kinds of new businesses (known as *e-commerce* to Wall Street types), and eBay is one of its few superstars. The reason is simple: It's the place where buyers and sellers can meet, do business, share stories and tips, and have fun. It's like one giant online party — and instead of bringing a dish, you sell it!

eBay *doesn't* sell a thing. Instead, the site simply does what all good hosts do — eBay creates a comfy environment that brings people with common interests together. You can think of eBay as the person who set you up on your last blind date (except the results are often a lot better). Your match-making friend doesn't perform a marriage ceremony, but does get you in the same room with your potential soul mate. eBay puts buyers and sellers in a virtual room and lets them conduct their business safely within the rules that eBay has established.

All you need to do to join eBay is fill out a few forms online and click — congratulations, you're a member with no big fees or secret handshakes. Chapter 2 eases you through the registration process. Once you register, you can buy and sell anything that falls within the eBay rules and regulations.

All About Auctions

The value of an item is determined by how much someone's willing to spend to have it. That's what makes auctions exciting. eBay offers several different kinds of auctions — but for the most part, they all work the same way. An *auction* is a unique sales event where the exact value of the item for sale is not known, and as a result, there's an element of surprise involved, not only for the bidder (who may end up with a great deal), but for the seller (who may end up making a killing). A seller fills out an electronic form and sets the auction up, listing a *minimum bid* he or she is willing to accept for the item. Think of an auctioneer at Christie's saying, "The bidding for this diamond necklace begins at $5,000." You could bid $4,000, but it won't do you much good. Sellers can also set a *reserve price* — sort of a financial safety net that protects them from losing money on the deal. We explain how this all works later in this chapter.

Bidders duke it out over a period of time (sometimes three days, but usually a week or even longer) until one comes out victorious. Usually, the highest bidder wins. The tricky thing about participating in an auction (and the most exciting aspect) is that no one knows the final price an item goes for until the last second of the auction.

Traditional auctions

Did you ever hear those motor-mouthed auctioneers raising the price of an item until they say "going once, going twice, sold?" They're conducting *traditional* auctions, and the majority of items sold on eBay are sold this way. The beauty of eBay is you don't have to sweat out translating what these auctioneers are saying, everything is done very quietly. Traditional auctions are simple: The highest bidder takes home the prize.

Reserve-price auctions

Unlike a *minimum bid,* which is required in any eBay auction, a *reserve price* protects a seller from having to sell an item for less than it's actually worth. You may be surprised to see a 1968 Jaguar XKE sports car up for auction on eBay with a minimum bid of only a buck, but believe us, this savvy seller has put a reserve price on this car to protect himself from losing money. The reserve price allows sellers to set lower minimum bids, and lower minimum bids attract bidders. Unfortunately, if a seller makes the reserve price too high and it isn't met by the end of the auction, no one wins.

eBay charges a fee for sellers to run these autions. Nobody knows (except the seller and the eBay computer system) what the reserve price is until the auction is over, but you can tell from the auction page whether you're dealing with a reserve-price auction. If there have been bids on an item, a message also appears on the page saying whether the reserve price has been met. You can find out more about bidding on reserve-price auctions in Chapter 6 and setting up a reserve-price auction in Chapter 8.

Restricted-access auctions

If you're over 18 years of age and interested in bidding on items of an adult nature, eBay has an Adults Only category, which has restricted access. Although you can peruse the other eBay categories without having to hand over credit card information, you must have a credit card number on file with eBay to view and bid on items in this category. Restricted-access auctions are run the same as every other eBay auction. To bid on adult items, you first need to complete an authorization page using your User ID and password, which pops up automatically when you attempt access these kinds of items.

If you aren't interested in seeing or bidding on items of an adult nature, or if you're worried that your children may be able to gain access to graphic adult material, eBay's solved that problem by excluding adult-content items from easily accessible areas like the New Items and (ahem) Hot Items pages. Besides, children under the age of 18 aren't allowed to register for eBay and should be under an adult's supervision if they do wander onto the site.

If you're interested in bidding on adult merchandise, remember that legal statutes regulate the sale and distribution of adult materials. In other words, know the laws. See Chapter 8 for more on what's legal on eBay and what's not.

Private (mind-your-own-business) auctions

Some sellers choose to hold a *private auction* because they know that some bidders may be embarrassed to be seen bidding on a box of racy neckties in front of the rest of the eBay community. Others may go the private route because they are selling big-ticket items and don't want to disclose their financial status.

Private auctions are run like traditional auctions except that each bidder's identity is kept secret. At the end of the auction, eBay provides contact info to the seller and to the high bidder, and that's it.

A Dutch auction can't be conducted as a private auction. You can send e-mail questions to the seller in a private auction, but you can't check out your competition because the auction item page shows the current bid price, but not the high bidder's User ID. Private auctions are quite civilized, but many eBay members have more fun knowing who they're waging a bidding war against.

Charity auctions: All for a good cause

A *charity auction* is a high-profile fund-raising auction where the proceeds go to a selected charity. Most people don't wake up in the morning wanting to own the shoes that Ron Howard wore when he put his footprints in cement at Mann's Chinese Theater in Hollywood, but one-of-a-kind items like that are often auctioned off in charity auctions. (In fact, someone did want those shoes bad enough to buy them for a lot of money on eBay.) Charity auctions became popular after the NBC *Today Show* sold an autographed jacket on eBay for over $11,000

with the proceeds going to Toys for Tots. Charity auctions are run like most other auctions on eBay, but because they're immensely popular, bidding can be fierce and the dollar amounts can go sky-high. Ron Howard, Rosie O'Donnell, and other celebrities often use eBay to help out their favorite charities. We suggest that you visit these auctions and bid whenever you can. Charity auctions are a win-win situation for everyone. You can read more about celebrity auctions in Chapter 16.

Dutch auctions

Dutch auctions have nothing to do with windmills, wooden shoes, or sharing the check on a date. A *Dutch auction* allows a seller to put multiple, identical items up for sale. Instead of holding 100 separate auctions for 100 pairs of wooden shoes, a seller can sell them all together. As a buyer, you *could* elect to bid for one, three, or all 100 pairs. Unless you're running an alternative boutique (or know a giant centipede who needs all those clogs), we think you should bid on just one pair.

To bid on only one item in a Dutch auction, indicate the number "1" in the "Quantity you are bidding for" box, and type in the amount you wish to bid for that single item in the "Your maximum bid" box. eBay will read your bid as a single-item bid for that auction. For more on Dutch auctions, see Chapter 6.

So You Wanna Sell Stuff

If you're a seller, creating an auction page on eBay is as simple as filling out an online form. You write in the name of your item, a short description, add a picture if you want to, set your price, and voilà — it's auction time. eBay charges a small fee ($.25 to $2.00) for the privilege. When you list your item, millions of people from all over the world can take a gander at it and place bids. All you do is sit back and watch the bids come in. With a little luck, a bidding war could break out and drive the bids up high enough for you to turn a nice profit. After the auction, you deal directly with the buyer, who sends you the money. Then you ship the item. Go out and meet your friendly mail carrier, courteously accept your check, and grin wildly all the way to the bank. Abracadabra — you just turned everyday household clutter into cash! And if you want to, you can run as many auctions as you want, all at the same time. To get info on deciding what to sell, leaf through Chapter 8; to find out how to set up an auction, jump to Chapter 9, and to get the scoop on advanced selling strategies, roll on over to Chapters 12 and 13.

So You Wanna Buy Stuff

If you're a collector or you just like to shop for bargains, you can browse 24 hours a day through the items up for auction in eBay's thousands of categories, which range from Antiques to Writing Instruments. Find the item you want, do a little research on what you're buying and who's selling it, place your bid, and keep an eye on it until the auction closes.

Take a look at Chapter 5 for info on searching for items to bid on. When you see an item you like, you can set up a bidding strategy and let the games begin. Chapter 6 gives you bidding strategies that can make you the winner. When you win the auction, you can get expert advice about completing the transaction from Chapter 7. You can bid as many times as you want on an item, and you can bid on as many auctions as you want.

Research for Fun and Profit

eBay's awesome search engine allows you to browse through countless *categories* of items, all up for sale. As a buyer, you can do some comparison shopping on that special something you just can't live without or just browse around until something catches your eye. If you're a seller, the search engine allows you to keep your eye on your competition and get an idea of how hot your item is — that way you can set a competitive price. To find out more about using search options and categories, check out Chapters 3 and 5.

The search engine even lets you find out what other people are bidding on. From there you can read up on their *feedback rating* (eBay's ingenious honor system) to get a sense of how good their reputations are — even before you deal with them.

eBay's Role in the Auction Action

Throughout the entire auction process, eBay's computers keep tabs on what's going on. When the auction is over, eBay takes a small cut of the final selling price and introduces the seller to the buyer (and vice versa) through e-mail. At this point, eBay's job is pretty much over, and they step aside.

Most of the time, everything works great, everybody's happy, and eBay never has to step back into the picture. But if you happen to run into trouble in paradise, eBay can help you settle the problem, whether you're the buyer or the seller.

eBay also regulates members with a detailed system of checks and balances known as *feedback,* which we talk about in Chapter 4. The grand plan is that the community polices itself. Don't get us wrong — eBay does jump in when sketchy activity comes to light, but the people who keep eBay most safe are the buyers and sellers who have a common stake in conducting business honestly and fairly. Every time you sell something or win an auction, eBay members have a chance to leave a comment about you. You should do the same for them. If they're happy, the feedback is positive; otherwise, the feedback is negative. Either way, feedback sticks to you like glue.

Building a great reputation with positive feedback ensures a long and profitable eBay career. Negative feedback, like multiple convictions for grand theft auto, is a real turnoff to most folks and can make it hard to do future business on eBay.

If you get four negative feedback messages, eBay can suspend your buying and selling privileges. You can find out more about how eBay protects you in Chapters 14 and 15.

Features and Fun Stuff

So eBay is all about making money, right? Not exactly. The folks at eBay aren't kidding when they call it a community — a place where people with similar interests can compare notes, argue, buy and sell, and meet each other. Yes, people have gotten married after meeting on eBay. (Take a guess how friends bought them wedding gifts!)

Setting up shop and getting to know the neighborhood

The eBay Home page, shown in Figure 1-1, is your automatic link to all the cool stuff you can see and do on eBay. You can conduct searches, take bearings on what's happening, and get an instant link to the My eBay page, which helps you keep track of every auction item you have up for sale or have a bid on. You can read more about the eBay Home page in Chapter 3 and find out more about My eBay in Chapter 4.

Figure 1-1: The eBay Home page, ground zero for all your auction needs.

Chatting it up

eBay has about two dozen specific chat boards whose topics range from advertising to trading cards. So if you have no idea what that old Mobil gas station sign you found in your grandfather's barn is worth, just post a message on the Advertising chat board. Somewhere out there is an expert with an answer for you. Your biggest problem is deciding whether to keep the sign or put it up for auction. Those are good problems to have!

One of our favorite chat rooms is eBay's Wanted Board. Here's a fun posting we came across while looking around on this board:

> *I am looking for a vintage Charlie Brown and Snoopy bedspread. It has Peanuts characters around the edges and Charlie Brown hugging Snoopy in the middle (large picture). If anyone is willing to sell this item, please e-mail me or auction it off. Thanks.*

We're happy to report this posting worked. Two weeks later, the bedspread hunter got a tip from an eBay user that one was up for auction. Today Charlie Brown and Snoopy are resting comfortably in her home. If there's an item you want out there somewhere, someone on eBay knows how to find it. For more about posting messages and chat rooms, visit Chapters 5 and 15.

SafeHarbor

SafeHarbor is sort of the catch-all for information and services about making deals on eBay safer — and what to do if deals go sour. We don't like to think about it, but sometimes, despite your best efforts to be a good eBay user, you find buyers or sellers don't keep their word — unscrupulous louts sometimes do invade the site and try to pull scams, and you may buy an item that isn't as it was described, or you may spend months waiting for the winner of your auction to send you payment. Sometimes even honest members get into disputes. SafeHarbor is an excellent resource when you need questions answered or you need a professional to come in and handle an out-of-hand situation. Chapter 14 tells you all about SafeHarbor.

Computers: How High-Tech Do I Go?

You don't have to know a lot of fancy computer mumbo-jumbo to do well on eBay, but you do have to have a computer. Read this section for info on what you need and how to get it, and move on to Chapters 12 and 13 if you're looking for advanced technical strategies that can really zip you into the eBay stratosphere.

If you're in the market for a computer, you can buy or lease a new, used, or refurbished system, depending on your computing needs. If you want more information on buying a computer than we give you here, a painless place to find it is in *Buying a Computer For Dummies* by Dan Gookin. If you're in the market for an upgrade, grab *Upgrading and Fixing PCs For Dummies,* 4th Edition, by Andy Rathbone. Both books are published by IDG Books Worldwide, Inc. (Uncanny, isn't it?)

You need access to the Internet to get into the eBay scene, whether you decide to go with a new computer or a used one. Remember that you should find one with a good modem and enough memory and speed to work efficiently on the Internet. See "Buying a new computer," coming up next. You won't have far to look.

Buying a new computer

Even though the following list is geared mainly toward the purchase of new PCs and Macs, which you can get for around a thousand bucks, you should read this info even if you think you might want a used computer:

✔ Look for a computer with a good memory. Remember that 1950s horror movie, *The Blob?* The more time you spend using your computer, the more stuff you want to save on your hard drive. The more stuffed your hard drive, the more Blob-like it becomes. A hard drive with at least 4 gigabytes of storage space should keep your computer happy, but you can get hard drives as big as 10GB. We recommend you buy the biggest hard drive you can afford because no matter how large your hard drive is, you'll find a way to fill it up.

✔ Make sure you have a fast modem. Your modem connects your computer to the Internet using your telephone line. The faster the modem the more information it sends and receives every second (it transfers data over phone lines at a rate called "kilobytes per second" or just plain "K". Older modems were rated by "baud," as in 1,200 or 2,400 baud). Translation: With a fast modem, your computer snags a lot more info and makes good use of the online time you're paying for. And you don't have to wait forever for your monitor to show you what you want to see. A 56K modem is standard equipment these days, especially if you plan on using a lot of digital images (photographs) to help sell your items (we tell you how to do that in Chapter 12).

✔ A color monitor that has at least a 15-inch screen. Any smaller and you'll have a hard time actually seeing the auctions and images.

✔ A CPU with at least a 333-MHz (megahertz) processor. This is not as fast as the 400- to 500-MHz processors on the market, but for what you need it to do on eBay — create a completed Web page on your monitor while handling other chores (such as running other software) at the same time — it's fast enough. If you want lightning-fast speed (imagine a Daytona 500 race car with jet assist) you have to move up to the 400- to 500-MHz range. Systems with that kind of speed can cost around $2,000 and more.

✔ A CD-ROM drive is also standard equipment. You use the CD-ROM drive to load new software programs into your computer from compact discs. The top-end models even play DVD movies on your computer, but we think you'll be so entertained by eBay, you might as well skip the frills and save the bucks.

✔ A keyboard. The basic one is fine. They do make funky ergonomic models that are split in the middle. But if the good old standard keyboard feels comfortable to you, stick with it.

✔ A pointing device, usually a mouse. Some laptops come with touchpads or trackballs designed to do the same thing — give you a quick way to move the pointer around the screen so you can select options by clicking.

Chairman of the baud

Maybe you've heard about "baud rate" in computer-speak. What is it exactly, and where did it come from? It's named after J.M.E. Baudot, a Frenchman who created a telegraph code in 1880 that rivaled Morse code. Unfortunately Baudot's code was dismissed at the time, and the world adopted Morse code instead. *Baud,* however, lived on as a unit of measure for how fast a telegraph could transmit dots and dashes. By the 1980s, it had become an approximate measure of how much information a modem could transmit every second. As modems got faster and faster,

"baud rate" was gradually eclipsed by *kilobits per second* (or *Kbps*), which is what the "K" in "56.6K" stands for — thousands of bits per second.

Mr. Morse's code, by the way, had a great run until 1999, when Morse code was officially abandoned as the standard nautical means of emergency communication. It seems satellites and computer technology put an end to the dashing dot man's claim to fame. Forevermore, S.O.S. is D.O.A! Until you hear it again....

Buying a used computer

If you don't have a computer yet, and don't want to spend a lot of money, you can start by investigating the used market. There are thousands of perfectly good used machines floating around looking for a caring home. You can pick up a Pentium for a few hundred dollars, and it will serve your budding eBay needs just fine. Same holds true for used Apple PowerPCs or 7110/66 models. Make sure a monitor is included in the purchase price; sometimes you need to buy them separately.

If you buy used from a computer reseller, be sure to ask whether there is still a warranty on the system. Also, ask a lot of questions about the potential of upgrading the system with more memory later on.

Buying a refurbished computer

If you don't feel comfortable buying a used machine, you may want to consider a factory-refurbished model. These are powerful new machines that were returned to the manufacturer for one reason or another. The factory fixes them up nice and spiffy, and sweetens the deal with a terrific warranty. Some companies even offer optional, extended, on-site repairs. What you're getting is a new computer at a deep discount because they can't be legally resold as "new."

Don't mail this postcard

Here's an item that did very well on eBay: A *Titanic* postcard, dated 1912, Germany, in very good condition. A rare and unusual card for the serious collector. It shows the Statue of Liberty (which indicates the card was printed before the disaster), showing the ship entering New York Harbor. Unfortunately, this never took place due to the sinking. The later printings of the card obviously were amended to reflect the unexpected change of events. A must-have for the serious collector. This postcard's starting price was $9.95, and it sold on eBay for $120!

Timing is all, after all.

For the most part, "refurbished" computers are defined as those that were returned by customers, units with blemishes (scratches, dents, and so on), or evaluation units. The factories rebuild them to the original working condition, using new parts (or sometimes used parts that meet or exceed performance specs for new parts). They come with warranties (60 to 90 days depending on the manufacturer) that cover repairs and returns. Warranty information is available on the manufacturers' Web sites. Be sure to read it before you purchase a refurbished computer.

Major computer manufacturers like Compaq, Dell, IBM, Hewlett-Packard, and Apple provide refurbished computers. Unfortunately, they only ship within the United States.

Because the inventory of refurbished computers changes daily (as do the prices), there's no way of telling exactly how much money you can save by buying refurbished instead of new. We suggest finding a new computer system you like (and can afford) in a store or catalog, and then comparing it with refurbished systems. If you're thinking about buying from the Web or a catalog, don't forget to include the cost of shipping when you add up the total price. Even with shipping costs, however, a refurbished computer may save you between 10 percent and 30 percent, depending on the deal you find.

Other purchasing options

When it comes to buying computer equipment, you have several options. You can go the conventional store route (CompUSA, Circuit City, Sears) or you can buy through a catalog (*MacWarehouse, PC Connection*). These options are just fine, and with a little research, you can often get good deals there. You can also lease computer systems and find great (even amazing) deals on eBay. If you think a whole new computer system is beyond your needs but you still want to get hooked up to eBay in your own home, WebTV may be the ticket. For more info, tune in *WebTV For Dummies,* 2nd Edition, by Brad Hill (from IDG Books Worldwide, Inc., but you knew that).

You may think we're putting the cart before the horse with this suggestion, but you can get a really good deal on a cheap computer system by signing on to eBay *before* you buy your computer. You can get online at a local library or ask to borrow a friend's computer. We've seen listings for Pentium 100 machines with a CD-ROM drive, a modem, a monitor, and a 5GB hard drive, all for $400. Often such systems also come fully loaded with software.

You can also find the bits and pieces of a computer you need to upgrade on eBay. If you have a good used computer without a modem (or if you have a really old, obsolete modem with a glacier-like speed of 1,200 baud or even less), you can upgrade to a pretty fast 28.8K model for about ten dollars by watching eBay's auctions carefully. If you plan on using a lot of digital images (photographs) to help sell your items (we tell you how to do that in Chapter 12), you do need to get a 56.6K modem, which you can find on eBay for $40 to $50. Considering the reasonable price, it certainly makes sense to buy the fastest modem you can afford. (Of course, then you'd have to *have* a modem so you could connect and buy *another* modem . . . so you may want to sneak a peek at Chapter 12 first.)

You may have to keep checking in and monitoring the different auctions that eBay has going on; listings change daily. Go put in your best bid, and check back a week later to see whether you've won! (If you want to hurry up and register so you can bid, skip ahead to Chapters 2 and 5. We won't be insulted if you leave us for awhile now!)

No Computer? Connect to eBay on the Cheap

Yes, sometimes life is a Catch-22 situation. Say, for instance, your goal is to make some money on eBay so you can afford to buy a computer. Because you can't log on to eBay without a computer, you can't make the money — right? Well, not exactly. Here's how you can start selling and bringing in some cold hard cash for that shiny new (or not-so-shiny used) hardware.

Libraries: From Dewey decimal to eBay

If you haven't been to your local library lately, you may be surprised that most libraries are fully wired with computers that can connect to the Internet. Right now, 80 percent of all American libraries offer computer access to the public. They've come a long way since the card catalog file and the Dewey decimal system. (Remember those?) Some libraries don't even require you to have a library card if you want to use a computer. Others limit the amount of time you can spend online and the sites you can log on to (often it's just the "adult" sites that are blocked). eBay is considered fair game, and exploring it is even considered research.

The upside of using the library's computer is that it's free. The downside is you may have to wait for some kid to finish doing research for a term paper on the ceremonial use of yak milk.

Commercial cyber-outlets

If, for some reason, you strike out at the public library (or you're tired of the librarian *shhhhshing* you as you cheer your winning bids), your friend threw you out of the house, and your boss is watching you like a hawk, you can use a commercial outlet to kick off your eBay career.

National chains like Kinko's — or your favorite local Cyber-Coffee café — offer computer usage at an hourly rate. Kinko's offers computers (both PC and Mac) that can get you online for around $12 per hour or 20 cents per minute. There are no restrictions — you get full access to the Internet and can enjoy all of the elements of eBay. You can conduct your auctions by posting them and checking back a week later after they're finished. You can also watch for great computer deals on eBay that you may want to bid on.

Time is money, and an hour flies by fast when you're having fun online. Before you sit down and the clock starts ticking, make sure you're well organized and know exactly what you want to accomplish during that session. At $12 an hour, you don't want to spend a lot of time surfing for items on eBay for fun. You can do that when you own your own system. The money you save now can help you get there.

Hooking up from work

If you get a long lunch break at work, or you have to kill time waiting for clients to call back, you may want to get started on eBay from your work computer. But give it a lot of thought before you do. Pink slips can come unbidden to those who run auctions on company time!

Before you even consider tinkering with a workplace computer, check with your boss or MIS person. The last thing you want to do (and it may *be* the last thing before they show you the door) is crash your company computer system by messing with the hardware!

Choosing an ISP

Okay, so you bought (or found a way to access) a computer, and you're ready to surf over to eBay. Hold on a minute — before you can start surfing, you need access to the Internet. (Details, details.) The most common way is through an *ISP,* or *Internet service provider,* such as America Online (AOL), Earthlink, MSN (Microsoft Network) or any of the commercial Internet enterprises out there today. If you don't already belong to one of these, don't worry, they're really easy to join.

When you buy a new or factory-refurbished computer, you're hit with all kinds of free trial offers that beg you to "Sign up now, get 30 hours free!" If you already own a computer and need to find an ISP, many of the big commercial ISPs give away millions of free registration CD-ROMs — we're sure you can find a few. They're everywhere! We have a friend who painted all her free CD-ROMs and hung them on her Christmas tree. Another sawed them in half and made a very unattractive cyber-belt. (Martha Stewart would never approve.)

If you're not sure which ISP to go with, your best bet may be to start with AOL. AOL is the largest ISP around, and it's easy to find and easy to use. If you're not happy with AOL down the road, you can easily cancel your membership and sign up with a different company.

To join an ISP, just load the freebie registration disc into your CD-ROM drive and follow the registration steps that appear on your computer screen. Have your credit card and lots of patience handy. With a little luck and no computer glitches, in less than an hour you'll have an active account and instant access to e-mail and the Internet.

Here are some built-in features that big-name ISPs offer to new users:

- ✔ **Powerful web browsers.** Browsers are software programs that let your computer talk to the Internet.

- ✔ **Local toll-free telephone numbers.** The last thing you want is long-distance charges while connected to eBay for hours.

- ✔ **E-mail software.** Short for *electronic mail*, e-mail lets you send and receive messages electronically.

- ✔ **Easy registration features.** The best are short, sweet, and painless.

- ✔ **A vast database of information and activities.** Each ISP offers chatrooms, news forums, research areas, online magazines, special events, and shopping sites.

- ✔ **A storage area for your digital pictures.** We explain this in detail in Chapter 12.

Browsing for a browser

When you join a commercial ISP, those good folks give you a browser for free. A *browser* is the software program that lets your computer talk to the Internet. It's like having your own private cyber-chauffeur. Type in the address (also known as the *URL,* for *Uniform Resource Locator*) of the Web site you'd like to visit, and boom, you're there. For example, to get to eBay's home page, type **www.ebay.com** and press Enter. (It's sort of a low-tech version of "Beam me up, Scotty!" — and almost as fast.)

The two most popular browsers (they are what Coca-Cola and Pepsi are to the cola wars) are Netscape Navigator and Microsoft Internet Explorer. Both programs are powerful and user-friendly. Figures 1-2 and 1-3 show you these browsers. (Sit, browser! Now shake! *Good* browser!)

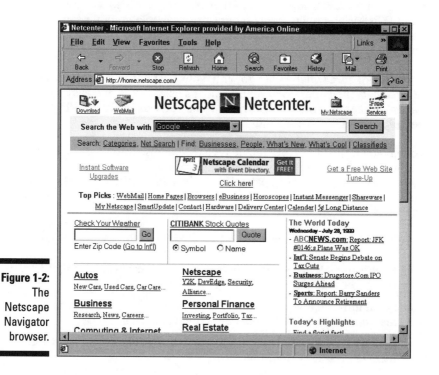

Figure 1-2: The Netscape Navigator browser.

When you join an ISP, you get either Microsoft Internet Explorer or Netscape Navigator for free. If you need more information (or you want to make sure you're using the most up-to-date version of the software) you can get it online.

✔ For Microsoft Internet Explorer, go to www.microsoft.com.

✔ For Netscape Navigator, go to www.netscape.com.

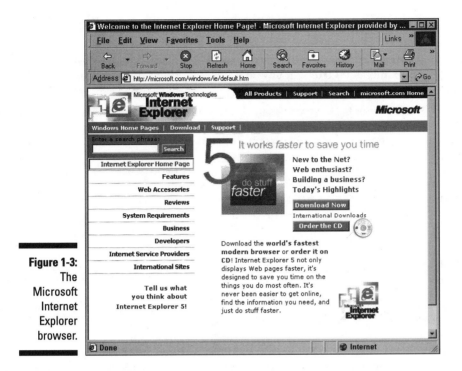

Figure 1-3:
The
Microsoft
Internet
Explorer
browser.

Hooking up on e-mail

Once you have access to the Internet, you need access to e-mail. If you have your own computer and an ISP, then you probably have e-mail access automatically. But if you're logging on to the Internet from the library or a friend's house, you should look into setting up e-mail for free.

Yahoo! and Hotmail are two of the most popular e-mail providers around. Both are free and secure, and signing up is a snap. We like Yahoo! because it has a Mail Alert feature, which allows you to instruct Yahoo! to contact you via your pager when you have new e-mail.

You can join Yahoo! e-mail at yahoo.com. You can join Hotmail by going to hotmail.com.

Whether you sign up for e-mail at Hotmail, Yahoo!, or any other service or ISP (Internet service provider), following some common-sense rules can help you protect your account:

✔ **Select a password that is difficult to guess.** Use letter-and-number combinations or nonsensical words that nobody else knows. Don't use common names or words relating to you (like your street name).

> ✔ **Keep passwords secret.** Nobody will ever ask for your password online — if somebody does, you can bet it's a scam. *Never give it out.*
>
> ✔ **If you get an e-mail with an attachment (another file attached to your e-mail message) from an unknown person, don't open it.** The attachment could contain a virus.
>
> ✔ **Don't respond to "spam" mail.** *Spam* is online slang for harassing, offensive, or useless-but-widely-distributed messages. If you ignore such junk, the sender will probably just give up and go away.

For more info on using e-mail, a ready resource is (you guessed it) *E-Mail For Dummies,* 2nd Edition, by John R. Levine, Carol Baroudi, Margaret Levine Young, and Arnold Reinhold (from IDG Books Worldwide, Inc. — how *did* we know that?). Also check out Chapter 13 for some additional online privacy tips.

Extra Gizmos You're Gonna Want Later

We suggest you first get your feet wet on the Web before you buy the extras. But when you've graduated from eBay "newbie" status, you might want to consider investing in a couple of extra devices for the longer run. Digital cameras and scanners can help make your time on eBay a more lucrative and fun adventure. (We explain how to use digital technology in your auctions in more detail in Chapter 12.)

No fuss, no muss — the digital camera

Even though digital cameras are dropping in price, they're still a major investment; You certainly don't need a digital camera when you start trading on eBay, but as your experience as a trader advances, you may want to consider buying one. A picture is worth (at last count) about *two* thousand words (inflation, you know). A good digital snapshot of your item — available for all the online world to see — can increase your exposure to prospective buyers.

Scanning the globe

Using a scanner to create digital pictures of your items — which you can then post on eBay — is an alternative to using a digital camera. Scanners cost much less to purchase than cameras. Prices range from under $100 for a basic model to several thousand bucks for sophisticated versions.

You may pay less initially for a scanner than you would for a digital camera, but remember to factor in the cost of developing film. Then decide which piece of equipment is likely to be more economical for you in the long run.

Chapter 2

The Bucks Start Here: Signing Up on eBay

. . . .

In This Chapter

▶ Using eBay's easy forms (the shape of things to come)

▶ Getting up close and personal about privacy

▶ Identifying with User IDs and passwords

▶ Learning the ropes (eBay rules and regs)

. . . .

*Y*ou've probably figured out by now that you sign on to eBay electronically, which means you don't *really* sign on the proverbial dotted line as folks did in days of old before computers ran the world. Nowadays, the art of scribbling your signature has become as outdated as 8-track tapes (although you *can* still get 8-track tapes on eBay if you're feeling nostalgic).

Compared to finding a prime parking space at the mall in a snowstorm, signing up for eBay is a breeze. About the toughest thing you have to do is type in your e-mail address correctly.

In this chapter, you find out everything you need to know about registering with eBay. We give you tips on what information you have to disclose and what you should keep to yourself. Don't worry — this is an open-book test. You won't need to memorize state capitals or multiplication tables.

Sign in, Please — Register with eBay

No, you won't have to wear one of the tacky "Hello My Name Is" stickers on your shirt after you sign in, but eBay needs to know some things about you before it grants you your membership. You and several other folks will be roaming around eBay's online treasure trove (or garage sale, depending where you wind up); it wants to keep track of who's who. So, keeping that in mind, sign in, please!

You don't have to be a rocket scientist to register on eBay, but you can *buy* a model rocket or something bigger after you do. The only hard-and-fast rule on eBay is that you have to be 18 years of age or older. Don't worry, the Age Police won't come to your house to card you; they have other ways to dis-creetly ensure that you're at least 18 years old. (*Hint:* Credit cards do more than satisfy account charges.) If you're having a momentary brain cramp and you've forgotten your age, just think back to the *Brady Bunch* TV show. If you can remember watching the original episodes of our favorite show of the 1970s, you're in! Head to the eBay Home page and register. The entire process takes only a few minutes.

We did a quick search on eBay and found 139 *Brady Bunch* items listed, including autographed pictures, dolls, and books. After you register, just type **Brady Bunch** in the search field of the Home page and see how many items you can dig up, and then skip to Chapter 5 for more research tips. Your results will vary from ours. That's normal.

Registering is free and fun (and fast)

Before you can sign up for eBay, you have to be connected to the Web. If you're confused about what particular computer hardware, software, and Internet services you need, it's Chapter 1 to the rescue. If you're already connected, you're ready to sign up.

Just type **www.ebay.com** in your browser, press Enter, and your next stop is the eBay Home page. Right there, next to the New Users image where you can't miss it, is the Registration link shown in Figure 2-1. Click on it and let the sign-up begin. You can also get to the Registration form by clicking one of eBay's Fab Four links. Check Chapter 3 for details.

Figure 2-1:
Click on
this link to
register —
it's free!

This part of eBay is like window-shopping. It's free until you buy something.

The Register button links you to the first of the eBay Registration pages. To register, first choose your country. Follow these steps to complete this page:

1. **Scroll down the list and choose the country you happen to be in today.**

    You have many nations to choose from; we highly recommend your homeland (it *does* have to be on this planet; Klingons are out of luck).

2. Make sure the box that says "SSL" has a check mark in it.

SSL (Secure Sockets Layer) enables you to have a secure (encrypted) connection to eBay because a bunch of really smart techie-types made it that way. We could tell you how SSL works, but bottom line, it *does* work; trust us and use it. The more precautions you take, the harder it is for some mega-caffeinated high-school kid to hack into your files.

3. Click on the button that says "Begin the registration process now."

Now you're transported through a series of registration pages. Figure 2-2 shows you the first registration page.

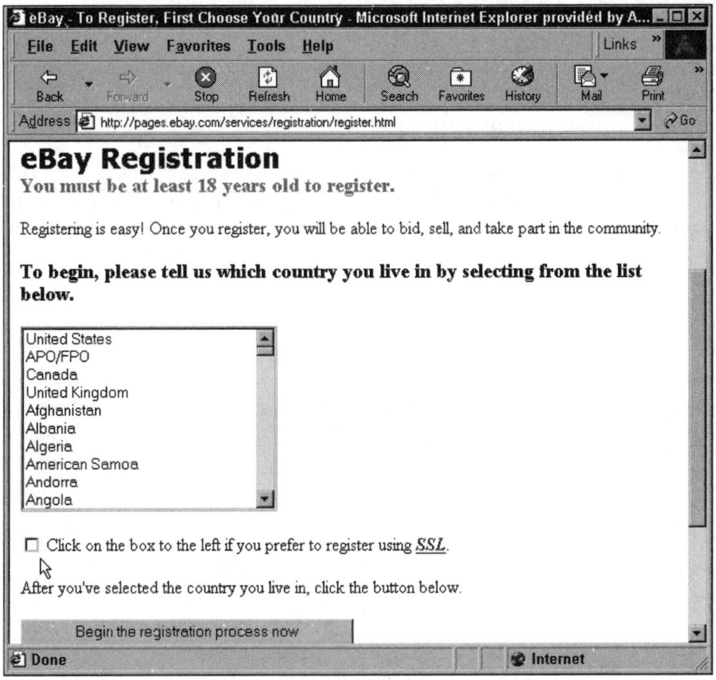

Figure 2-2: The first eBay registration page.

Required information — so, what's your sign?

At the top of the next page, eBay briefly outlines the registration process for you and asks you to fill out some required (and not-so-required) information, shown in Figure 2-3. Here's what eBay wants to know about you:

✔ Your e-mail address (yourname@bogusISP.com).

✔ Your full name, address, and primary telephone number. All this information is kept by eBay in case it needs to contact you.

---

eBay internationale!

eBay now has Web sites in the United States, the United Kingdom, Canada, Germany, and Japan. The vast majority of eBay users are from the United States, but the international membership is growing daily. On eBay's registration page, you can see a list that has more countries on it than the United Nations. Really! eBay lists 226 nations and territories, but the United Nations has only 185 member countries. You find in the list a "Where's Where" of the world, including countries from Australia to Zimbabwe. You can even register from Jan Mayen, a Norwegian island in the Arctic Ocean. That would be a feat, because Jan Mayen is an uninhabited meteorological station. (Maybe this is where retired weatherman should go to hide out after years of wrong predictions . . . ?)

✔ How you first heard about eBay.

✔ Your *promotional priority code,* if any. The term refers to a number that another Web site may have assigned to you, offering a discount in your initial eBay transactions. If you don't have a promotional priority code, leave this area blank.

✔ You can also include, if you want, a secondary phone number and a fax number.

Figure 2-3:
The eBay registration form, Step 1.

*Optional information —
getting to know you*

To wind up the registration process, some optional questions allow you to fill
in your self-portrait a bit for your new pals at eBay.

Although eBay doesn't share member information with anyone who isn't a
registered user, you don't have to answer these optional questions if you
don't want to.

Figure 2-4 shows you the optional questions eBay asks. You decide what you
feel comfortable divulging and what you want to keep personal. They ask for
this information because they want a better picture of who is actually using
the Web site. In marketing mumbo-jumbo it's called *demographics,* studying
statistics that characterize a group of people who make up a community. In
this case, it's the eBay community.

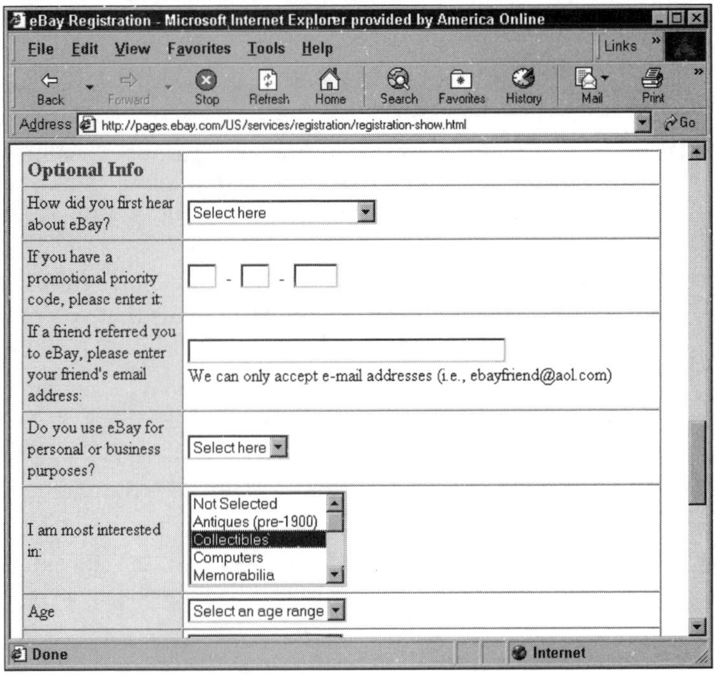

Figure 2-4:
Enter
optional
info here.

![eBay Registration screenshot showing the Optional Info form with questions including "How did you first hear about eBay?", "If you have a promotional priority code, please enter it:", "If a friend referred you to eBay, please enter your friend's email address:", "Do you use eBay for personal or business purposes?", "I am most interested in:", and "Age"]

Don't tell anyone, but your info is safe with eBay

eBay keeps most personal information secret. The basics (your name, phone number, city, and state) go out only to answer the specific request of another *registered* eBay user, law enforcement, or members of Verified Rights Owners (eBay's copyright-watchdog program). Other users may need your basic access info for several reasons — a seller may want to verify your location, get your phone number to call you regarding your auction, or double-check who you really are. If somebody does request your info, you get an e-mail from eBay giving you the name, phone number, city, and state of the person who made the request.

Here is the optional information eBay asks for — and some tips on how to respond to it:

- ✔ **If a friend referred you to eBay, please enter your friend's e-mail address.** If a friend referred you, we suggest you enter that person's e-mail address. Although eBay may not be offering any freebies for referrals at the moment, it may someday — and your buddy will be the lucky beneficiary of such goodwill.

- ✔ **Do you use eBay for personal or business purposes?** Sometimes this isn't easy to answer. If you're registering for fun but think you could turn buying and selling into a business, you may not be sure. It's okay to skip this one.

- ✔ **I am most interested in . . .** This is a good question to answer. eBay has the software to keep track of categories of items that you're interested in, so it doesn't hurt to let them know for their future planning.

- ✔ **Age.** If you feel comfortable letting your age float out into cyberspace where it's visible, go ahead and tell 'em; otherwise you can skip this one.

- ✔ **Education: Select an education.** You get the usual choices, high school, college, graduate school, and other. (Hmm, does Starfleet Academy count as "other"?)

- ✔ **Annual household income.** Fill it in *if* you want to (eBay states that this info is kept anonymous), but we think this information is too personal; if you're not comfortable with it, skip it.

- ✔ **Are you interested in participating in an eBay survey?** Not right away, of course — they're just asking for future reference. eBay's surveys are always anonymous and have no impact on your transactions, so if one shows up in your e-mail, go ahead and take it if you have time. Otherwise, don't sweat it.

- ✔ **Gender.** This is our favorite question because if you don't fill it out, it defaults to "unspecified" (which is great if you're an amoeba).

Registered eBay users can request the name, phone number, city, and state of other users for business purposes only. If you want more info about getting info, stroll discreetly over to Chapter 13, which goes into detail on privacy issues.

Check your work and confirm registration

Think back to your second-grade teacher who kept saying, "Class, check your work." Remember that? She's still right! Review your answers. If everything is accurate, then click once on the Continue button at the bottom of the page. If you've made a mistake, go back and fix it using the Review Registration Information page, shown in Figure 2-5.

Figure 2-5:
Use this
part of the
form to
review your
registration
information.

eBay Registration - Microsoft Internet Explorer provided by America Online

File Edit View Favorites Tools Help   Links »

Back   Forward   Stop   Refresh   Home   Search   Favorites   History   Mail

Address http://cgi4.ebay.com/aw-cgi/eBayISAPI.dll   Go

Please Review The Following Information

E-mail address	ebay4dummy@aol.com	to be verified in Step 2
Full name	Marsha Collier	OK
Address	1234 Anywhere St	OK
City	Northridge	OK
State	CA	OK
Zip Code	91355	OK
Country	United States	OK
Primary phone #	(818) 555 - 5555	OK

Click the Back button on your browser if you need to make any changes.

Click submit (please click only once) to complete Step 1 of the eBay registration process.

Please wait a few seconds for the next page to load. Clicking the submit button more than once may invalidate your confirmation information.

Done   Internet

If eBay finds a glitch in your registration, you end up back at the top of the registration page. If you put in a wrong e-mail address, eBay has no way of contacting you. You won't hear a peep from them until you go through the whole registration process all over again.

On a slow day, it takes eBay less than an hour to e-mail you with a confirmation notice. If you register on a busy day, it can take much longer. Unfortunately, you have no way of knowing just how busy eBay is. If you're ready to start on eBay as soon as possible, we suggest that you register in the evening and check your e-mail the following morning. Your confirmation message will get processed, we promise.

Get your confirmation e-mail

When you receive the eBay registration confirmation e-mail, print it out. What's most important is the confirmation code. If you lose that number, go back to the eBay Registration page and follow Step 2.

With your confirmation number in hand, head back to the eBay Registration page and click on the Step 3 Confirm Your Registration link or go to

```
pages.ebay.com/services/registration/reg-confirm.html
```

Do you solemnly swear to . . . ?

On the Confirm Your Registration Part 1 page, shown in Figure 2-6, you take an oath to keep eBay safe for democracy and commerce. You promise to play well with others, not to cheat, and to follow the golden rules. No, you're not auditioning for a superhero club, but don't ever forget that eBay takes this stuff very seriously. You could be kicked off eBay or worse. (Can you say "Federal investigation"?)

The craze that began with AW

Back in 1994, when eBay founder Pierre Omidyar had the idea to start a Web auction, he named his first venture Auction Web. The "aw" in many of eBay's URL addresses refers to the original name that eventually evolved into eBay. For example, `listings.ebay.com/aw/listings/list/category357/index.html` is the address that takes you to the Antiques: Folk Art category page (note the "aw" in the middle).

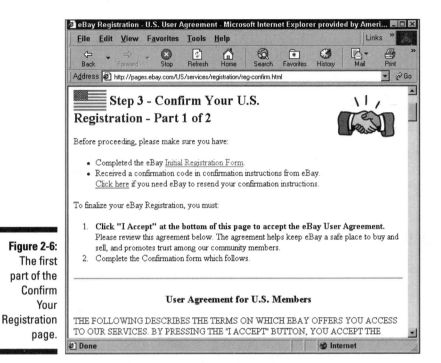

Figure 2-6:
The first
part of the
Confirm
Your
Registration
page.

So you don't have to deal with the legalese, we give you the bottom line:

✔ You understand that every transaction is a legally binding contract. (Click on the User Agreement link at the bottom of the Home page or in the Help section under Community Standards for the current eBay Rules and Regulations.)

✔ You state that you can pay for the items you buy and the eBay fees that you incur. (Chapter 8 fills you in on how eBay takes its cut of the auction action.)

✔ You understand that you're responsible for paying any taxes. (Chapter 8 covers paying the government piper.)

✔ You understand that if you sell prohibited items, eBay will forward your personal information to law enforcement for further investigation. (Chapter 8 explains what you can and can't sell on eBay — and what eBay does to sellers of prohibited items.)

eBay makes clear that it is just a *venue,* which means it's a *place* where people with similar interests can meet, greet, and do business.

When everything goes well, the eBay Web site is like a school gym that opens for Saturday swap meets. At the gym, if you don't play by the rules, you can get tossed out. But if you don't play by the rules on eBay, the venue gets un-gymlike in a hurry: eBay has the right to get state and federal officials to track you down and prosecute you. But fair's fair; eBay updates users by e-mail of any updates in the user agreement.

If you're a stickler for fine print, head to this address for all the *p*s and *q*s of the latest policies:

```
pages.ebay.com/help/community/png-user.html
```

Because we know that you, as a law-abiding eBay member, will have no problem following the rules, go ahead and click on the I Accept button at the bottom of the page, which takes you to Part 2 of Confirm Your Registration.

Sprint to the finish

Finally, after all this talk about confirming your registration, you actually get to do it! On the Confirm Your Registration Part 2 page, shown in Figure 2-7, follow these steps:

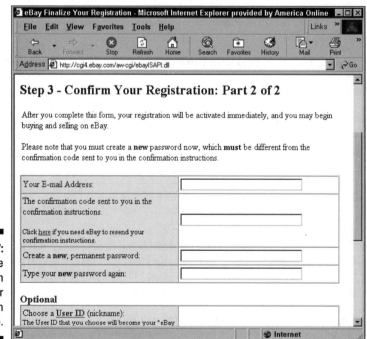

Figure 2-7:
Part 2 of the
Confirm
Your
Registration
page.

1. **Start at the eBay Registration page.**

2. **Click the Confirm your Registration button.**

3. **Re-enter your e-mail address.**

4. **Enter the confirmation code eBay sent you, and then promptly forget it (no, noooo . . .)!**

   If you lose your confirmation code, you can click just below the line on this page to have eBay re-send it to you.

5. **Early in the registration process, make up a permanent password when requested to. Reconfirm your password by typing it again.**

   For more information on choosing a password, see the next section, "A quick word about passwords."

6. **Choose a User ID for yourself.**

   For more information on making up a User ID for yourself, see the "Choosing a User ID" section later in this chapter.

7. **Click the Complete your Registration button.**

   Figure 2-8 shows you what your completed registration looks like.

Figure 2-8: You've completed your registration!

You're all set! (And if you think *that* was the fun part, just wait. . . .)

A quick word about passwords

Picking a good password is not as easy (and twice as important) as it may seem. Whoever has your password can (in effect) "be you" on eBay — running auctions, bidding on auctions, and leaving dangerous feedback for others. Basically, such an impostor can ruin your eBay career — and possibly cause you serious financial grief.

As with any online password, you should follow these common-sense rules to protect your privacy:

✔ Don't pick anything too obvious, such as your birthday, your first name, or your Social Security number. (***Hint:*** If it's too easy to remember, it's probably too easy to crack.)

✔ Make things tough on the bad guys — combine numbers and letters and create nonsensical words.

✔ Don't use words from the dictionary — they're too easy to figure out.

✔ Don't give out your password to anyone — it's like giving away the keys to the front door of your house.

✔ If you even suspect someone has your password, immediately change it by going to the following address:

```
pages.ebay.com/services/myebay/selectpass.html
```

✔ Change your password every few months just to be on the safe side.

Choosing a User ID

eBay gives you the option of picking your User ID. (If you don't choose one, then your e-mail address becomes your default User ID.) Making up a User ID is our favorite part. If you've never liked your real name (or never had a nick-name), here's the chance to "correct" that situation. Have fun. Consider choosing an ID that tells a little about yourself or items that you like to col-lect, like NYTEACHER or LOVELUCY (for you *I Love Lucy* buffs). Of course, if you move to Los Angeles or get really tired of Ricardo-and-Mertz memora-bilia, you may regret too narrow a User ID. Figure 2-9 shows the User ID box on the registration page.

Figure 2-9:
The User ID
box.

Choose a <u>User ID</u> (nickname):
The User ID that you choose will become your "eBay name" that others see when you participate on eBay. You can create a name or simply use your email address.

Examples "wunderkid", "jsmith98", "jeff@aol.com".

You can call yourself just about anything; you can be silly or creative, or boring. But remember, this is how other eBay users will know you. So here are some common-sense rules:

- ✔ Don't use a name that would embarrass your mother, like "Tightwad."

- ✔ Don't use a name that's too weird, such as "Scam-Man." If people don't trust you, they won't buy from you.

- ✔ Don't use a name with a negative connotation. (Even if you're a *Sanford and Son* junkie, don't use "Junkman.") People may think that's what you're selling!

- ✔ eBay doesn't allow spaces in User IDs, so make sure the ID makes sense when putting two or more words together. One eBay user we know wanted to use the name of her company, Gang of One. When she listed it and the spaces between the words disappeared, "Gang of One" ended up being "gangofone," which looks like some exotic disease caused by a telephone. She decided to rethink her User ID. (Gee, can't think why . . .)

If you're dying to have several short words as your User ID, you can use *underscores* to separate them, as in "Tin_sign_king", but we don't recommend it. Trying to type this kind of User ID when you're involved in a frenzied, last-minute bidding war will slow you down and may even lead to carpal tunnel syndrome with all those keystrokes!

You can change your User ID (once every 30 days) if you want to, but we don't recommend it. People will come to know you (and your eBay reputation) by your User ID. If you change your ID, your past plays tagalong and attaches itself to the new ID. Also, if you change your User ID too many times, people may think you're trying to hide something or you're in the Witness Protection Program.

To change your User ID, click on the My eBay link at the top of most eBay pages. From the My eBay login page, click on the Change My User ID link, fill out the boxes, and click on the Change User ID button. You now have a new eBay identity.

eBay also has some User ID rules to live by:

- ✔ No offensive names (like "&*#@guy")

- ✔ No names with "eBay" in them (It makes you look like you work for eBay, and they take a dim view of that.)

- ✔ No names with "&" (even if you *do* have both "looks&brains")

- ✔ No names with @ (like "@Aboy")

- ✔ No case-sensitive names (like "SuZiEq")

- ✔ No names of one letter (like "Q" — James Bond might be shaken *and* stirred by this — who would supply all the great spy gadgets?)

✔ No symbols other than letters A–Z and numbers 0–9. The only symbols you can use are the underscore (_) or the dollar sign ($), which is bad news if you're the Artist Formerly Known as Prince.

 When you pick your User ID, make sure it isn't a good clue for your password. If you use *Natasha* as your User ID, don't pick *Boris* as your password. Even Bullwinkle could figure that one out. Also, try to avoid having a User ID that's too similar to your e-mail address — unless you don't mind sharing your e-mail address with anyone who browses the site, including non-eBay members. See Chapter 13 for more on Privacy.

Your license to deal (almost)

After you click on the Complete your Registration button, you get a big ol' `Welcome to eBay`. You are now officially a *newbie*, or eBay rookie. The only problem is that you're still at the window-shopping level. (And even that isn't a problem if you're a little short on cash right now.)

Now is a great time to explore some of eBay's nooks and crannies, get a look at the rules and regulations, read some of the chat boards, spend some time getting familiar with the overall lay of the eBay land, and after a while, win a few auctions.

Once you're ready to go from window-shopper to item-seller, you just zip through a few more forms, and before you know it, you can start running your own auctions on eBay.

Chapter 3

There's No Place Like the Home Page

In This Chapter

▶ Getting the lay of the land

▶ Using the eBay Home page's links and icons

▶ Getting the first word on searches

▶ Checking out featured auctions and other fun stuff

The writer Thomas Wolfe was wrong: You *can* go home again — and again — at least on eBay you can! Month after month, millions of people land at eBay's Home page without wearing out the welcome mat. The eBay Home page is the front door to the most popular auction site on the Internet.

Everything you need to know about navigating eBay begins right here. In this chapter, we take the grand tour through the areas you can reach right from the Home page with the help of links.

What Is the Home Page?

The eBay Home page is shown in Figure 3-1 and includes the following key areas:

✔ A navigation bar at the very top with six eBay links that can zip you straight to any of the many eBay areas.

✔ A Search window that — like the Search link in the menu bar — helps you find the items or information that you want.

✔ Four destination links that tell you a little more about eBay, get you started on selling or buying items, and registering with eBay.

✔ A list of auction categories.

✔ Links to featured auctions, fun stuff like charity auctions, and information about what else is happening on eBay.

Figure 3-1:
The eBay
Home page.

Do not adjust your computer monitor. You're not going crazy. You may notice that a link was on the eBay Home page yesterday and is gone the next day. The links on the eBay Home page change often to reflect what's going on — not just on the site, but in the world. If you look at the Home page on February 14 and again in the first week of July, for example, you'll see different links.

This Bar Never Closes

The *navigation bar* is at the top of the eBay Home page, and lists six eBay links that take you directly to any of the different eBay areas.

Using the navigation bar is kind of like doing "one-stop clicking." You can find this bar at the top of every page you travel to on eBay. When you click on one of the six links, you get a subnavigation bar under it with specific links to other important places.

Think of links as expressways to specific destinations. Click just once on a link, and the next thing you know, you're right where you want to be. You don't even have to answer that annoying old question, *When are we gonna get there?*, from the kids in the backseat.

Here, without further ado, are the six navigation bar links and where they take you:

✔ **Browse:** Takes you to the page that lists featured auctions, hot items, big-ticket (pricey) items, and all the main categories on eBay. From this page you can link to any one of the millions of items up for auction on eBay. (Chapter 6 briefs you on the fine points of Featured Auctions. Hot Items can be found in Chapter 9; more details of the auction categories are in this chapter.

✔ **Sell:** Takes you to the Sell Your Item form that you fill out to start your auctions. We explain how to navigate this form in Chapter 9.

✔ **Services:** Takes you to the eBay Services Overview page. Here you can find links to pages that tell you all about buying and selling, registration pages, the feedback forum, eBay's SafeHarbor program, the My eBay page, and the About Me page. eBay registration is covered in Chapter 2; we clue you in on how feedback works (and how the My eBay page helps you) in Chapter 4. In Chapter 14, we show you how to protect yourself using the SafeHarbor program; Chapter 12 helps you create your own personal About Me page.

✔ **Search:** Takes you to the eBay main Search page. Because close to two million items are up for auction at any given time, finding just one (say, an antique Vermont milk can) is no easy task. The main search page includes five specific searches (see "Exploring Your Home Page Search Options" later in this chapter). You can also search for other members from this link, and get information about their feedback (more on that in Chapter 6). In addition, the subnavigation bar links you to Personal Shopper (eBay's way of helping you find what you're looking for; more about that in Chapter 16).

✔ **Help:** Takes you to the eBay Help Overview page, which offers links to buyer-and-seller guides, personal account information, community standards (rules and regulations and prohibited items) and useful information like a glossary. They even have a search window here for help topics. See Chapter 15 for more details on finding eBay help online.

✔ **Community:** Takes you to a huge page where you find links to eBay News and Chat pages where you can find the latest news and announcements, chat with fellow traders in the eBay community, find charity auctions, read eBay's online newsletter *eBay Life,* and visit the eBay store. Chapters 15 and 16 tell you how to use these resources.

At the top of almost every eBay page, you find three small (but powerful) links that are just as important as the links on the navigation bar:

✔ **Home:** Takes you right back the Home page. Use this link from any other page when you need to get back to the Home page right away.

✔ **My eBay:** Takes you to the link that can access your personal My eBay page where you keep track of all your buying and selling activities, account information, and favorite categories (more about My eBay in Chapter 4).

✔ **Site Map:** Takes you around the eBay world. Every link available on eBay is listed here. If you're ever confused about finding a specific area, come to the Site Map. If a link isn't listed here, it's not on eBay. Yet.

Exploring Your Home Page Search Options

There's an old Chinese expression (that we updated!) that says, "Every journey begins with the first eBay search." Very wise words. You can start a search from the Home page in one of two ways:

✔ Use the Search window. It's right there at the top of the Home page and it's a fast way of finding item listings.

✔ Use the Search button on the navigation bar. This takes you to the main search page where you can do all kinds of specialized searches.

Both options give you the same results. The instructions we offer in the next two sections about using these search methods are just the tip of the eBay iceberg. You can find more in-depth search suggestions in Chapter 5.

Any time you see the words tips or more tips, you know you're about to get some useful information. Just click on the tips link on eBay, and you're off to explore eBay's Search Tips page. The Search Tips page offers distilled wisdom on wording your searches so you get optimum results.

Peering through the Home page Search window

To launch a title search right from the Home page, follow these steps:

1. **Type a description of the item you're looking for in the Search window.**

2. **Click the Search button.**

   The results of your search appear on-screen in a matter of seconds. Figure 3-2 shows you the search window.

You can type just about anything in this box and get some information. Say you're looking for *Star Trek* memorabilia. If so, you're not alone. The television show premiered on September 8, 1966, and even though it was cancelled in 1969 because of low ratings, *Star Trek* has become one of the most successful science fiction franchises in history. If you like *Star Trek* as much as we do, you can use the Search window on the eBay Home page to find all sorts of *Star Trek* stuff.

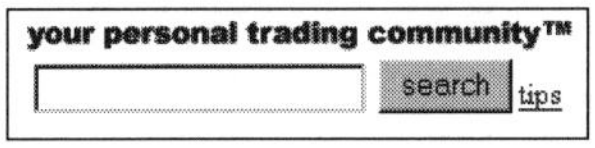

Figure 3-2:
The Search window on the eBay Home page.

The problem is that even if you type in something like **Shatner** (for *Star Trek* series star William Shatner) in the Home page Search box, you may get swamped with tons of auctions that match your search criteria.

When you search for popular items on eBay (and a classic example is *Star Trek* memorabilia), you may get inundated with thousands of auctions that match your search criteria. Even if you're traveling at warp speed, you could spend hours checking each auction individually ("Scotty, we need more power now!") If you're pressed for time like the rest of us, eBay has not-so-mysterious ways to narrow down your search so finding a specific item is much more manageable. Skip ahead to Chapter 5 now if you want to learn some techniques that can help you slim down those searches and beef up those results.

Going where the Search button takes you

One of the most important buttons on the navigation bar is the Search button. When you press this button, you're whisked away to the main search page, which promptly presents you with five different search options. Each option enables you to search for information in a different way. Here's how the five search options on the menu can work for you:

✔ **By Title:** The Title Search option is shown in Figure 3-3. Actually, the title "Title Search" is almost a misnomer, because you don't have to have a formal title, just a subject name. Type in the name of an item (for example, **Superman lunchbox** or **antique pocket watch**), click on Search, and you can see how many are available on eBay.

If this sounds a lot like using the Search window on the Home page, you're right — the two searches return exactly the same results — except this detailed eBay feature gives you more search options.

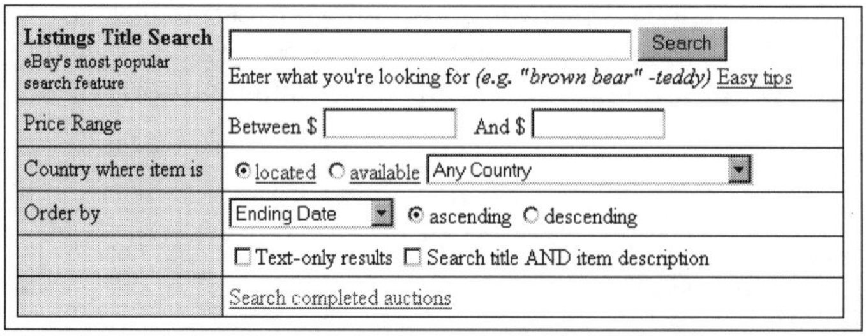

Figure 3-3:
A Title
search on
eBay's
Search
page.

Listings Title Search eBay's most popular search feature	[ ] [Search]
	Enter what you're looking for *(e.g. "brown bear" -teddy)* Easy tips
Price Range	Between $ [ ] And $ [ ]
Country where item is	⊙ located ○ available [Any Country ▼]
Order by	[Ending Date ▼] ⊙ ascending ○ descending
	☐ Text-only results ☐ Search title AND item description
	Search completed auctions

✔ **By Item Number:** Every item that's up for auction on eBay is assigned an item number, which is displayed under the item name on the auction page. The Item Number section of the Search page enables you to search for an item using the item number. All you have to do is type the number, click on Search, and away you go. To find out more about how individual auction pages work on eBay, spin through Chapter 6.

✔ **By Seller:** Every person on eBay has a personal User ID (the name you use to conduct transactions). We explain how you get and use them in Chapter 2. Use a Seller search if you liked the merchandise from a seller's auction and you want to see what else the seller has for sale. Type the seller's User ID or e-mail address, and you get a list of every auction that person is running.

✔ **By Bidder:** For the sake of practicality and convenience, User IDs help eBay keep track of every move a user makes on eBay. If you want to see what a particular user (say, a fellow *Star Trek* fan) is bidding on, use the Bidder search. Type in a User ID in the Bidder search window, and you get a list of everything the user is currently bidding on, as well as how much he or she is bidding. (If that seems a little too public, consider that people at live auctions usually know who's bidding on what, and it works out fine.) We show you how to use the Bidder search option as a strategic buying tool in Chapter 6. Forgetful bidders use this feature, typing in their own User IDs, if they can't remember what they bought and lost all the paperwork.

✔ **Completed Search:** To find an item that sold on eBay in the past, use the Completed Search. Type in the name of an item, and you get a list of items of this type that have been sold in the last 30 days, as well as what they sold for. You can use this type of search to strategize your asking price before you put an item up for auction.

AUCTION ANECDOTE

The "As Seen on TV" popularity game

Over the years, collectibles from classic television shows have spawned a cottage industry of buying, selling, and trading. Today, decades after these shows went into syndication, you can gauge how popular they remain on eBay. Here's our very unscientific TV rating system, based purely on how many items relating to a particular show were available on eBay one day when we were nosing around. (Note: The numbers change daily, so the results you get may vary. Just like gas mileage!)

1.	*I Love Lucy*	353 Items
2.	*M*A*S*H*	220 Items
3.	*Happy Days*	163 Items
4.	*Charlie's Angels*	117 Items
5.	*Man from U.N.C.L.E.*	97 Items
6.	*Beverly Hillbillies*	70 Items
7.	*Get Smart*	58 Items
8.	*I Dream of Jeannie*	33 Items
9.	*Rockford Files*	12 Items
10.	*Night Court*	1 Item

Using the "Fab Four" Home Links

Ladies and gentlemen, we'd like to introduce the "Fab Four." No, not Paul, John, George and Ringo. We're talking about the four links on the eBay Home page, shown in Figure 3-4. A click on one of these links takes you to some of the most important places on eBay. (Of course, if you happen to be looking for Beatles memorabilia, you've come to the right Web site.)

Figure 3-4:
The Fab
Four home
links.

welcoMe
What is eBay?
How do I bid?
How do I sell?
Register, it's free!

✔ **What is eBay?:** This link takes you to the page that gives you a basic overview and links about eBay. There's also a nifty help window where you type in your questions, click on the Search button, and faster than the Amazing Kreskin, eBay comes up with helpful answers for you. This help window is also found on two other Fab Four Home links:

✔ **How do I bid?** This link takes you to a six-point checklist on how to place bids on eBay. There's even a link to take you to the Feedback Forum, which we explain for you in Chapter 4.

✔ **How do I sell?** This link takes you to a four-point selling checklist and includes a quick link to the Sell Your Item form (which you have to fill out to begin your auctions). If you want to jump-start your selling career, go ahead to Chapter 9 and see how to fill out this form.

✔ **Register — It's free!** This link takes you to the New User Registration page. If you haven't been there yet, skip back to Chapter 2 to get the quick and painless facts of easy eBay registration. When you're done, you can start buying and selling stuff in earnest.

There are four other links on the Home page, which give you express service to several key parts of the site:

✔ **Sell Your Item** takes you to the Sell Your Item form.

✔ **Get News and Chat** takes you to the Community Overview page.

✔ **New Users Click Here** takes you to the Help Basics page.

✔ **Register It's Free and Fun** takes you to the eBay Registration form.

Maneuvering through Categories

So how does eBay keep track of the millions of items that are up for auction at any given moment? The brilliant minds at eBay decided to group items into a nice, neat little storage system called *categories*. The Home page lists around a dozen categories at any given time, as shown in Figure 3-5, but currently eBay lists thousands of categories, ranging from Antiques to Writing Instruments. And don't ask how many subcategories (categories within categories) they've got — we can't count that high.

Figure 3-5:
The
Categories
list on the
eBay Home
page.

categories
Antiques (58760)
Books, Movies, Music (340194)
Coins & Stamps (95604)
Collectibles (783303)
Computers (85406)
Dolls, Figures (50566)
Jewelry, Gemstones (100162)
Photo & Electronics (45316)
Pottery & Glass (149440)
Sports Memorabilia (311430)
Toys, Bean Bag Plush (259348)
Miscellaneous (230722)
all categories...

Well, okay, we *could* list all the categories and subcategories currently available on eBay in this book — if you wouldn't mind squinting at a dozen pages of really small, eye-burning text. Besides, a category browse is an adventure that's unique for each individual, and we wouldn't deprive you of it. Suffice to say that if you like to hunt around for that perfect something, you're in browsing heaven now.

Here's how to navigate around the categories:

1. **Click on the category that interests you.**

   If you don't find a category that interests you among the dozen on the Home page, simply click the "all categories" link, and you're off to the Listings page. You get not only a pretty impressive page of main categories, but also a list of featured auctions. If you're ready to get really serious, click on the Category Overview link to see *every* category and subcategory available on eBay — on a page loaded with small type like an eye chart's last lines. We recommend reading it with both eyes open!

   When you look at the categories and subcategories listed on eBay, you see a number in parentheses next to each heading, shown in Figure 3-6. That's the number of items currently up for auction within that category. Happy hunting.

2. **After the category page builds, find a subcategory that interests you and keep digging until you find what you want.**

   For example, if you're looking for items honoring your favorite television show, click on the Collectibles category. The page that comes up includes scores of subcategories plus hundreds of item-specific categories, ranging from women's shoes to Elvis. Scroll down the page until you see the Memorabilia category. Click on it, and it takes you to a page with many links including the Television subcategory. If you click on Television, you're off to the Collectibles:Memorabilia:Television page. There you find Featured Auctions at the top of the page, and all the current TV auctions under them. Little *icons* (pictures) next to the listings tell you more about each item — whether it's pictured (the camera), a hot item (the red chili pepper), a new item (the sunburst), or shows up in eBay's Gallery (the picture frame).

   By the way, we have lots more to say about Featured Auctions and Hot Items in Chapter 9.

3. **When you find an item that interests you, click on the item, and the Full Auction page pops up on your screen.**

   Congratulations — you've just navigated through several million items to find that *one* TV-collectible item that caught your attention! You can instantly return to the Home page by clicking on its link at the top of the page (or return to the Listings page by clicking on the Back button at the top of your browser).

Excuse me, do you have any Don Ho cocktail glasses?

As a matter of fact, we do! eBay adds new categories all the time to meet the needs of its users. For example, some specialized categories have popped up recently — with some interesting items:

- **Ethnographic:** Tribal masks, Kenyan drums, a Tibetan Prayer Wheel, an ebony walking cane, and a hat from Thailand.

- **Firefighting:** A firehose nozzle, an antique leather fireman's helmet (sorry, no antique leather firemen — yet), a West Virginia Fire Department badge, and a German fireman-shaped beer stein.

- **Vanity Items:** An Art Deco nail buffer, a child's hairbrush from the 1950s, a set of vintage hat pins, an antique curling iron, and a lady's compact made by Hudnut.

- **Weird Stuff:** Gag lotto tickets, antique artificial arm, skeleton wedding cake couple, a genuine hummingbird nest, a 1960s lava lamp, and a stuffed chicken collection.

- **Hawaiiana:** A coconut monkey bank, a hula-girl table lamp, a set of Don Ho cocktail glasses (See? They *do* exist!), an antique Hawaiian wedding shirt, and a Diamond Head surfing trivet.

Near the bottom of every subcategory page you can see the line `For more items in this category, click these pages.` The page numbers can fast-forward you through all the items in that subcategory. So if you feel like browsing around page 120 without going through 120 pages individually, just click on number 120, and you are presented with the items on that page (their listings, actually). You can also click on the arrows at the top of the page to go back and forth one page at a time, as shown in Figure 3-6. Happy viewing!

If you're a bargain hunter by habit, you may find some pretty weird stuff while browsing the categories and subcategories of items on eBay — some of it super-cheap, some of it (maybe) just cheap. Remember that (as with any marketplace), you're responsible for finding out as much as possible about an item before you buy — and preferably before you bid. So if you're the type who sometimes can't resist a good deal, ask yourself what you plan to *do* with the pile of garbage you can get for 15 cents — now, before it arrives on your doorstep. Chapter 6 offers more information on bidding with savvy, and remember: A pile of garbage is only a bargain if you're *looking* for a pile of garbage.

Previous   Next

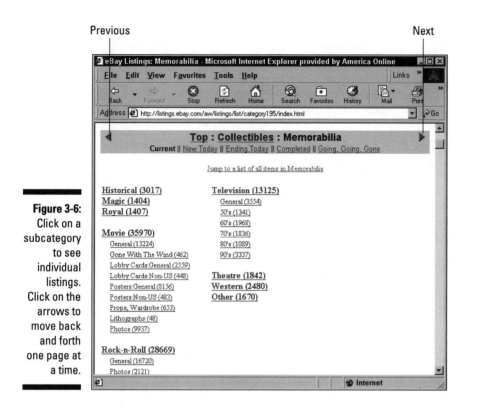

Figure 3-6: Click on a subcategory to see individual listings. Click on the arrows to move back and forth one page at a time.

Using the Featured Auctions Link

Know the old saying, "Money talks, everything else walks?" Here on eBay, money talks pretty loudly. In the center of the Home page, you see a list of the auctions eBay's featuring at the moment. eBay usually posts six featured items at any given time, and rotates items throughout the day; as many sellers as possible get a shot at being in the spotlight. When you click on the Featured Auctions button, you're instantly beamed to eBay's Featured Auction section, as shown in Figure 3-7.

You can find everything from Las Vegas vacations to Model-T Fords to diet products on the Featured Auctions page. Featured auctions are not for mere mortals with small wallets. They've been lifted to the exalted Featured status because sellers shelled out more money to get them noticed. Bidding on these items works the same way as on regular items. All you need to get your auction featured is $99.95, plus a few minutes to fill out a Featured Auction form. See Chapter 9 if you have an item that all eyes must see.

![eBay Listings - Microsoft Internet Explorer provided by America Online](screenshot)

| File | Edit | View | Favorites | Tools | Help | | Links |

Address: http://listings.ebay.com/aw/listings/list/featured/index.html

Current || New Today || Ending Today || Going, Going, Gone

Featured Auctions   You are on page **1** of 17.   Next Page ▸

Current   📁 = Gallery   📷 = Picture   🔥 = Hot!   🔆 = New!

Status	Item	Price	Bids	Ends PDT
📷	RAREST N.YEAR Excl.Mickey+Minnie beaniesCHEAP	$32.99	-	08/07 13:25
	WINDOWS 95 SR2 W/FAT32 & BOOT DISK & FREE PC!	$1.00	-	08/07 13:00
📷	POTTY TRAINING BOOK "PERSONALIZED"	$10.90	-	08/07 12:55
📁 📷	1000 ITEMS That SELL FAST Merch. LIQUIDATION	$320.00	-	08/04 12:54
📷	REAL HAUNTED HOUSE SOUNDTRACK! - THEME PARK!! 🔥	$9.95	-	08/07 12:47
	PHOTO INK JET GLOSSY PAPER on Sale @ $2.49!!! 🔥	$2.49	-	08/07 12:25
📁 📷	NEW -STATE- QUARTER -BOOK- 1999-2003 🔆	$3.75	-	08/07 12:25
📷	1997-98 Michael Jordan Bulls Game Worn Jersey 🔆	$8600.00	-	08/04 12:24

🌐 Internet

Figure 3-7:
The
Featured
Auctions
page.

The Featured Auctions page contains many expensive items, also called *big-ticket* items. (You can reach all big-ticket items from the Browse subnavigation bar.) Sellers who put up high-priced items have been around the block a few times and make it clear that they will verify each bid on the item. That means if you place a bid on that 1997 GMC Suburban with 36,000 miles and no dents, be prepared to get a phone call from the seller. The seller may ask you to prove that you can actually pay for the car — or insist that you go through an escrow service. Nothing personal; it's strictly business.

To find out more about how escrow services work, study up on Chapter 6. The bottom line is that Sally the Seller's item and money are on the line (not to mention her reputation); she can lose out if she doesn't protect herself. If you want an expensive Featured Auction item badly enough, you have to be willing to accept Sally the Seller's terms.

Hanging Out in the Gallery

When you get far enough into a category (for example, Antiques: Musical Instruments), the subnavigation bar offers you the option to either browse all of the items in the subcategory or to "shop with pictures!" Click on the

Gallery Items link (shown in Figure 3-8) to be taken to eBay's version of an auction catalog like the ones at conventional auction houses like Sotheby's. eBay's Gallery features pictures, also called *thumbnails,* of auction items. Scan the thumbnails until you find an item that interests you; click on the thumbnail, and you're taken to that item's auction page.

Figure 3-8:
Click on this
link to go to
the Gallery.

home | my eBay | site map

| Browse | Sell | Services | Search | Help | Community |

| all items | gallery items | ← shop with pictures!

You bid on Gallery items the same way as you would at traditional auctions. The only difference is that eBay charges the seller an extra $.25 to hang up an item in the Gallery. (Jump over to Chapter 9 to find out how to get your item in the door of this exclusive club.)

Finding Out What's Happening, Dude

The eBay community is constantly changing. To help you get into the swing of things right away, eBay provides a special link (shown in Figure 3-9) that takes you right to the current word on the latest eBay changes and special events.

Figure 3-9:
Get the
latest news
on eBay
events by
clicking on
these links.

fun sTuff

"From our homepage to your hometown"
Get up to speed on the eBay Tour!

Join eBay and Kruse for the 29th annual Auburn Fall Collector Car Auction!

cool happenings...

You *can* get there from here — lots of places, in fact:

✔ A rotating list of special-interest links changes at least once a day. (Half the fun is getting a closer look at pages you haven't seen.)

✔ Special money-saving offers from third-party vendors can be a boon if you're on the lookout for a bargain.

✔ eBay charity auctions like Rosie O'Donnell's. Charity auctions are a great way for memorabilia collectors to find one-of-a-kind (and authentic) items. Winning bids contribute to programs that help kids. (Chapter 6 tells you more about what you can bid on — and the good you can do with your checkbook.)

The Home page's list of happenings, fun stuff, and charity auctions *does* change daily — so check back often to keep current.

Bottoming Out

At the very bottom of the page is an unassuming group of links (shown in Figure 3-10) that provide more ways to get to some seriously handy pages.

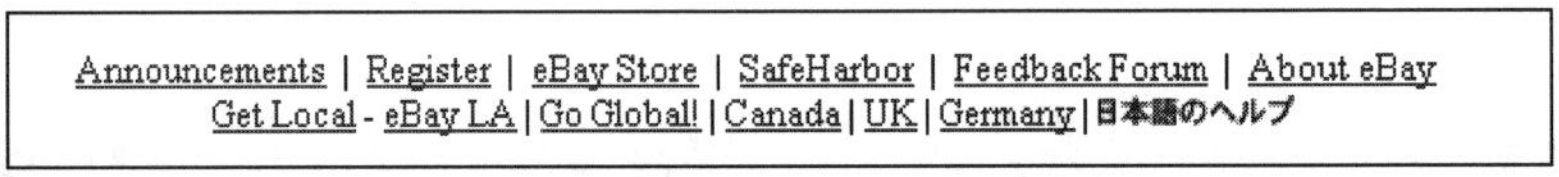

Figure 3-10:
Last but not necessarily least — the bottom links.

Announcements | Register | eBay Store | SafeHarbor | Feedback Forum | About eBay
Get Local - eBay LA | Go Global! | Canada | UK | Germany | 日本語のヘルプ

✔ **About eBay:** Click on this link to find out about eBay the company, get their press releases, company overview and stock information. You can also find out about eBay community activities and charities and even apply for a job at eBay.

✔ **SafeHarbor:** This link takes you to SafeHarbor, where concerns about fraud and safety are addressed. It's such an important eBay tool that we dedicate an entire chapter to the SafeHarbor program. Before buying or selling, it's a good idea to brush up on what's available in Chapter 14.

✔ **eBay Store:** This link enables you to browse and buy eBay merchandise.

✔ **Jobs:** Click here if you want to work *for* eBay instead of *through* eBay.

✔ **Get Local:** Click here if you want to search, buy, and sell in a specific region.

✔ **Go Global:** Click here to get answers to frequently asked questions about selling outside the United States.

✔ **Canada, UK, Germany, or Japan:** Click on one of these, and you jet off to eBay sites in these countries. (Remember: Once you leave eBay U.S.A., you're subject to the contractual and privacy laws of the country you're visiting.)

On other eBay pages, the bottom navigation bar looks a little different — it includes even more links so that you can cruise the site quickly without necessarily having to use the navigation bar.

Chapter 4

My Own Private eBay

*W*e know eBay is a sensitive kind of '90s company because it gives all users plenty of personal space. This space is called the My eBay page, and it's your private listing of all your activities on eBay, sort of a "This is your eBay life." We think it's the greatest organizational tool around and want to talk to somebody about getting one for organizing life outside eBay.

In this chapter we show you how you can use the My eBay page to keep tabs on what you're buying and selling, find out how much money you've spent, and add categories to your own personalized list so you can get to any favorite eBay place with just a click of your mouse. We give you the ins and outs of feedback — what it is, why it can give you that warm, fuzzy feeling, and how to manage it so that all that cyber-positive reinforcement doesn't go to your head.

The My eBay Page

Using your My eBay page makes keeping track of your eBay life a whole lot easier. And getting there is easy enough. To find the My eBay page once you've registered on eBay, follow these steps:

1. **On the top of any eBay page, click on the My eBay link on the upper right.**

   You're magically whisked to the eBay Services My eBay login page.

   Figure 4-1 shows you the eBay Services link that transports you to your My eBay page.

Figure 4-1:
The My eBay services link with the My eBay link highlighted.

home | my eBay | site map

| Browse | Sell | Services | Search | Help | Community |

| overview | registration | buying & selling | my eBay | about me | feedback forum | safe harbor |

You don't have to be on the eBay Home page to find My eBay. As you maneuver around the Web site, the My eBay link follows you like Mona Lisa's eyes.

2. Type in your User ID and Password.

If you forget your eBay User ID, you can type in your e-mail address instead. Your User ID appears in any search results, posts, or pages that come up using your e-mail address.

3. Before you click on the Enter box, look over the list that says Display Options and select the items that you want to appear on your My eBay page.

We discuss display options later in this chapter.

4. Click on the Enter button to accept the Display Options you've chosen.

Don't confuse the My eBay page with the About Me page. The About Me page is a personal home page that you can create to let other eBay members know about you, but you don't have to use it if you don't want to. We tell you all about the About Me page in Chapter 12.

At the bottom of the My eBay Services page dwell some extremely handy links. Although (as a new eBay member) you won't need to do all this stuff right away, you can use 'em to update your critical registration information, change your User ID, password, or e-mail address, and specify how much information you want eBay to e-mail to you.

Choosing Your My eBay Display Options

So what are all these Display Options, anyway? eBay created this feature to help you manage your searches, your account balance, and your participation in auctions. Choosing your options by pointing and clicking is a little like ordering dinner at a Chinese restaurant — choose what you want and pass the soy sauce.

The first time you enter the My eBay Services page, you see that all the Display Options boxes have checks in them. You can customize those options by clearing checks from the boxes (one click per box does it). Watch the options that you don't want disappear — is that power, or what?

If you're having trouble deciding what you want displayed on your My eBay page, Table 4-1 gives you the lowdown on what happens when you point and click on each option.

Table 4-1	Display Options for Your My eBay Page
Select This Option	*To See This on Your My eBay Page*
Favorite Categories	Displays links to your Favorite item listings.
Recent Feedback	Displays the last three Feedback Comments about you.
Account Balance	Displays what you currently owe eBay and links you to locations where you can get info on payments, credits, and refunds.
Selling Items	Lists every auction in which you are currently selling items.
Bidding Items	Lists every auction in which you are currently bidding on items.
Seller/Bidder List Options	Lists the number of days you want an auction listed on your page after it's ended. It can be sorted eight different ways. We suggest sorting by ending time, the default choice.

After you set your options, there's also an area to update your eBay information. A link to click to:

✔ Change your User ID

✔ Change your password

✔ Change your registration information (should you change your address or phone number)

✔ Report a change of e-mail address

✔ Change your "notification parameters" (what e-mails and/or notifications you wish eBay to send to your mailbox)

When you finally get to your My eBay page, save yourself a lot of work — use your browser to bookmark your My eBay page as a favorite. It'll save you a lot of keystrokes later on. Some folks even make their My eBay pages their browser home pages, so they can see it the minute they log in! That's dedication.

My Account

When you first explore your My eBay page, you'll see that your eBay account has "not been activated." The eBay folks only charge you a fee when you list something to sell; they collect again after it's sold. It doesn't cost you a nickel in fees to look around or sign up — or even buy. We have more on how eBay charges you for its services in Chapter 8.

When you first sign up on eBay (see Chapter 2), eBay gives you a $10 line of credit for your first month. You can start buying and selling all you want, but if you go over $10 in eBay fees, your credit line is cut off until you sign up for a payment plan. You do that from your My eBay page. Figure 4-2 shows you what the My Account section of the My eBay page is all about.

The My Account section of your My eBay page gives you six links for dealing with money.

Figure 4-2:
The My
Account
section of
the My eBay
page.

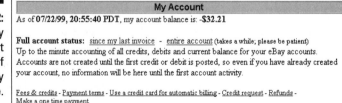

From the My Account section of the My eBay page you can look up every detail of your account history, as well as make changes to your personal preferences (such as how and when you want to pay fees). If you think eBay owes you money, you can do a refund request from here as well. Before you jump into the money game, you might want to review the links eBay gives you to manage your money and what they do:

   ✔ **Fees and Credits.** Click here to get a complete explanation of the eBay fee structure.

   ✔ **Payment Terms.** Click here to get a complete explanation on how eBay collects its fees.

✔ **Use a Credit Card for Automatic Billing.** If you want to use VISA or MasterCard to pay your monthly eBay fees, click here and fill in the information. You can also change billing information here at any time. Every month eBay charges your credit card for fees you've incurred the previous month. You can see these charges on your credit card statement as well as on your eBay account.

When you give eBay your credit card information, it takes about 24 hours for them to verify it.

✔ **Credit Requests.** If you sell an item and the buyer backs out (usually this is even rarer than a blue moon), you can at least get a refund on some of the fees that eBay charges you as a seller. These are the Final Value Fees; they're based on the selling price of the item. This place on the form is where to let eBay know what they owe you. Just click on the Final Value Fee Credit Request Form link, type in your User ID and Password, click on the Submit button, and fill out the online form.

Before you can collect a Final Value Fee refund, the following conditions must apply:

- After your auction, you have to allow bidders at least seven business days to contact you.

- You can apply for the refund for up to 60 days after the auction has ended.

- The auction must have received at least one winning bid. If you held a reserve auction, at least one bid must have met or exceeded the reserve price. For more on setting up a reserve auction, see Chapter 9.

✔ **Refunds.** If you have prepaid your account and have money in it that you're not planning to use, you can get it back by clicking on the refund link. You need to print out the form on the page, fill it out, and then either fax it or send it by mail to eBay.

✔ **Make a One-Time Payment.** If you're antsy about giving out your credit card information, or don't have a credit card, you can send eBay the information by mail. To do so, you need an eBay Payment coupon, which you can get by typing in your User ID and Password, clicking on either the Check or Money Order or Credit Card payment buttons, printing out the coupon page, and following the directions. Just that easy, just that simple.

We recommend that if you make one-time payments, you make sure that you've sent eBay enough money to cover your anticipated sales. Most sellers who pay by mail send their payments about two weeks before they think their money will be needed.

The downside of paying eBay fees by check or money order is that you are charged if you bounce a check, miss a payment, or use Canadian dollars instead of U.S. dollars. You're supposed to get an e-mail invoice at the end of the month, but even if you don't, eBay expects to be paid on time. A word to the wise: Keep close tabs on your account status if you choose to pay this way.

No matter what payment option you choose, you can check your account status at any time. Your account status lists all of your transactions with eBay over the last two months. If you want a more detailed account, you can click on the Entire Account link on your My eBay page and see a record of every transaction you've ever done.

When you choose to see your Entire Account, eBay may take a little while to put all of your transactions on your screen. How long depends on the number of auctions you've run on eBay. Don't be alarmed. eBay's just sifting through the endless list of completed auctions that have been run on the site. Just another example of why people say the *www* in Internet addresses really stands for "World-Wide Wait!"

We check our account status about once a month just to double-check that all the numbers add up. We recommend that you check your account status often, especially if you plan to do a lot of selling on eBay.

My Favorites

Part of the fun of eBay is actually searching around for stuff that you'd never in a million years think of looking for. (Can you say "invigorating magnetic shoe insoles"? A guy was actually auctioning off 500 of them!)

Wacky stuff aside, most eBay users spend their time hunting for specific items — say, Barbies, Elvis memorabilia, or U.S. stamps. That's why eBay came up with the My Favorites area of your My eBay page.

Whenever you view your My eBay page, you see a list of four of your favorite categories. Because eBay isn't psychic, you have to tell it what you want listed.

You can only choose four categories to be your favorites, and with almost 2,000 categories to choose from, make your choices count. If you're having a hard time narrowing down your category picks, don't worry, your choices aren't set in stone. You can change your favorites list whenever you want. Chapter 3 offers details on eBay categories.

To choose your favorite categories and list them on your My eBay page, follow these steps:

1. **Go to My Favorites and click on the "here" link.**

   The link takes you to the User Preferences page.

2. **Scroll down the User Preference page to the Favorite Category 1 heading.**

   You see four separate windows each containing category listings. These windows contain all of eBay's categories and subcategories and sub-subcategories and sub-sub-subcategories. A rub-a-dub-dub, tons of categories in the subs!

3. In the far left column, click the category you want.

Click the category you want in the left-hand column. Automatically, the column to the right changes to reflect more choices based on what main category you selected. Be sure to highlight the categories and subcategories you want, as shown in Figure 4-3.

Figure 4-3:
Changing
your
Favorite
Categories
in the User
Preference
section of
the My eBay
page.

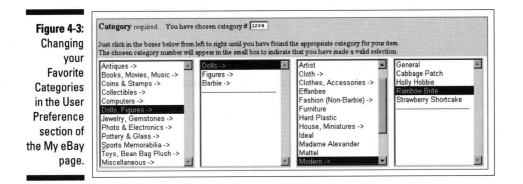

4. Continue across from left to right.

Depending on your choices, you might have to scroll through each window to find the subcategory you are looking for. Once you've completed your choice, a number will appear in the window at the top. That's your category number.

5. Repeat this process for Favorites Categories 2 through 4.

If you don't want to use all four choices, just delete any numbers in the chosen category window.

6. Click on the Submit button at the bottom of the page.

Your favorite categories will appear on your My eBay page within five minutes of your submission.

How specific you get in choosing your favorites depends on how many items you want to see. The more you narrow down your focus, the fewer items you'll have to wade through. The more general your favorite, the broader range of items for you to view. Since we know specifically what we are looking for, we narrow down our favorites choice. And like hem-lengths, you can change your favorites as often as you like.

My Favorites time frame

Just below your favorites, as shown in Figure 4-4, are five options for screening your favorites. Which link you choose to view auctions depends on what kind of information you're looking for. Whether you're doing some preliminary searching on a category or monitoring the last few days (or minutes) of an auction, there's a link that sorts auctions and meets your needs best.

Here's a list of the sorting options and when to use them.

- ✔ **Current:** Shows you every item currently being auctioned in the category, with the newest items shown first. If you want to look at all of the current auctions for a category, you end up with a gazillion pages of items awaiting sale in a particular category for the next week. If you want to sort though it all, go ahead, you may find something you like.

- ✔ **New Today:** Shows you every item that was put up for auction today. The little "new" icon (picture) next to the item tells you the item was listed today.

- ✔ **Ending Today:** Shows you every auction that is closing today. The ending time is printed in red.

If you're pressed for time, we suggest you use a category link, such as New Today or Ending Today. These links automatically narrow down the number of listed auctions to a manageable number. For more information on narrowing down searches on eBay, see Chapter 5.

- ✔ **Completed:** Shows you every auction that ended in the last two days. If you had your eye on an item that was for sale last week but you didn't want to buy it then, you can check in to see how the auction went by clicking on the Completed link. The Completed link gives you a good idea of how the market is going for an item, which helps you plan your own buying.

- ✔ **Going, Going, Gone:** Shows you every auction that's ending in the next five hours, all the way down to the last few seconds. A great way to find items you can bid on down to the wire.

When you view auctions from the Going, Going, Gone link, remember that eBay only updates this page every hour or so, so be sure to read the "auction ends" time. (Use our eBay time conversion chart to decipher your time difference.) Due to this same hourly update, sometimes the going-going-gone items actually *are* gone — the auction has ended.

Figure 4-4:
The My
Favorites
categories
display
option on the
My eBay
page, showing a few of
our favorite
places.

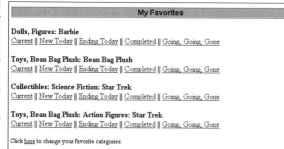

Houston, we don't have a problem

Here's an item we wish we'd sold.

Neil Armstrong signed NASA portrait w/COA (Certificate of Authenticity). A very clean 8x10 color NASA portrait signed and inscribed by Neil Armstrong, the first human on the Moon. In recent years Armstrong has been very reclusive and difficult to obtain in any form. There are many forgeries being offered, so buyer beware.

Many believe (including me) that Neil Armstrong's autograph will be among the most important of the twentieth century. Just think of it. He was the first human to step onto another celestial body. This feat may never happen again and certainly not in our lifetimes. Comes with a lifetime COA. The starting price was $10, and this portrait sold on eBay for $520!

Got the time? eBay does. Click on the Check eBay official time (you can find it on any subcategory page). The eBay clock is so accurate that you can set your watch to it! And you may want to, especially if you plan to get a last-second bid in before an auction closes. After all, eBay's official time is, um, *official*.

All Sorts of Sorting: Keeping Track of Your Auction Items

If you want to keep tabs on the items you're selling and bidding on (and why wouldn't you?), start thinking about how to sort them *before* you start looking for the first item you want to bid on. That's also pretty good advice for planning your own first auction.

Sorting auction items using My eBay

Sometimes it seems that eBay gives you too many options. There are eight — count 'em, eight — ways to sort items you're selling and bidding on from the My eBay page. That gives you a lot of options to think about, dwell on, and ponder. Each sorting method does pretty much the same thing, so pick the one that catches your eye and don't lose any sleep over your choice. After all, life's too short — and here you can change anything with a click of your mouse (wish the rest of life were like that). Table 4-2 goes into more detail about sorting methods.

Table 4-2	Sorting Methods and What They Do
Sort by	**Does This**
Item	Lists items alphabetically by what they're called.
Start $	Lists items by their opening prices.
Current $	Lists items by current highest bid. This listing changes often.
Reserve $	Lists items by the secret reserve price you set when you started the auction (only for items you're selling). See more on reserve auctions in Chapter 9.
Quant	Lists items according to how many are available. For example, if you're bidding on an item in a Dutch auction, anywhere from 2 to 100 of exactly the same items may be auctioned at the same time. (See Chapter 6 and 9 to see how Dutch auctions work.)
Bids	Lists items by the number of bids they've received.
Start	Lists items based on when the auction began.
End PDT	Lists items based on when the auction finishes. This is one that eBay automatically chooses for you if you don't select one on your own. This is the way most people view their lists.

All auctions on eBay are based on Pacific Daylight or Standard Time, depending on the time of year. This is true whether you live in sunny California, or Vitamin-C-rich Florida, or anywhere else in the world.

One thing you must decide is how long you want eBay to keep information about the items you're buying and selling on your My eBay page. You can keep information for as long as 30 days. Click on My eBay at the top of the page to get to the My eBay services page. Just type in the number of days you want to hang on to information into the box under Seller/Bidder List Options heading, as shown in Figure 4-5.

How long you keep buying and selling information on your My eBay page depends on, well, how much you buy and sell. If you're selling 200 items a month, your page will be loaded, and you'll have to do a lot of looking to find what you want. You may want to shorten the list by limiting the number of days (once an auction is over and you did the transaction, you really don't need to keep it around). If you're buying or selling just a few items, going the full 30 days won't overwhelm your My eBay page.

Figure 4-5:
The Seller/
Bidder List
Options.

Seller/Bidder List Options:
Days worth of ended auctions you want shown: 2 (max 30)

Staying organized on your own

Yeah, we're going to bug you about printing stuff out — not because we're in cahoots with the paper industry, but because we care! The best way to protect yourself is to keep good records on your own. Don't depend on eBay to cover you — not that they *don't* care — but this is your money, so keep a close eye on it!

Now don't become a pack rat and overdo it, but here's a list of important documents we think you should print and file whether you're a buyer or a seller:

- ✔ Auction pages as they appear when they close
- ✔ Bank statements indicating any payment you receive that doesn't clear
- ✔ Insurance or escrow forms
- ✔ Refund and credit requests
- ✔ Receipts from purchases you make for items to sell on eBay

Always, always, *always* save any and every e-mail message you receive about a transaction, whether you buy or sell. Also save your *EOAs* (End of Auction) e-mails that eBay sends. For more information about EOAs and correspondence etiquette after the auction's over, see Chapters 7 and 10.

Why should you save all this stuff? Here are some reasons:

- ✔ Even if you're buying and selling just a couple of items a month on eBay, you need to keep track of who you owe and who owes you money.
- ✔ Good e-mail correspondence is a learned art — but if you reference item numbers, your e-mail is an instant record. If you put your dates in writing — and follow up — you've got yourself a nice, neat paper trail.
- ✔ Documenting the transaction through e-mail will come in handy if you ever end up in a dispute over the terms of the sale.
- ✔ If you sell specialized items, you can keep track of trends and who your frequent buyers are.
- ✔ Someday the IRS might come knocking on your door, especially if you buy stuff for the purpose of selling it on eBay. Scary, but true. For more tax information, take a look at Chapter 8.

Keeping up the easy way

The way we keep our auctions organized is with a spreadsheet. You can set up a spreadsheet to keep track of who paid, who didn't, your expenses, and your profits. In Chapter 19, we write about some software that can help you stay organized.

When it comes to e-mail and documents about transactions, we say that after you've received your feedback (positive, of course), you can dump it. If you get negative feedback (how could you?), hang on to your paperwork for a little longer. You won't get much negative feedback because we know you're a polite and respectable person — so you have room at the bottom of a drawer for a few papers, don't you? You can find out more about feedback later in this chapter. Use your discretion, but generally you can toss the paperwork from a bad transaction after it's reached some sort of resolution.

Once a month, we do a seller search on ourselves and print out our latest eBay history. You can also check on eBay selling history by using My eBay and printing out items on selling item details by using the Details link. Chapter 5 tells you more about doing seller searches, organizing your searches, and starting files on items you want to track.

My Feedback

You know how they say you are what you eat? On eBay, you are what your feedback says you are. Your feedback is made up of comments — good, bad, or neutral — that people leave about you (and you leave about others). In effect, they're commenting on your overall professionalism (even if you're an eBay hobbyist with no thought of using it professionally, a little businesslike courtesy can ease your transactions with everyone). These comments are the basis for your eBay reputation.

When you get your first feedback, the number that appears next to your User ID is your feedback rating, which follows you everywhere you go in eBay, even if you change your User ID. It's stuck to you like glue. The thinking behind the feedback concept is that you wouldn't be caught dead in a store that has a lousy reputation. So why on earth would you want to do business on the Internet with someone who has a lousy reputation?

Nice shades!

For the first 30 days after you change your User ID (which you can do anytime, as Chapter 2 shows) — eBay sticks you with a pair of sunglasses that stays next to your User ID every time it appears on eBay (as when you bid, run an auction, or post a message on any of the chat boards).

So why the sunglasses? eBay calls them "Shades." They're sort of a friendly heads-up to others that you're a new user or have changed your User ID. You still have all the privileges that everybody else has on eBay while you're breaking in your new identity. Remember: The shades are nothing personal, just business as usual.

You're not required to leave feedback, but because it's the benchmark by which all eBay users are judged, we think you should leave feedback comments every time you complete a transaction.

Every time you get a positive comment from a user who hasn't commented before, you get a point. Every time you get a negative rating, you lose a point. Neutral comments rate a zero. eBay even has what it calls the Star Chart, as shown in Figure 4-6, which rewards those with good-and-getting-higher feedback ratings.

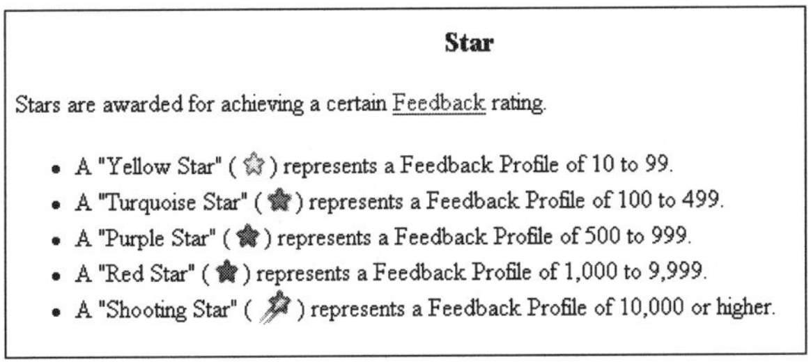

Figure 4-6: Ready for your close-up? Become a star with the eBay Star Chart.

Star

Stars are awarded for achieving a certain <u>Feedback</u> rating.

- A "Yellow Star" (☆) represents a Feedback Profile of 10 to 99.
- A "Turquoise Star" (★) represents a Feedback Profile of 100 to 499.
- A "Purple Star" (★) represents a Feedback Profile of 500 to 999.
- A "Red Star" (★) represents a Feedback Profile of 1,000 to 9,999.
- A "Shooting Star" (🌠) represents a Feedback Profile of 10,000 or higher.

The flip side (or "dark side" to you fans of *Star Wars*) of the star system is negative numbers. If you get nailed with negative feedback comments, your star is swiped by eBay, and you're condemned to hang out with Darth Vader and his gang.

eBay riddle: When is more than one still one? Gotcha, huh? The answer is, when you get more than one feedback message from the same person. Confused? This should help: You can sell one person a hundred different items, but only the first feedback that person leaves for you counts toward your rating. In this case, the other 99 Feedback Comments appear in your Feedback Profile, but your rating only increases by one (or decreases by one if it's a negative comment). eBay does this to keep the rating system honest. (One gush per member, no matter how terrific you are.)

Anyone with a -4 rating has his or her eBay membership terminated. Remember, just because a user may have a 750 feedback rating, it doesn't hurt to click the number after the name to double-check the person's eBay ID card. Even if someone has a total of 1,000 feedback messages, 250 of them *could* be negative. Our experience suggests that if you're dealing with anyone whose name shows a rating of less than zero, you may expect to *get* just that (*caveat emptor* big-time).

You can get to your personal Feedback Profile page right from your My eBay page by clicking on the link that invites you to *See all feedback about me in the Feedback section.*

Feedback comes in three exciting flavors, positive, negative, and neutral:

✔ **Positive feedback.** Someone once said, "All you have is your reputation." Reputation is what makes eBay function. If the transaction works well, you get positive feedback; whenever it's warranted, you should give it right back. To observe some typical positive feedback in its natural habitat, see Figure 4-7.

Figure 4-7:
Positive
feedback
message.

User: ⬜⬜⬜ ⭐ Date: 07/28/99, 10:02:04 PDT	Item: 129033398
Praise: Friendly emails, swift payment, excellent addition to the eBay community! A++	

✔ **Negative feedback.** If there's a glitch (for instance, it takes six months to get your Charlie's Angels lunchbox, or the seller substituted a rusty Thermos for the one you bid on, or you never got the item), you have the right — some would say *obligation* — to leave negative feedback, as shown in Figure 4-8.

Figure 4-8:
Negative
feedback.

User: ⬜⬜⬜ ⭐ Date: 01/27/98, 11:18:16 PST
Complaint: Won $1900 worth before Xmas, asked me to send ALL COD... never accepted package!

✔ **Neutral feedback.** Neutral feedback can be left if you feel "so-so" about a specific transaction. It's the middle-of-the-road comment. Say you bought an item that had a little more wear and tear on it than the seller indicated, but you still like it and want to keep it. You can post a neutral comment, as shown in Figure 4-9.

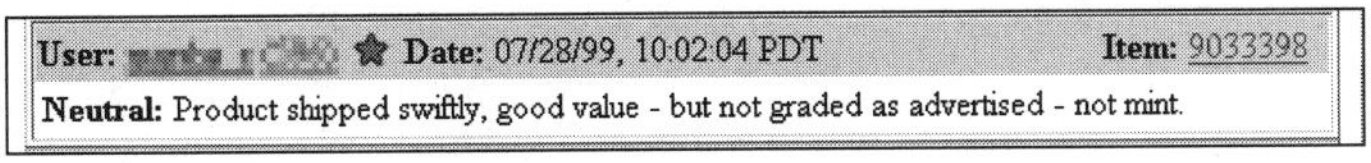

Figure 4-9:
Neutral
feedback.

User: ▓▓▓▓ ▓▓▓▓ ★ Date: 07/28/99, 10:02:04 PDT   Item: 9033398
Neutral: Product shipped swiftly, good value - but not graded as advertised - not mint.

How to get positive feedback

If you're selling, here's how to get a good rep:

✔ Establish contact with the buyer (pronto!) after the auction ends. (See Chapter 10.)

✔ After you've received payment, send out the item quickly. (See Chapter 10.)

✔ Make sure your item is exactly the way you described it. (See Chapter 9.)

✔ Package the item well and ship it with care. (See Chapter 10.)

✔ React quickly and appropriately to problems — say, the item's lost or damaged in the mail, or the seller's slow in paying. (See Chapter 10.)

If you're buying, try these good-rep tips:

✔ Send your payment out fast. (See Chapter 7.)

✔ Keep in touch with the seller with e-mails. (See Chapter 7.)

✔ Work with the seller to resolve any problems in a courteous manner. (See Chapters 7 and 10.)

How to get negative feedback

If you're selling, here's what to do to tarnish your name big-time:

✔ Tell a major fib in the item description. (Defend truth, justice, and legitimate creative writing. See Chapter 9.)

✔ Take the money but "forget" to ship the item. (Who did you say you are? See Chapter 15.)

✔ Package the item poorly so that it ends up smashed, squashed, or vaporized during shipping. (To avoid this pathetic fate, see Chapter 10.)

If you're buying, here's how to make your rep a serious mess:

- ✔ Bid on an item, win the auction, and never respond to the seller. (Remember your manners and see Chapter 6.)

- ✔ Send a personal check that bounces and never make good on the payment. (See Chapter 15 and don't pass "Go.")

- ✔ Ask the seller for a refund because you just don't like the item. (Remember how to play fair and see Chapter 7.)

The Feedback Profile page

At the bottom of the feedback section is a link, see all feedback about me. Click it, and you end up at the Feedback Profile page. Think of the Feedback Profile page as your eBay report card. Your goal is to get straight *As* — in this case, all positive feedback. As you accumulate feedback, you get a numerical rating similar to a grade-point average. (Unlike a real report card, you don't have to bring it home to be signed!) We explain how the number system works in the "Ratings Game" section later in this chapter.

Here's what's on the Feedback Profile page:

- ✔ **Your User ID.** Your eBay nickname appears, followed by a number in parentheses — the total of the Feedback Comments you have received.

- ✔ **Your Overall Profile Makeup.** This area sums up the positive, negative, and neutral Feedback Comments people have left for you.

- ✔ **Summary of Most Recent Comments.** This box is a scorecard of your Feedback for the last six months.

- ✔ **Feedback Links.** These links take you to other feedback-related areas.

  - • **Leave Feedback** is where you leave feedback for others.

  - • **Feedback Forum** is where you can get any of your feedback questions answered.

  - • **Respond to Comments** allows you to comment about feedback others have left about you.

Figure 4-10 shows the Feedback Profile page.

eBay View User Feedback for newforcecc - Microsoft Internet Explorer provided by Ame... ▢▢✕

File   Edit   View   Favorites   Tools   Help   Links »

⇦   ⇨   ⊗   ▣   ⌂   @   *   🕰   ▤▾   🖨
Back   Forward Stop   Refresh Home   Search   Favorites History   Mail   Print

Address http://cgi2.ebay.com/aw-cgi/eBayISAPI.dll?ViewFeedback&userid=newforcecc   ▾ ⟜Go

Overall profile makeup

696 positives. **631** are from unique
users and count toward the final
rating.

4 neutrals. **4** are from users no
longer registered.

0 negatives. **0** are from unique
users and count toward the final
rating.

e**b**Y **ID card**   newforcecc (631)
                                 ☆

Summary of Most Recent Comments

	Past 7 days	Past month	Past 6 mo.
Positive	21	109	456
Neutral	0	0	1
Negative	0	0	0
Total	**21**	**109**	**457**

Auctions by newforcecc

Note: There are 4 comments that were converted to neutral because the commenting users are no longer registered.

You can leave feedback for this user. Visit the Feedback Forum for more info on feedback profiles.

If you are newforcecc (631) ☆, you can respond to comments in this Feedback Profile.

Items 1-25 of 700 total

🌐 Internet

Figure 4-10:
The
Feedback
Profile page,
your eBay
report card.

Reading your feedback

Your eBay reputation is at the mercy of the one-liners the buyers and sellers
leave for you in the form of Feedback Comments. Each box contains the User
ID of the person who left you feedback, the date and time feedback was left,
and whether the feedback was praise (in green), negative (in red) or neutral
(black).

Your My eBay page lists the most recent three Feedback Comments you
received. To see all of them, you have to go to your Feedback Profile page.

The Feedback box contains these reputation-building (or -trashing) ingredients:

- ✔ The User ID of the person who sent it. The number in parentheses next
  to the person's name is the number of Feedback Comments he or she
  has received.
- ✔ The date and time the feedback was posted.
- ✔ The item number of the transaction that the feedback refers to.
- ✔ The feedback the person has left about you.

Anyone can leave non-transaction feedback for anyone else on eBay. Because non-transaction feedback doesn't refer to a specific auction, it won't have an item number associated with it. eBay does not permit negative comments on non-transaction feedback. Only positive or neutral comments are accepted. The system is set up so you can only leave negative feedback with an item number. When checking another user's feedback, make sure the majority of positive feedback is transaction-related, and look at Chapters 6 and 15 for more info.

A positive or negative comment can also change to a neutral comment in your Feedback Profile if the person who left the post decides to quit or is suspended by eBay. Don't be surprised if you see this happen to you as well; it happens to everybody and in no way reflects upon you. (In response to a flood of complaints, however, the eBay powers-that-be are rethinking their policy. Stay tuned!)

Leaving feedback with finesse

Believe it or not, writing feedback well takes some practice — it isn't a matter of saying things, it's a matter of saying *only the appropriate things*. Think carefully about what you want to say because once you submit feedback, it stays with the person for the duration of his or her eBay career. It cain't be erased nohow, no siree!

You can leave feedback for any eBay member, for any reason, even if you haven't had a transaction with that member. Although we think you should always leave feedback, especially at the end of a transaction, it isn't mandatory. Think of leaving feedback as voting in an election — if you don't leave feedback, you can't complain about lousy service.

Extra, extra, read all about it

Normally, we say, keep your business private. But not when it comes to feedback. The default setting is for public viewing of your feedback. This way everyone on eBay can read all about you.

If you want to make your feedback a private matter, you need to go to the Feedback Forum and click on the link Make Feedback Changes Public or Private and reset to Private.

We think hiding your feedback is a bad idea. You want people to know that you're trustworthy;

being honest and up-front is the way to go. If you hide your feedback profile, people may suspect that you're covering up bad things. It's in your best interest to let the spotlight shine on your feedback history.

It's your rep, your money, and your experience as an eBay member. It's wise to keep in mind that all three are always linked.

eBay says to make feedback "factual and emotionless." You won't go wrong if you comment on the details (either good or bad) of the transaction. The last thing you want is to appear in any way biased, because then your credibility can come into question. If you have any questions about what eBay says about feedback, click on the Services link at the top of every eBay page, then click on the Feedback Forum on the subnavigation bar that automatically appears (or go to the User Agreement by clicking on the link at the bottom of every eBay page).

In the real world (at least in the modern American version of it), anybody can sue anybody else for slander or libel at any time; this holds true on the Internet, too. It's a good idea to be careful not to make any comments that could be libelous or slanderous. eBay is not responsible for your actions, so if you are sued because of negative feedback (or anything else you've written), you're on your own. The best way to keep yourself safe is to stick to the facts and don't get personal.

If you're angry, take a breather *before* you type out your complaints and click on the Leave Comment button. If you're convinced that negative feedback is necessary, try a "cooling-off" period before you send comments. Wait an hour or a day; see whether you feel the same. Nasty feedback based on pure emotion can make you look vindictive (even if what you're saying is perfectly true). And speaking of safety features you should know about feedback, you might want to study up on these:

✔ Remember that feedback, whether good or bad, is (above all) *sticky*. eBay won't remove your feedback comment if you change your mind later. Be sure of your facts and consider carefully what you want to say.

✔ Before you leave feedback, see what other people had to say about that person. Click on the link See the Feedback profile of an eBay user in the Profile Forum. See whether what you're thinking is in line with the comments others have left.

To get to an eBay user's Feedback Profile page quickly, click on the number in parentheses beside the eBay user's name. This number is a link that takes you immediately to the place where you can review previous feedback about the user (and leave your own).

✔ If you want to relate feedback to a transaction, you must leave your feedback comment within 60 days of the end of the auction. After 60 days have passed, any comments are treated as non-transactional.

✔ Your comment must be a maximum of 80 letters long, which is really short when you have a lot to say. Before you start typing, organize your thoughts and use common abbreviations to save precious space.

✔ Before posting negative feedback, try to resolve the problem by e-mail or telephone. You may discover that your reaction to the transaction is based on a misunderstanding that can be easily resolved. Maybe your item arrived late because of a massive snowstorm, or because the seller went on vacation and you forgot that he or she told you about it.

✔ eBay users generally want to make each other happy — so use negative feedback *only as a last resort*. See Chapters 7 and 9 for more details on how to avoid negative feedback.

If you do leave a negative comment that you later regret, you can't remove it. You *can* go back and leave an explanation or a more positive comment, but think twice before you blast.

Here's how to leave Feedback Comments:

1. **If you're on the user's Feedback Profile page, click on The Leave Feedback link** (refer to Figure 4-10).

   The Leave Feedback page is shown in Figure 4-11.

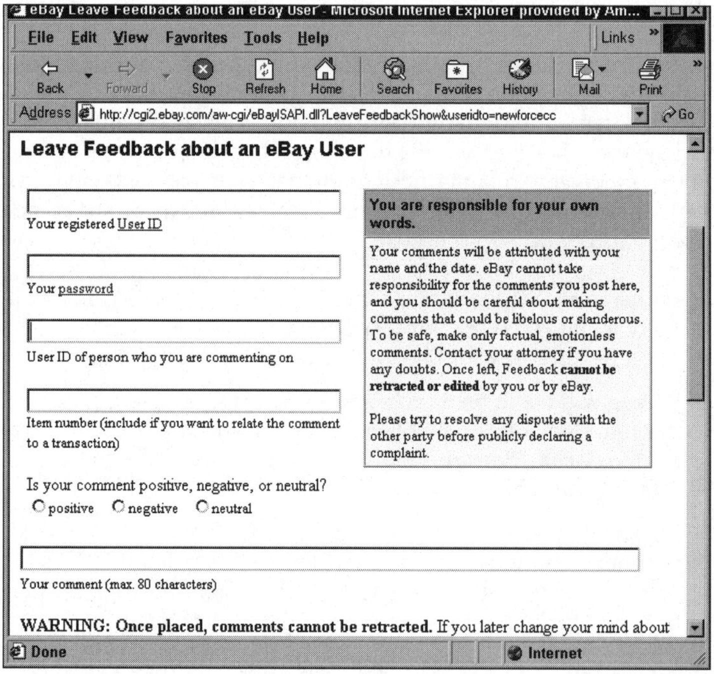

Figure 4-11:
The Leave
Feedback
page.

You can also leave feedback from the Feedback Forum page or on the Items page of a completed auction. Get to the Feedback Forum from the main navigation bar by clicking on Services and then clicking on Feedback Forum on the subnavigation bar. Click on the link that invites you to Leave Feedback about an eBay User.

Mincing words: The at-a-glance guide to keeping it short

eBay likes to keep things simple. If you want to compliment, complain, or take the middle road, you have to do it in 80 characters or less. That means your comment needs to be short and sweet (or short and sour if it's negative, or sweet and sour if you're mixing drinks or ordering Chinese food). If you have a lot to say but you're stumped about how to say it, we offer you a few examples for any occasion. String them together or mix and match!

Positive feedback:

- Very professional
- Quick e-mail response
- Fast service
- A+++
- Exactly as described
- Wonderful merchandise
- Smooth transaction
- Would deal with again
- An asset to eBay
- Highly recommended

Negative feedback:

- Never responded
- Deadbeat
- Steer clear!
- BAD!
- Beware track record
- Do not do business here
- Not as described
- Watch out — you won't get paid

Neutral feedback:

- Slow to respond but item as described
- Item not as described, but seller made good
- Paid w/MO (money order) after check bounced
- Lousy communication, but item came OK

2. **Enter the required information.**

   Always include the item number if your feedback relates to an auction. (You can also leave feedback at the Item page of a completed auction.)

3. **Choose whether you want your feedback to be positive, negative, or neutral.**

To see what your last feedback was for someone else, start at the Feedback Forum and click on Review feedback you have left about others. Type your User ID and password in the boxes, click on the View Feedback button, read what you've said about others, and either agree or blush.

The bed hasn't left the building!

Not all unusual items rock. One seller offered a five-piece bedroom set from Elvis Presley's Los Angeles home — complete with a king-size bed, night stands, dresser, chest of drawers, available authentication — and a starting price of $15,000. Nobody bid; the set didn't sell.

You have the last word — use it!

After reading feedback you received from others, you may feel compelled to respond. If the feedback is negative, you may want to defend yourself. If it's positive, you may want to say *Thank you*.

To respond to feedback:

1. **In the feedback section of your My eBay page, click on the Review and respond to feedback about me link.**

   You are transported to the Review and respond to feedback left for you page, shown in Figure 4-12.

2. **When you find the feedback you want to respond to, click on the small icon of an envelope with an arrow.**

   Figure 4-7 shows a positive feedback comment and the location of the icon you use to respond to it.

3. **Type your password into the appropriate box.**

   Always keep your password a secret. If you suspect somebody may know your password, change it before that person has a chance to sign in as you and ruin your reputation. (For more on selecting and protecting your level of privacy, see Chapters 1 and 13.)

4. **Type in your response.**

   Keep your response brief and to the point. If you're sorry, say so. If everything worked out fine in the end, make nice and leave a positive comment.

Feedback scams

As in the real world, there are people who won't play fair. At eBay, the feedback system is sacred. Because it's such a critical part of the integrity of the eBay community, the folks at eBay don't want anyone messing with the system. They know all the scams, and if you try them, you'll be "going, going, gone" faster than you can imagine. Here are the feedback scams they look for.

Some folks with bad reputations will try to hide by using another User ID or a different e-mail address to post positive feedback. That's a huge eBay sin. Then there's feedback "bombing."

That's when someone leaves negative feedback through a second account or another person unrelated to the transaction. As you might imagine, the eBay community takes an amazingly dim view of such nasty hi-jinks.

Feedback "extortion" is another no-no. That's leaving negative feedback based on a transaction *outside* eBay (such as an ex-spouse taking the favorite cat). Those who try this ugly stuff are shown the eBay equivalent of the ejection seat.

For further advice on eBay safety, check the SafeHarbor guidelines in Chapter 14.

Figure 4-12:
Respond to feedback left for you by clicking on the small envelope icon.

Part II

Are You Buying What They're Selling?

The 5th Wave   By Rich Tennant

"My gosh, Barbara, if you don't think it's worth going a couple of weeks without dinner so we can afford to bid on that small Mediterranean island we saw on eBay, just say so!"

In this part . . .

*O*nce you have an idea how to get around the eBay
site, you probably want to get started. You've come
to the right place. Here you find all the information you
need to start bidding on (and winning) auctions.

While eBay is a lot more fun than school, you still have to
do your homework. After you've registered to become an
eBay member (in Part I), you can place a bid on any item
you see. But first you have to find it . . . and then maybe
find out what it's worth. And what happens when you do
win? In this part, we show you how to find the items you
want without sifting through every single one of eBay's
millions of auctions. We also give you an insider's look at
determining the value of a collectible, determining how
much you're willing to spend, and using the right strategy
to win the item at just the right price. When the auction's
over, you can follow our advice to make things go smooth
as silk. Watch the positive feedback come pouring in!

Chapter 5

Seek and You Shall Find: Research

- -

In This Chapter

▶ Getting sound real-world buying advice

▶ Getting solid online buying advice

▶ Checking out other information sources for savvy buyers

▶ Conducting a narrow-minded search on eBay

- -

*T*hink of walking into a store and seeing thousands of aisles of shelves with millions of items on them. Browsing the categories of auctions on eBay can be just as pleasantly boggling, without the prospect of sore feet. Start surfing around the site and you instantly understand the size and scope of what's for sale here. You may feel overwhelmed at first, but these clever eBay folks have come up with lots of ways to help you find exactly what you're looking for. Once you figure out how to find the items you want to bid for on eBay, you can protect your investment-to-be by making sure that what you find is actually what you're looking for.

Of course, searching is easier if you have an idea of what you're looking for. In this chapter we offer first-time buyers some expert collecting tips and tell you how to get expert advice from eBay and other sources. We also show you tips for using the eBay turbo search engine from a buyer's perspective.

The best advice you can follow as you explore any free-market system is *caveat emptor* ("let the buyer beware"). Although nobody can guarantee that every one of your transactions will be perfect, research items thoroughly before you bid so you don't lose too much of your hard-earned money — or too much sleep.

General Online Tips for Collectors

If you're just starting out on eBay, chances are you like to shop and you also collect items that interest you. You'll find out (pretty early in your eBay adventures) that a lot of people online know as much about collecting as they do about bidding — and some are serious contenders.

How can you compete? Well, in addition to a well-planned bidding strategy (covered in Chapter 6), knowing your stuff gives you a winning edge. We've collected the opinions of two collecting experts to get the info you need about online collecting basics. (If you're already an expert collector but want some help finding that perfect something on eBay so you can get ready to bid, you've got it — "Looking to Find an Item? Start Your eBay Search Engine" — later in this chapter.) We also show you how one of those experts puts the information into practice, and we give you a crash course on how items for sale are (or should be) graded.

The experts speak out

Bill Swoger runs a Burbank, California, collectibles store — Blast From the Past, a place where GI Joe guards the honor of Barbie, and Underdog is still trying to take his place next to Batman and Superman. Bill knows eBay well; he currently makes about 80 percent of his sales (some 250 items) at the online auction site. His Web site (`www.tvandmoviestuff.com`) plays a big role in his business. And Lee Bernstein — an antiques-and-collectibles dealer who operates (as you might expect) Lee Bernstein Antiques and Collectibles from her home base in Schererville, Indiana — not only frequents eBay, but also has her own Web site (`www.eLee.com`). Bill and Lee offer these tips to collectors new to eBay:

- ✔ **Get all the facts before you put your money down.** Study the description carefully. It's your job to analyze the description and make your bidding decisions accordingly. Find out whether all original parts are included and if the item has any flaws. If the description says that the Fred Flintstone figurine has a cracked back, e-mail the seller for more information.

- ✔ **Don't get caught up in the emotional thrill of bidding.** First-time buyers (known as *Under-10s* because they have less than 10 transactions under their belts) tend to bid wildly, using emotions instead of brains. If you're new to eBay, you can get burned if you just bid for the "thrill of victory" without thinking about what you're doing.

  We think that determining an item's value is important. But because values are such flighty things (values depend on supply and demand, market trends, and all sorts of other cool stuff), we recommend that you get a general idea of the item's value and use this ballpark figure to set a maximum amount of money you're willing to bid for that item. Then *stick* to your maximum and don't even think about bidding past it. If the bidding gets too hot, there's always another auction. To find out more about bidding strategies, Chapter 6 is just the ticket.

- ✔ **Know what the item should cost.** Buyers used to depend on *price guides* — books on collectibles and their values — to help them bid. Bill says price guides are becoming a thing of the past. Sure, you can find a guide that says a *Lion King* poster in excellent condition has a book price of $75, but if you do a search on eBay, you'll see that they're actually selling for $40 to $50.

When your search on eBay turns up what you're looking for, average out the current prices that you find. This gives you a much better idea of what you need to spend than any price guide can.

✔ **Timing is everything, and being first costs.** In the movie-poster business, if you can wait three to six months after a movie is released, you'll get the poster for 40 to 50 percent less. The same goes for many new releases of collectibles. Sometimes you're wiser to wait and save money.

✔ **Be careful of pre-sell items.** Sometimes you may run across vendors selling items that they don't have in stock at the moment but that they'll ship to you later. For example, before *Star Wars Episode I: The Phantom Menace* came out, some vendors ran auctions on movie posters they didn't have yet. If you bid and won, and for some reason they had a problem getting the poster, you'd be out of luck. Don't bid on anything that can't be delivered after your check clears.

✔ **Being too late can also cost.** Many collectibles become more difficult to find as time goes by. Generally, as scarcity increases, so does desirability and value. Common sense tells you that if two original and identical collectibles are offered side-by-side, with one in like-new condition and the other in used condition, the like-new item will have the higher value.

✔ **Check out the seller.** Check the rating feedback (the number in parentheses next to the person's User ID) a seller has before you buy. If the seller has many comments with very few negative ones, chances are good that this is a reputable seller. For more on feedback, check out Chapter 4.

Although eBay forbids side deals, an unsuccessful bidder may (at his or her own risk) contact a seller after an auction is over to see if the seller has more of the item in stock. If the seller is an experienced eBay user (a high transaction-related feedback rating is usually a tip-off) and is interested in the bidder's proposition, he or she may consider selling directly to a buyer. See Chapter 6 for more details, but don't forget that eBay strictly prohibits this behavior. If you conduct a side deal and are reported to eBay, you could be suspended. Not only that, but buyers who are ripped off by sellers in away-from-eBay transactions shouldn't look to eBay to bail them out. They're on their own.

✔ **If an item comes to you broken in the mail, contact the seller to work it out.** The best bet is to request insurance (you pay for it) before the seller ships the item. But if you didn't ask for it, it never hurts to ask for a refund (or a replacement item if available) if you're not satisfied. Chapter 10 offers the lowdown on buying shipping insurance, and Chapter 14 provides pointers on dealing with transactions that go sour.

Go, Joe: Following an expert on the hunt

Bill looks for specific traits when he buys GI Joe action figures. Although his checklist is specific to the GI Joe from 1964 to 1969, the information here can help you determine your maximum bid, (or whether an item's even worth bidding on) before an auction begins. As you find out in Chapter 6, the more you know before you place a bid, the happier you're likely to be when you win.

Bill's checklist can save you considerable hassle:

- ✔ **Find out the item's overall condition.** For GI Joe, look at the painted hair and eyebrows. Expect some wear, but overall, a collectible worth bidding on should look good.

- ✔ **Be sure the item's working parts are indeed working.** Most GI Joe action figures from this period have cracks on the legs and arms, but the joints should move and any cracks should not be so deep that the legs and arms fall apart easily.

- ✔ **Ask if the item has its original parts.** Since you can't really examine actual items in detail before buying, e-mail the seller with specific questions relating to original or replacement parts. Many GI Joe action figures are rebuilt from parts that are not from 1964 to 1969. Sometimes they even have two left or right hands or feet! If you make it clear with the seller before you buy that you want a toy with only original parts, you'll be able to make a good case for a refund if it arrives rebuilt as the Six-Million-Dollar Man. Chapter 6 has plenty of tips on how to protect yourself before you bid — and Chapter 14 has tips on what to do if the deal goes bad.

- ✔ **Ask if the item has original accessories.** A GI Joe from 1964 to 1969 should have his original dog tags, boots, and uniform. If any of these are missing, you will have to pay around $25 to replace each missing item. If you are looking to bid on any other collectible, know in advance what accessories came as standard equipment with the item, or you'll be paying extra just to bring it back to its original version.

- ✔ **Know an item's value before you bid.** A 1964 to 1969 vintage GI Joe in decent shape, with all its parts, sells for $125 to $150 without its original box. If you're bidding on a GI Joe action figure on eBay and you're in this price range, you're okay. If you get the item for less than 125 bucks, congratulations — you've nabbed a bargain.

- ✔ **If you have any questions, ask them *before* you bid.** Check collectors' guides, research similar auctions on eBay, and enlist the expertise of people like Bill Swoger. You probably have someone as knowledgeable as Bill in your hometown, but you can also let your fingers do the walking and visit Bill's Web site, www.tvandmoviestuff.com.

Making the grade

Welcome to our version of grade school without the bad lunch. One of the keys to establishing value is knowing an item's condition, typically referred to as an item's *grade*. Table 5-1 lists the most common grading categories used by collectors. The information in this table is used with permission from (and appreciation to) Lee Bernstein (www.eLee.com) and can also be found on the eBay Web site.

Table 5-1	Grading Categories	
Category (also known as)	*Description*	*Example*
Mint (M, Fine, 10, Mint-In-Box or MIB)	A never-used collectible in perfect condition with complete packaging (including instructions, original attachments, tags, and so on) identical to how it appeared on the shelf in the original box.	Grandmother got a soup tureen as a wedding present, never opened it, and stuck it in her closet for 50 years.
Near Mint (NM, Near Fine, Like-New, 9)	The collectible is perfect but no longer has the original packaging, or the original packaging is less than perfect. Possibly used, but must appear to be new.	Grandmother used the soup tureen on her 25th anniversary, washed it gently, then put it back in the closet.
Excellent (EX, 8)	Used, but barely. Close to and often mistakenly interchanged with Near Mint. May have very *minor* signs of wear.	Grandma liked to ring in the New Year with a cup of soup for everyone.
Very Good (VG, 7)	Looks very good but has defects, such as a minor chip or light color fading.	If you weren't looking for it, you might miss that Grandma's tureen survived the '64 earthquake, as well as Uncle Bob's infamous ladle episode.
Good (G, 6)	Used, with defects. More than a small amount of color loss, chips, cracks, tears, dents, abrasions, missing parts, and so on.	Grandma had the ladies in the neighborhood over for soup and bingo every month.
Poor (P or G-, 5)	Barely collectible, if at all. Severe damage, heavy use.	Grandma ran a soup kitchen.

Grading is subjective. "Mint" to one person may be "Very Good" to another. Always ask a seller to define the meaning of the terms used. Also, be aware that many amateur sellers may not really know the different definitions of grading and may arbitrarily add "Mint" or "Excellent" to their item descriptions.

Don't let a Poor rating scare you away from an item's potential. Yes, the item for sale may be in far worse condition than the one you've got — but it may have the part you're missing!

Finding More Collecting Information

Hey, the experts have been buying, selling, and trading collectible items for years. But just because you're new to eBay doesn't mean you have to be a "newbie" for decades before you can start bartering with the collecting gods. We wouldn't leave you in the cold like that — and neither would eBay — you can get information on items you're interested in, as well as good collecting tips, right on the eBay Web site. You can also search the rest of the Web or go the "old-fashioned" route and check the library (yes, libraries are still around).

Visiting eBay's online library

eBay's free public library offers online buying and collecting tips from experts. You can see what they have to say under the Inside Scoop and Front page headings in the library section. The categories that offer collecting advice include these:

- ✔ Antiques
- ✔ Coins and stamps
- ✔ Computers

The ultimate family station wagon for sale

Need a lift? Drive in style in a 1977 Cadillac Fleetwood Hearse. Only 91K miles! Fully loaded: V8, P/S, P/B, P/W. Gray & Black w/Black interior. Good engine, good brakes, five extra tires, and a stereo system. Buyer must pick up after check clears.

This hearse sold on eBay for $600, and now the Addams family has a new set of wheels!

    ✔ Dolls and figures (including figurines)

    ✔ Jewelry and gemstones

    ✔ Photography and electronics

    ✔ Pottery and glass

    ✔ Sports memorabilia

    ✔ Toys and bean-bag plush collectibles

To find Inside Scoop, shown in Figure 5-1, go to the eBay Home page and follow these steps:

1. **Click on the Community link on the navigation bar at the top of the page.**

   You're taken to the Community Overview page.

2. **Click on the Library link on the subnavigation bar to see listings for all the categories offering collecting information.**

3. **Click on the Inside Scoop Link for a category you're interested in and start reading.**

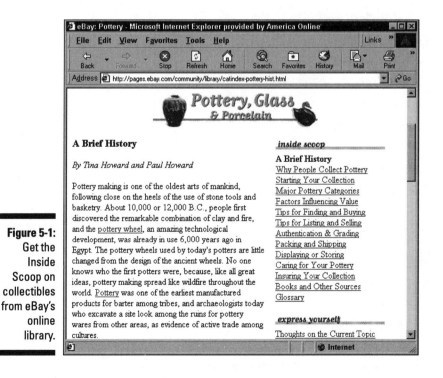

Figure 5-1:
Get the
Inside
Scoop on
collectibles
from eBay's
online
library.

Searching other places online

If you don't find the information you need on eBay, don't go ballistic — just go elsewhere. Even a site as vast as eBay doesn't have a monopoly on information. The Internet is filled with Web sites and Internet auction sites that can give you price comparisons and information about cyber-clubs.

Your home computer can connect to powerful outside servers (really big computers on the Internet) that have their own fast-searching systems called *search engines*. At this moment, if something is out there and you need it, you can find it right from your home PC in just a matter of seconds. Here are some of the Web's most highly regarded search engines or multi-search engine sites:

- AltaVista (www.altavista.com)
- Dogpile (www.dogpile.com)
- Excite (www.excite.com)
- EZ-Find (www.theriver.com/TheRiver/Explore/ezfind.html)
- Galaxy (www.einet.net/galaxy.html)
- HotBot (www.hotbot.com)
- Inference Find (www.infind.com)
- Infoseek (www.infoseek.com)
- The Internet Sleuth (www.isleuth.com)
- Lycos (www.lycos.com)
- MetaCrawler (www.go2net.com/search.html)
- ProFusion (www.profusion.com)
- WebCrawler (www.webcrawler.com)
- Yahoo! (www.yahoo.com)

The basic process of getting info from an Internet search engine is pretty simple:

1. **Go to the site.**

2. **Find the text box next to the button labeled "Search" or something similar.**

3. **Click in the text box.**

   You see a blinking cursor.

4. **Type in a few words indicating what you're interested in.**

Be specific. The more precise your entry, the better your chances of finding what you want. Look for tips, advanced search, or help pages on your search engine of choice for more information about how to narrow your search.

5. **Click on the Search (or similar) button, or press Enter on your keyboard.**

   The search engine returns with a page that lists how many pages had the requested information and includes brief descriptions and links to the first group of pages (say, for example, the first 20 pages found). You'll find links to additional search pages at the bottom if your search finds more listings than can fit on one page (and if you ask for something popular, like *Star Wars,* don't be surprised to get thousands of replies).

You should always approach information on the Web with caution. Not everyone is the "expert" they'd like to be. Your best bet is to get lots of different opinions, then boil 'em down to what makes sense to you. And remember — *caveat emptor.* (Is there an echo in here?)

For more on using Internet search engines, allow us to recommend *Internet Searching For Dummies,* by Brad Hill, or *Researching Online For Dummies,* by Reva Basch (both IDG Books Worldwide, Inc.; they may look vaguely familiar).

Finding other sources of information

If you're interested in collecting a particular item, you can get a lot of insider collecting information without digging too deep:

✔ **Go to other places on eBay.** eBay's chat boards and bulletin boards (covered in detail in Chapter 15) are full of insider info. The eBay community is always willing to educate a "newbie."

✔ **Go to the library.** Books and magazines are great sources of info. At least one book or one magazine probably specializes in your chosen item. For example, if old furniture is your thing, *Antiquing For Dummies,* by Ron Zoglin and Deborah Shouse (IDG Books Worldwide, of course) can clue you in to what antique collectors look for. Before you know it, people will be coming to you for expert advice!

If you find a magazine that looks interesting in the library, try entering the title in your search engine of choice. You may just find that the magazine you just got out of your mailbox has also gone paperless — you can read it online.

✔ **Go to someone else in the know.** Friends, clubs, and organizations in your area can give you a lot of info. Ask your local antique dealer about clubs you can join and see how much info you end up with.

Testing, testing . . . how long *does* a search take on eBay?

Having a massive search engine is a matter of necessity at eBay — millions of items are up for auction at any given time — and often an easy, fast search makes all the difference between getting and not getting. After all, "time is money," and eBay members tend to be movers and shakers who don't like standing still.

So, how long do searches really take on eBay? We put it to the test. In the search window of the eBay Home Page, we typed in **1933 Chicago Worlds Fair Souvenir Pennant** and let 'er rip.

The search engine went through 1.5 million general items and 647 World's Fair items and gave us our one specific item in just eight seconds. (Now, if the wizards at eBay could only figure out a way to find that disappearing sock that always escapes from clothes dryers, they'd really be on to something!)

By the way, that slightly wrinkled felt pennant got four bids and sold for $17.50, in case you're in the market for one!

Looking to Find an Item? Start Your eBay Search Engine

NEWS FLASH! Dateline: Silicon Valley, 1999: It's official. Through billions of dollars of research and development, millions of man- (and woman-) hours, incredible advances in miniaturization, and really good rebate programs, people around the world can now actually find a needle in a haystack with a personal computer that costs under a thousand bucks. The needle that has been lost for centuries has now been found, and we can finally put that threadbare cliché to rest. In a related story, haystacks are now tragically missing. They are golden yellow in color, stand about 5 feet tall, and have straw-like features. Check your local television station for more details.

Okay, we made up that news flash, but when you've done your research and you're ready to buy, the powerful eBay search engine can help you find whatever you're collecting — even if that's needles from haystacks.

eBay has lots of cool ways to search for items (sample 'em in Chapter 3). The five main options are

- Searching by title
- Searching by item number
- Searching by seller

✔ Searching by bidder

✔ Searching through completed auctions

No matter which search option you use, you can access the five search options by clicking on the Search link on the navigation bar at the top of any eBay page. Each search option can provide a different piece of information to help you find the right item from the right seller at the right price.

If you want to be thorough in your eBay searches, we recommend that you conduct searches often. And when you find a particularly juicy item or sub-category, don't forget to print it out, bookmark it, write down where the nugget was so you can find it again, or use Personal Shopper. See Chapter 6 for more info on keeping a paper trail, and see Chapter 16 for more on Personal Shopper.

Title search

When you conduct a Title search, the search engine looks for every auction on eBay that has the title you're looking for. The title is (as you might expect) just another word or group of words for what you call the item. For example, if you're looking for an antique silver ice tea spoon, just type **silver ice tea spoon** into the search window.

Clicking the Search button starts the process, but don't click the button quite yet. You can narrow your search down further by adding info about

✔ **What price range you want to see:** Type in the price range you're looking for and eBay searches the specific range between that low and high price. If money is no object, then leave this box blank — and loan us 20 bucks.

✔ **What country you'd like searched:** You can select any country (searches from Afghanistan to Zimbabwe, no kidding!) or narrow it down to the United States or Canada. Don't forget that you have to pay for shipping, so if you don't want to pay to ship a heavy ice-shaving machine from Hungary to Hoboken, New Jersey, stick close to home. You also have the choice of narrowing down your country search with "located" or "available" selections. By selecting "located," the search engine looks for items from the specific country you entered in the box. Selecting "available" gets you search results for items within your own country, or from international sellers willing to ship to you.

✔ **In what order you want your results to appear:** If you click on "ascending," the search engine gives you the results so that the most recent auctions appear first on the list.

✔ **Whether you want the search engine to check through item titles alone or check *both* item titles *and* item descriptions:** We suggest that you use Search Title *and* Description. You get more information that way.

✔ **Search completed auctions:** Click on this link to jump down to the bottom of the search page. We explain searching through completed auctions later in this section.

Okay, *now* you can click on the Search button. In a few seconds, you see the fruits of all the searching you've been doing. (Wow, you're not even perspiring.)

Figure 5-2 shows our Title search with all of this information filled out, and Figure 5-3 shows the results.

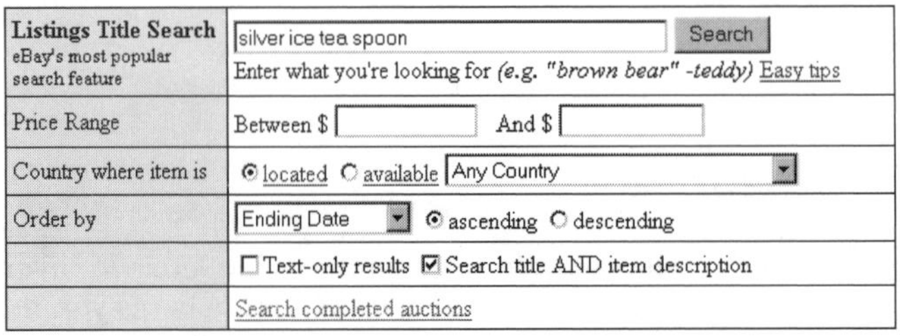

Figure 5-2:
A Title search for a "silver ice tea spoon" with specifications entered.

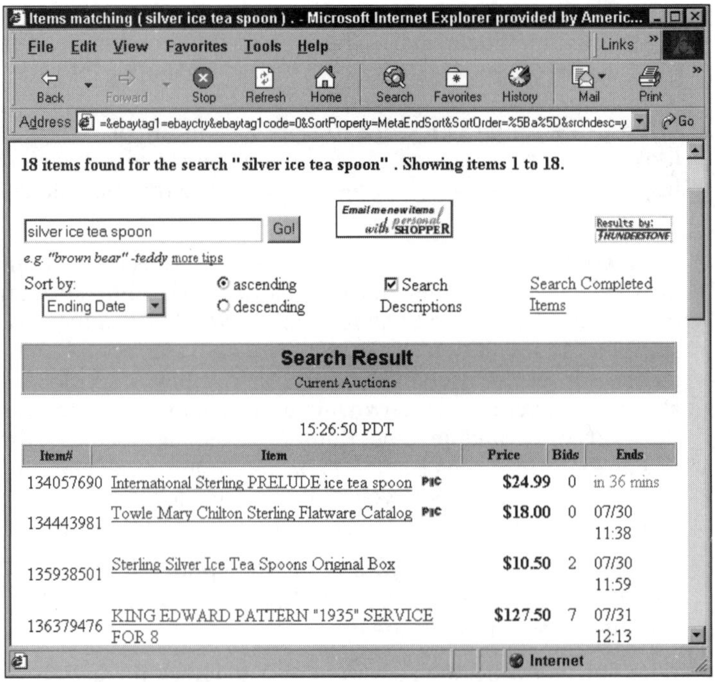

Listings Title Search	silver ice tea spoon	Search
eBay's most popular search feature	Enter what you're looking for *(e.g. "brown bear" -teddy)* Easy tips	
Price Range	Between $ [ ] And $ [ ]	
Country where item is	⊙ located ○ available Any Country ▾	
Order by	Ending Date ▾ ⊙ ascending ○ descending	
	☐ Text-only results ☑ Search title AND item description	
	Search completed auctions	

Figure 5-3:
The results of the quest for a silver ice tea spoon.

Items matching (silver ice tea spoon) . - Microsoft Internet Explorer provided by Americ...

File Edit View Favorites Tools Help — Links

Back Forward Stop Refresh Home Search Favorites History Mail Print

Address =&ebaytag1=ebayctry&ebaytag1code=0&SortProperty=MetaEndSort&SortOrder=%5Ba%5D&srchdesc=y ▾ Go

18 items found for the search "silver ice tea spoon" . Showing items 1 to 18.

silver ice tea spoon [Go!]

e.g. "brown bear" -teddy more tips

Sort by: ⊙ ascending ☑ Search Search Completed
Ending Date ▾ ○ descending Descriptions Items

Search Result

Current Auctions

15:26:50 PDT

Item#	Item	Price	Bids	Ends
134057690	International Sterling PRELUDE ice tea spoon **Pic**	**$24.99**	0	in 36 mins
134443981	Towle Mary Chilton Sterling Flatware Catalog **Pic**	**$18.00**	0	07/30 11:38
135938501	Sterling Silver Ice Tea Spoons Original Box	**$10.50**	2	07/30 11:59
136379476	KING EDWARD PATTERN "1935" SERVICE FOR 8	**$127.50**	7	07/31 12:13

Internet

Next to item listings you often see the words *new* and *pic. New* means the listing is brand new (this icon stays on for the first 24 hours an item is listed), and *pic* means the seller included a digital picture along with the item description.

Item number search

All items put up for auction on eBay are assigned an item number. Using an item number is extremely handy if you don't want to wade through a Title search again as you follow an auction or find out about auctions that have closed. Sure, you can type **LARGE ESTATE TANZANITE & PAVED DIAMOND RING** into the Title Search form again and again, but once you've found one, all you have to do is enter the 9-digit item number in the Item Number (#) search box to find it again, which is a lot simpler. Trust us.

The Item Number Lookup search form, shown in Figure 5-4, is simple to use:

1. **Type the item number in the Item Number (#) box.**

2. **Click on the Search button.**

Figure 5-4:
The Item
Number (#)
search box.

Item Number Lookup Use only if you have the item number (#)	Item Number (#) [ ] Search

Seller search

The Seller Search box, shown in Figure 5-5, gives you a list of all the auctions a seller is running and is a great way to keep a list of people you have successfully (or unsuccessfully, if you're trying to avoid them) done business with in the past. It's also a strategy that eBay users use to assess the reputation of a seller. You can find out more about selling strategies in Chapter 8. To use the Seller Search option, follow these steps:

Figure 5-5:
The Seller
Search box.

Seller Search Find all items currently listed by a specific seller	marsha_c Search User ID or email address of seller. See your favorite seller's listings.
Include bidder emails	⊙ No ○ Yes
Completed items too?	○ No ○ All ○ Last Day ○ Last 2 Days ⊙ Last Week ○ Last 2 Weeks
Order by	○ Newest first ○ Oldest first ⊙ Auction end ○ Current price
# of items per page	25 ▾

1. **In the Search window, type the eBay User ID or e-mail address of the person you want to learn more about.**

   User IDs and e-mail addresses can be used interchangeably anywhere on eBay. If you've forgotten one, use the other. They both work the same way.

2. **On the Include bidder e-mails line, tell eBay whether you want to see the e-mail address of other people bidding on auctions posted by the person for whom you are searching.**

   If you want these addresses, click the Yes option button. If not, click No. If you click Yes, then you have to fill out the User ID History and Email Address Request Form (shown in Figure 5-6) in two short steps:

   a. **Type in your own User ID and password.**

   b. **Click on the Remember me box.** This installs a *cookie,* a temporary file on your computer that reminds eBay of who you are so that for the remainder of this online session you don't have to submit your User ID and password every time you want someone's e-mail address.

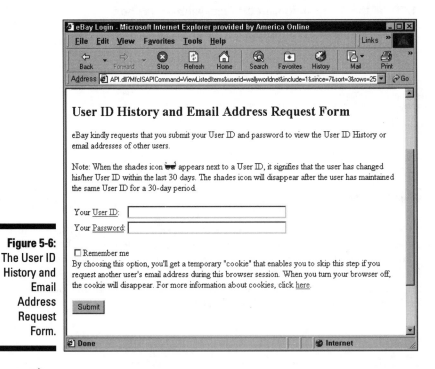

Figure 5-6:
The User ID
History and
Email
Address
Request
Form.

For more on eBay e-mail, privacy issues, and cookies, look at Chapter 13 (and don't think we didn't see your hand in the jar).

3. **If you don't want to see auctions that this specific user has conducted in the past, click No on the Completed auctions too? line.**

You can choose to see all current and previous auctions, auctions that have ended in the last day, last two days, last week, or last two weeks.

eBay only keeps past auction results active for 30 days; if you're looking for something auctioned 31 days (or longer) ago, sorry, no dice.

4. **Choose an Order by option to control how you want the results of your search to appear on your screen.** If you want to see the auctions that are closing right away, click on Sort by Auction End.

5. **Choose the number of results you want to see per page.**

   If the person you're looking up has 100 auctions up and running, you can keep from getting swamped by sheer quantity if you limit the number of results to 25 listings, spread over four separate pages. That allows you to narrow down what you want to see.

6. **Click Search.**

That's how a Seller search goes. Figure 5-7 shows the results page.

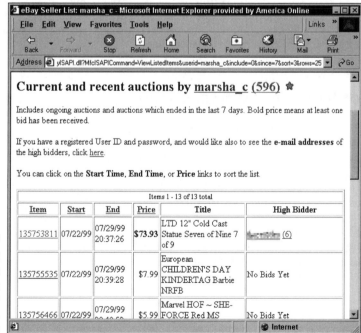

Figure 5-7:
The results
page from a
Seller
search.

A shorts story: Boxers or briefs?

Here's an actual eBay auction listing, mistakes and all (we swear we're not making this up):

"Will they help your game? Master's Golf Boxer Shorts. Size large, NO FLY,.Winner to pay shipping of $.65 Item is used, but in like good condition. Item is CLEAN and free of any odor. Any questions about any auction is gladly answered if the E-Bay item number is included. Those with out E-Bay number will not be answered. Thank You for Bidding,Good Luck. Opening bid $3.00."

Are you surprised that this item didn't sell? In short(s), we weren't.

Bidder search

The Bidder search option is unique because sellers and buyers alike use it when an auction's going on. They use it to figure out their best strategies. After all, money is the name of the game. For information on conducting a Bidder search, take a look at Chapter 6.

Completed auctions search

A completed auctions search returns results of auctions that have already ended. This is our favorite search option on eBay because you can use it as a strategic bidding tool. How? If you're bidding on an item and want to know if the prices are likely to go too high for your pocketbook, you can use this search option to compare the current price of the item to the selling price of similar items from auctions that have already ended.

You can also use this tool if you want to sell an item and are trying to determine what it's worth, how high the demand is, and if this is the right time to list the item. Chapter 9 offers the nuts, bolts, and monkey wrenches you need to set up your auction.

Here's how to do a Completed Auctions search:

1. **Type in the title name of the item you want to find.**

   You're asked how you want the results arranged.

2. **Tell eBay how you want the results arranged.**

AUCTION ANECDOTE

What's green, sounds great, and flies?

That's right — David Clark aviation headsets (those green ones pilots wear in the movies). We have a friend who needed a set for flight training. After doing research on what the headset costs new, he did a Completed Auctions search to see the selling prices of similar headsets in previous eBay auctions. Armed with the power of information, our friend was able to bid strategically on a current David Clark headset auction, which he won. Our friend paid $100 less than the cost of a new headset, *and* his winning bid was $25 less than the winning bid of the last headset that sold on eBay.

You have four options:

- Select Ending Date to see your search results listed by the date the auction ended.
- Select Starting Date to see your search results listed by the date the auction started.
- Select Bid Price to see a list of the final auction prices paid for an item.
- Select Search Ranking to see how many of your keywords in the title were hit during the search.

When you've made your choice, you see an Order by option.

3. **Select how you want your results ordered.**

   Click on the descending circle to see the most recent, most expensive, or most items first. Click on the ascending circle to see the last recently completed auctions, least expensive selling prices, and the least whatever else, first.

4. **Click Search.**

   Your search results appear on your screen in just a few seconds.

Figure 5-8 shows the Completed Auctions search box.

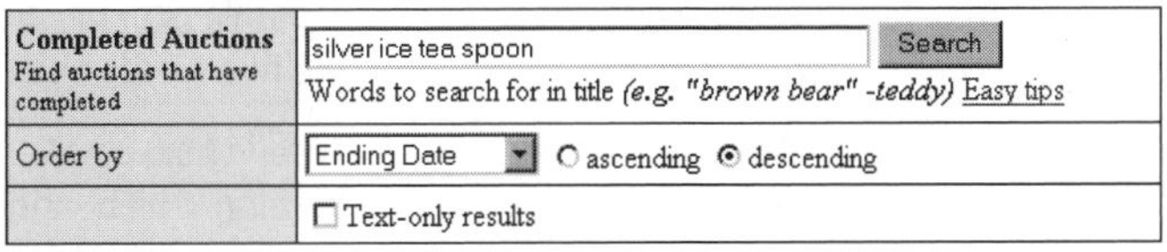

Figure 5-8: The Completed Auctions search box.

Completed Auctions Find auctions that have completed	silver ice tea spoon [Search]
	Words to search for in title *(e.g. "brown bear" -teddy)* Easy tips
Order by	[Ending Date ▼] ○ ascending ⊙ descending
	☐ Text-only results

Narrowing down your eBay search

Once you're familiar with each of eBay's search options, you need a crash course in what words to actually type into those nice little boxes. Too little information and you may not find your item — too much and you'll be overwhelmed with information. If you're really into Beanie Babies, you might be looking for Tabasco the Bull, for example. If you just search for Tabasco, you get swamped with results ranging from hot sauce to advertisements.

Some simple tricks can help narrow your eBay searches. Table 5-2 has the details.

Table 5-2	Symbols and Keywords for Conducting Searches with the eBay Search Engine	
Symbol	*Impact on Search*	*Example*
No symbol, multiple words	Returns auctions with all included words in title	**reagan letter** might return an auction for a mailed message from the former U.S. President, or it might return an auction for a mailed message from Boris Yeltsin to Ronald Reagan.
Quotes ("")	Limits search to items with the exact phrase inside the quotes	**"Wonder Woman"** returns items about the comic book/TV heroine. Caps and lowercase letters are regarded the same by the search engine. Using either gets you the same results.
Asterisk (*)	Serves as a wild card	**budd*** returns items that start with budd, such as Beanie Buddy, Beanie Buddies, or Buddy Holly.
Separating comma without spaces (a,b)	Finds items related to either item before or after comma	**kennedy,nixon** returns items with descriptions that relate to either Kennedy or Nixon.
Plus sign (+)	Results must have both items before + and after +	**chanel+purse** shows you every auction that has both Chanel *and* purse in the title, regardless of the order in which the two words appear.
Minus sign (-)	Excludes results with the word after -	Type in **box-lunch** (and you'd better not be hungry, because you may find the box, but lunch won't be included).

Symbol	Impact on Search	Example
At symbol and number 0 (@0)	Returns results with either of two examples that follow	**@0 ds9 "Deep Space Nine"** brings you auctions relating to the recently completed *Star Trek* spin-off TV series.
At symbol and number 1 (@1)	Returns results with two of three examples that follow	**@1 "Deep Space Nine" "Star Trek" "Next Generation"** should appeal to those with their own sets of Vulcan ears.
Pound symbol (#) followed by number	Searches for auctions with that number in the title	**#2000** gets you lots of stuff about the beginning of the new millennium (or the last year of *this* millennium, depending on your point of view).
Minus symbol and parentheses	Searches for auctions with words before parentheses, but excludes those with word(s) inside parentheses	**midge-(skipper,barbie)** means that auctions with the Midge doll won't have to compete for Ken's attention.
Parentheses	Searches for both versions of the word in the parentheses	**Beanie (pin,pins)** will search for Beanie pin or Beanie pins.

Here are additional tips to help you narrow down any eBay search:

- ✔ **Don't worry about capitalization:** You can capitalize proper names or leave them lowercase — the search engine doesn't care.

- ✔ **Don't use *and, a, an, or,* or *the*:** Called *noise words* in search lingo, these words are interpreted as part of your search unless you enclose them in quotes. So if you want to find something from *The Sound of Music* and you type in **the sound of music,** you may not get any results. Most sellers drop noise words from the beginning of an item title when they list it, just as libraries drop noise words when they alphabetize books.

Search within specific categories: This type of search further narrows down your results because you only search one niche of eBay, just the specific area you want. For example, if you want to find Tabasco the Bull, start at the Home Page and under the Categories heading, click on the link to Toys and Bean Bag Plush (you know — beanies). Unless a seller has accidentally misplaced an item, you won't find any hot sauce here. The only problem with searching in a specific category is sometimes an item can be in more than one place, like a Mickey Mouse infant snuggly. If you look for it in Disney items, you may miss it. It might be listed in infant wear.

Finding eBay Members: The Gang's All Here

With millions of eBay users on the loose, you may think it's hard to track folks down. Nope. eBay's powerful search engine kicks into high gear to help find other eBay members in seconds.

Here's how to find people or get info on them from eBay:

1. **From the main navigation bar found at the top of most eBay pages, click on the Search link.**

   This takes you to the main search page where you see three links pop up on the subnavigation bar. The links are Find Items, Find Members, and Personal Shopper.

2. **Click on the Find Members link.**

   This link takes you to the main Find Members page, where you can search for specific About Me pages (see Chapter 12 to find out how to create your own personal eBay Web page). Here you can also get a look at the Feedback Profile of a user (remember Feedback from earlier in this chapter? It *will* be on the exam . . . just kidding), or find the e-mail addresses and User ID histories of fellow eBay members (which comes in handy when you're bidding on items, as Chapter 6 avows), or get contact information.

3. **Fill in the appropriate boxes with what you're looking for and click on the Search (or, in some cases, the Submit) button to get the info you want.**

Clicking on the Personal Shopper link found on the subnavigation page takes you to the Personal Shopper login page where you start the process of registering for this free service. You tell eBay what items you're looking for and Personal Shopper does automatic searches for you. Then Personal Shopper lets you know when auctions that match your descriptions crop up. (Chapter 16 tells the tender story of signing up and getting the Personal Shopper link to unite you with the item of your dreams.)

Chapter 6

Bidding: Go Up the Creek but Take Your Paddle

● ●

In This Chapter

▶ Getting your plan together before you bid

▶ Finding out about the seller and your competition

▶ Placing a token bid

▶ Using canny strategies to win your auction item

▶ Avoiding bidder's remorse

● ●

*B*rowsing different categories of eBay, looking for nothing in particular, you spot that must-have item lurking among other Elvis paraphernalia in the Collectibles category. Sure, you *can* live without that faux gold Elvis pocket watch, but life would be so much sweeter *with* it. And even if it doesn't keep good time, at least it'll be right twice a day.

When you bid for items on eBay, you can get that same thrill that you would at Sotheby's or Christie's for a lot less money, and the items you win are likely to be *slightly* more practical than an old Dutch masterpiece you're afraid to leave at the framer's (Hey, you have to have a watch, and Elvis *is* the King).

In this chapter we tell you about the types of auctions available on eBay and run down the nuts and bolts of bidding strategies, and some tried-and-true tips that help give you a leg up on the competition.

The Auction Item Page

Because at any given point you have more than a million pages of auction item pages you can look at on eBay, auction item pages are the heart (better yet, the skeleton) of eBay auctions. No matter what kind of auction you're bidding on, the auction item page looks pretty much the same. Figure 6-1 shows a conventional item page. Here's a list of the stuff you see:

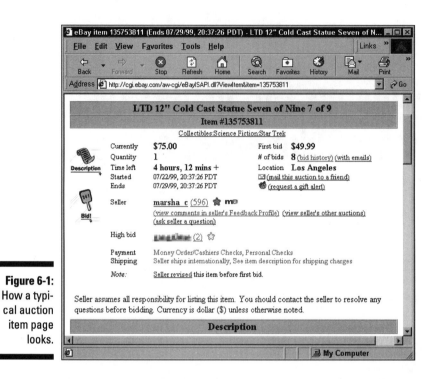

Figure 6-1:
How a typical auction item page looks.

✔ **Item name and number:** Identifies the item. Keep track of this info for inquiries later on.

If you have an interest in a particular type of item, take note of the words used in the item name (you're likely to see them again in future names). This will help you in narrowing down your searches.

✔ **Item category:** If you click on this category listing, you can do some comparison shopping. Similar items are often advertised in multiple categories. (Look at Chapter 5 for more searching strategies.)

✔ **Currently:** This indicates the dollar amount the bidding has reached — which changes throughout the auction as people place bids. Sometimes, next to the current dollar amount, you see `Reserve not yet met` or `Reserve met`. This means the seller has a set a *reserve price* for the item — a secret price that must be reached before a seller will sell an item.

If you don't see this listing on an auction item page, don't be alarmed. Not all auctions have reserve prices.

✔ **Quantity:** Tells how many items are available. If you see a number other than 1 in this place, then you're looking at a Dutch auction, which we explain later in this chapter. But if a seller is selling two Elvis watches for the price of one, then the item quantity still shows up as 1 (as in 1 set of 2 watches).

✔ **Time left:** Although the clock never stops ticking at eBay, you must continue to refresh your browser to see the time remaining on the official clock. This window tells you the time remaining in this particular auction, and right below it, when the auction started, and when it'll end.

Timing is the key in eBay bidding strategy (covered later in this chapter), so don't forget that because eBay world headquarters is in California, they use Pacific standard time or Pacific daylight time as the standard, depending on the season.

✔ **First bid:** The starting price set by the seller (sometimes called the minimum bid). This is the lowest price somebody can bid to get the auction going.

✔ **# of bids:** Tells how many bids have been placed. To use the number of bids to your advantage, you have to read between the lines. You can determine just how "hot" an item is by comparing the number of bids the item has received over time. Based on the amount of interest of an item, you can create a time strategy (which we talk about later in this chapter). Next to the # of bids are two links: (bid history) and (with emails). Click on (bid history) to find out who is bidding and what date and time bids were placed on this item. The dollar amount of each bid is kept secret until the end of the auction. Click on the (with emails) link to get the e-mail addresses of bidders (after you fill out the User ID History and Email Address Request Form, which pops up automatically).

Bidding is more an art than a science. Sometimes an item gets no bids because everyone's waiting until the last minute; then you see a flurry of activity as they all try to outbid each other (called *sniping,* which we explain later in this chapter). But that's all part of the fun of eBay.

✔ **Location:** Tells where the item is. Factor in the geographic location of a seller when you consider bidding on an item. If the item is in Australia (for example) and you're in Vermont, you may decide that you don't need that wrought-iron doorstop. Remember, you pay the shipping charges. Or, if the item is a town away, you might bid a little higher because you probably can do the transaction in person without any shipping and handling charges. Knowing exactly where the item is can help you calculate what shipping charges will be. (We tackle that in Chapter 10.)

✔ **Mail this auction to a friend:** You can tip off a buddy on a good find, get some advice from an antique or collecting expert, or run it by a friend who's been around the eBay block a few times and ask for strategy advice.

✔ **Request a gift alert:** If you won this auction but you're planning on giving the item to somebody else as a gift, click here to send them an electronic card from eBay. The card has the item description and a picture if one was used in the auction. It's a nice way of telling someone a gift is on the way and it costs nothing to send it. It can only be ordered after an auction has closed and the seller must have 10 or more feedback points.

✔ **Seller:** Gives you information about the seller. *Know thy seller* ranks right after *caveat emptor* as a phrase that pays on eBay. As we tell you a million times in this book, *Read the feedback!* (Okay, maybe not a million — it would drive the editors bonkers.) Human beings come in all shapes, sizes, and levels of honesty — and like any community, eBay has its share of good folks and bad folks. Your best defense is to read the seller's feedback. To the right of the seller's name is a number in parentheses, click on the number to view his or her eBay ID Card (kind of a report card of feedback for the last six months) and entire feedback history just below it. Read, read, and reread all the feedback (hey, we're getting *closer* to telling you a million times!) to make sure you feel comfortable doing business with this person. Just below the seller's name is a link to see other auctions he or she may be running- and another link that pops up an e-mail window so you can send a question. We give you a step-by-step guide on how these links work later in this chapter.

✔ **High bid:** Shows you the User ID of the current high bidder. It could be you if you placed a bid!

✔ **Payment:** Tells you the payment terms the seller has set. Usually it tells you to read the item description for more details. We explain how to read item descriptions later in this chapter.

✔ **Shipping:** Check here to see if the seller is willing to ship to your area. Sometimes sellers will not ship internationally, and they'll let you know here before you place a bid. Also, always check the item description for shipping charges and terms (which, except in rare instances, buyers have to pay).

Organization is the name of the game on eBay, especially if you plan to bid on multiple auctions while you're running auctions of your own. We figure you're in the bidding game to win, so start thinking about keeping track of your paperwork now. Print out a copy of the auction item page you're interested in bidding on. Chapter 7 offers tips on which paperwork you should definitely hang on to.

Does the horse know?

One seller offered a bracelet from the mid-1800s, 8 inches in diameter and made from links of woven horsehair (some rather worn, but generally in good condition). A horsehair "charm" dangled from a foot-long chain of links; the clasp was a woven ball-and-loop. The opening bid was $8, and this bracelet sold for $103.50!

Strategy: Beating the Devil in the Details

As with any sale — whether you find it at Harvey's Hardware, Bloomingdale's, or Kmart — carefully check out what you are buying. The auction page gives you links to help you know what you're bidding on — and whom you're bidding to buy from. If you take advantage of this convenience, you won't have many problems. But if you ignore these essential tips, you may end up unhappy with what you buy, the person you buy it from, and how much you spend.

Read the item description carefully

The *item description* is the most critical item on the auction item page. This is where the seller lists the details about the item being sold. Read this page carefully and pay close attention to what is, and isn't, written.

Don't judge a book by its cover — but do judge a seller by his or her item description. If the sentences are succinct, detailed, and well structured, you're most likely dealing with an individual who planned and executed the auction with care. It takes time and effort to post a good auction. If you see huge lapses in grammar, convoluted sentences, and misspellings, YOU MAYBE GONNA GET BURNT! Dig deeper and make sure you feel comfortable dealing with this person; decide for yourself whether he or she is out to sell junk for a quick buck or is part of eBay for the long term.

If there's a picture, take a good look. The majority of eBay sellers jazz up their auctions with photos of the item. The seller should answer a few general questions in his or her item description. If these questions aren't answered, that doesn't necessarily mean that the seller's disreputable — only that if you're really interested, you should e-mail the seller and get those answers before you bid. In particular, ask questions like these:

- Is the item new or used?
- Is the item a first edition or a reprint? An original or a reissue? (See Chapter 5 for tips on how to assess what you're buying.)
- Is the item in its original packaging?
- Is the item under warranty?
- What are the shipping charges and payment options, if any?
- If you're in a hurry to get the item, are delays likely? If so, what sort and how long?
- Can the seller guarantee you a refund if the item is broken?

✔ Who pays insurance on the item when it's shipped — you or the seller?

✔ What condition is the item in? Is it broken, scratched, flawed, or "mint?"

Most experienced collectors know that, depending on the item, a tiny scratch here or there may be worth the risk of making a bid. But a scratch or two may affect your bidding price. Look at Chapter 5 for more expert collecting advice.

✔ Is this item the genuine article or a reproduction, and if it's the real deal, does the seller have papers certifying its authenticity?

✔ What size is the item? (That fiberglass whale may not *fit* in your garage.)

If you win the item and find out the seller lied in the description, you have the right to return the item — but if you win the item and discover that you overlooked a detail in the description, the seller isn't obligated to take the item back.

Many sellers spell out, in their item descriptions, exactly how the item should be paid for and shipped. Check to see whether an actual shipping charge applies — and if so, how much it'll cost you.

The seller is obligated to describe the item honestly and in detail, so if your questions aren't answered in the item description, then for goodness' sake, e-mail the seller for the facts. If a picture is available, is it clear enough that you can see any flaws? What you see may not be what you get, so we suggest that you follow up with questions. (Look at our glossary for a list of abbreviations commonly used in item descriptions.)

How Swede it is!

A savvy eBay user we know benefited from a major seller-error. The seller titled his auction "Swede Star Trek Cast Jacket." Our friend checked out the item description and found that it was written with bad spelling and incoherent grammar, so she e-mailed the seller for more information. The seller explained that the jacket was a *suede* cast jacket given to the crew of the movie *Star Trek: Generations*. He had won it in a local radio contest, and it was brand new.

Because of the seller's mistake, there was only one bidder for this lovely green suede (silk-lined!) jacket, which our friend picked up for $150. Because of its *Star Trek* connection, the jacket is worth upwards of $400 to collectors. So, study the item page carefully. You may get lucky and find that errors can work to your benefit! (And a word to the wise: Check your own spelling and grammar carefully when you put an item up for sale!)

Get the scoop on the seller

We can't tell you enough that the single most important way you can make an auction go well is to *know who you're dealing with*. Apparently, the eBay folks agree with us; they help you get info on the seller right from the auction item page. We recommend that you take advantage of these links. Chapter 5 demonstrates how to conduct a thorough By Seller search.

- ✔ Click on the number beside the seller's User ID to get feedback history.

  OR

- ✔ Click on the "me" image next to "Seller" to view the seller's About Me page.

  AND

- ✔ Click on "View seller's other auctions" to take a look at what else they're selling.

Check the seller's feedback (message sound familiar?)

Check the seller's eBay ID Card and Feedback history. All together now — *check the feedback.* (Is there an echo in here?) What you find are (for the most part) the honest thoughts and comments of buyers from previous transactions. No eBay user has control over the comments others make, and feedback sticks to you like your high school "permanent record."

Read every piece of feedback — the good, the bad and the neutral — and, unless you're prepared to kiss your money good-bye, we recommend that you stay away from anyone with two or more negative comments.

eBay, like life, is full of shades of gray. Some sellers are unfairly hit with negative comments for something that wasn't their fault. If you suspect a seller's received a bum rap (after you've read all his or her positive feedback), send the seller an e-mail asking for an explanation of a spotty feedback record. Look at Chapter 4 for more on reading and leaving feedback.

The eBay Star Chart is a convenient, quick way to size up another eBay member. It can give you a solid sense of that person's professionalism. The Star Chart in Chapter 4 gives you a look at how eBay ranks star-quality eBay members.

The tale of the 3-plus-negative seller

A friend of ours took a risk and bid on an old Winchester rifle (now a banned item — see Chapter 8 for what you're allowed and not allowed to sell on eBay) without reading the seller's feedback. The seller had a (+3) next to his User ID, which is an okay rating. Good thing

our friend lost the auction. It turned out that the seller had a whopping 20 negative feedback messages. He had 23 positives, mostly posted by suspicious-looking names. Repeat after us: "Always read the feedback!"

Although scoping out an eBay member's ID card is *just that fast, just that simple,* you still need to take the time to read the feedback! (There's that echo again. Good thing it's a wise echo.) Someone with 500 positive feedback messages may look like a good seller, but if you take a closer look, you may find that his or her most recent 10 feedback messages are negative!

View the seller's other auctions

To find out what other auctions the seller has going on eBay, all you have to do is click on the corresponding link on the item page and you're whisked away to a list of the other auction pies the seller has a finger in. If the seller is running 25 auctions and has a good number of positive feedback comments, it says this person is serious about selling and is probably reliable. If the seller has no other auctions going, and has no current feedback, then you may want to do a more thorough investigation and conduct a By Seller search that will show you all their completed auctions in the last 30 days. See Chapter 5 for details.

Sellers often stick with one product. Look at a seller's other auctions, and you may learn more about auctions that feature the item you're interested in. If the seller is someone you like dealing with, look at the seller's other merchandise to see whether there's anything else you'd like to bid on.

Ask the seller a question

If anything about the auction is unclear to you, remember this one word: ASK. Find out all the details about that item before you bid. If you wait until you've won the item before you ask questions, you may get stuck with something you don't want. Double-checking may save you woe and hassle later.

You can find out more about payment options, shipping charges, insurance, and other fun stuff in Chapters 7 and 10.

If you're bidding on a reserve-price auction, don't be afraid to e-mail the seller and ask what the reserve is. Yeah, reserves are customarily kept secret, but there's no harm in asking — and some sellers may even tell you!

To ask a seller a question, follow these steps:

1. **Click the Ask Seller a Question link on the item page.**

   You're automatically taken to the User ID request page.

2. **Enter your eBay User ID and your password in the boxes provided.**

3. **Click the small "remember me" box.**

   This gives your computer access to the e-mail addresses of all registered eBay users throughout your current session — which can save you from repeating the rigmarole of finding e-mail addresses.

4. **Click Enter.**

   You automatically receive the e-mail address for the seller and a list of any other User IDs the seller may have had on eBay in the past.

   You can always change your User ID, but your past life (in the form of feedback messages) stays with you on eBay. Along with your feedback from your previous User ID, all your previous User IDs are listed as well.

5. **Click the seller's current e-mail address, fire off your questions, and send the e-mail.**

   Expect to hear back from the seller in a day. If it takes the seller more than a day or two to respond, and you get no explanation for the delay, think twice before putting in a bid.

Extend your scam antennae if the reply comes from an e-mail address that's *different* from the one to which you sent your question. The seller should include an explanation for the difference in addresses. If you don't see one, ask. And don't be afraid to ask for references. Fraudulent sellers often use several e-mail addresses to hide their true identity. There may be nothing wrong with having several e-mail addresses, but if you're getting a gut feeling the seller is playing hide-and-seek with addresses all over the place, *thank* your gut very much and rethink doing business with that person.

Get to know the high bidder

The User ID of the person the item would belong to if the auction ended right now is listed on the auction item page. Take a look at this name, because you may see it again in auctions for similar items. If the high bidder has lots of feedback, he or she may know the ropes — and be back to fight if you up the ante.

You can use the Bidder search option, shown in Figure 6-2, to find what the bidder's recent auction experience is. If you're bidding on an item, conducting a bidder search can be a valuable asset. You can size up your competition using this search option.

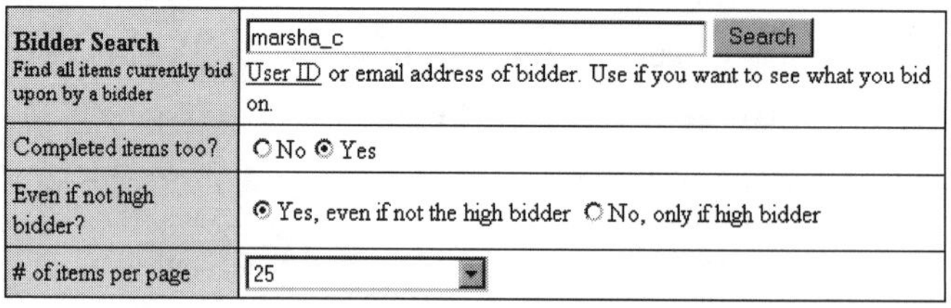

Figure 6-2:
Use the
Bidder
Search box
to get an
idea of the
competi-
tion's
auction
experience.

Bidder Search Find all items currently bid upon by a bidder	marsha_c Search
	User ID or email address of bidder. Use if you want to see what you bid on.
Completed items too?	○ No ◉ Yes
Even if not high bidder?	◉ Yes, even if not the high bidder ○ No, only if high bidder
# of items per page	25

To get the skinny on a bidder (whether it's slender or not), here's the move:

1. **Type in the User ID (or e-mail address) of the bidder you want to search.**

   eBay asks if you're interested in completed auctions.

2. **If you want to see auctions that this specific user has bid on in the past, click Yes on the Completed items too? line.**

   We think you should check completed auctions. They give you a sense of how often the user participates in auctions, and you can always e-mail some of the past sellers for comments on how they liked doing business with this person.

   Remember that eBay has a 30-day limit on the auction information it provides, so don't expect to see results from a year ago. By clicking on the item number in the Results, you can see when your main competition tends to bid, and then bid when you know they won't be looking.

3. **Tell eBay whether you also want to see the person's bid, even if not high bidder?**

   Clicking Yes means that you want to see the bidder's activity in every auction, even if the person is not the *current* high bidder. Clicking No limits the search to auctions where the bidder is the current top dog. We think you should check all of the bidder's auctions to see how aggressively he or she bids on items. You can also see how badly a bidder wants specific items.

4. **Choose the number of items you want to see per page.**

5. **Click Search.**

Figure 6-3 shows the results of a Bidder Search.

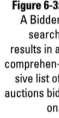

Figure 6-3:
A Bidder search results in a comprehensive list of auctions bid on.

> eBay Bidder List: marsha_c - Microsoft Internet Explorer provided by America Online

File   Edit   View   Favorites   Tools   Help   Links »

Back   Forward   Stop   Refresh   Home   Search   Favorites   History   Mail   Print

Address w-cgi/eBayISAPI.dll?MfcISAPICommand=ViewBidItems&userid=marsha_c&completed=1&all=1&rows=25   Go

Current and recent auctions bid on by marsha_c (596) ⭐

Includes ongoing auctions and auctions which ended in the last 30 days. Bold price means at least one bid has been received.

This list includes **all** auctions marsha_c (596) ⭐ has bid on, and in some cases may no longer be the high bidder.

You can click on the **Start Time**, **End Time**, or **Price** links to sort the list.

Items 1 - 17 of 17 total

Item	Start	End	Price	Title	High Bidder
137405872	07/26/99	08/02/99 11:35:25	**$21.05**	TREND FORECASTER BARBIE (NRFB) CC# OK	marsha_c
135961748	07/23/99	07/30/99 12:58:28	**$11.50**	"Back Street"1961 vhs Susan Hayward, J.Gavin	marsha_c
133904393	07/19/99	07/26/99 09:07:26	**$6.03**	"Hugo Pool" Alyssa Milano movie poster MINT!	marsha_c(*)
132495847	07/16/99	07/23/99 08:28:58	**$20.50**	HUGO POOL w/ Alyssa Milano Sean Penn *RARE*	marsha_c(*)

My Computer

You may be tempted to try to contact a bidder you're competing with so you can get information about the person more easily from feedback. Or you may consider requesting the bidder's contact information from eBay. Doing either is not only bad form, doing so could also get you suspended. Don't do it.

Find out the item's bidding history

The *bidding history,* shown on the auction item page, lists everybody who is bidding on an item. You can see how often and at what time bids were placed, but you can't see *how much* each bidder bids until the auction ends. Look at Figure 6-4 to see a typical bidding history list.

Pay attention to the times bidders are placing their bids, and you may find that, like many eBay users, the people bidding in this auction seem to be creatures of habit, making their bids about once a day and at a particular time of day. They may be logging on before work, during lunch, or after work. Whatever their schedules, you have great info at your disposal in the event that a bidding war breaks out — just bid after your competition traditionally logs out, and you increase your odds of winning the auction.

eBay Item Bid History - Microsoft Internet Explorer provided by America Online

File Edit View Favorites Tools Help   Links »

Back Forward Stop Refresh Home Search Favorites History Mail Print

Address http://cgi3.ebay.com/aw-cgi/eBayISAPI.dll?ViewBids&item=140297512

eBay bid history for Beautiful St. John Knit Aqua Dress. NEW (item #140297512)

If you have questions about this item, please contact the seller at the User ID provided below. Seller assumes all responsibility for listing this item.

```
Last bid for this item:        $142.50
Date auction ends:             08/11/99, 09:35:00 PDT
Date auction started:          08/01/99, 09:35:00 PDT
Seller:                        ▓▓▓▓▓▓▓ (21) ☆
First bid at:                  $44.95
Number of bids made:           11 (may include multiple bids by same bidder)
```

```
marsha_c (600) ★
        Last bid at:        $142.50
        Date of bid:        08/11/99, 09:25:47 PDT

▓▓▓▓▓▓ (0) 👓
        Last bid at:        $140.00
        Date of bid:        08/11/99, 09:25:05 PDT
```

Figure 6-4:
The bid history tells you the date and time at which bidders place their bids.

Early in an auction, there may not be much of a bidding history for an item, but that doesn't mean you can't still check out the dates and times a bidder places bids. Check out all of the previous auctions a bidder has bid on and see if you find a pattern by conducting a By Bidder search. Check out "Get to know the high bidder," earlier in this chapter.

Factoring in the Extras

Before you think about placing a bid on an item, you should factor in the financial obligation you have to make. In every case, the maximum bid you place *won't* be all you spend on an item. We recommend that you look closely at the payment methods the seller's willing to accept, and also factor in shipping, insurance, and escrow costs. If you only have $50 to spend, you shouldn't place a $50 bid on a fragile item that will be shipped a long distance because often the buyer (that would be you) pays for shipping and insurance. In addition, if you live in the same state as the seller, you may have to pay sales tax if the seller is running an official business.

Payment methods

Several payment options are available, but the seller has the right to refuse some forms of payment. Usually, the form of payment is laid out in the item's description. If it isn't, e-mail the seller and get a clear idea of your additional costs *before* you place a bid.

The forms of payment available to you are these:

- ✔ **Credit card:** Paying with a credit card is our favorite payment option, one that's mainly offered by businesses and dealers. We like that credit cards are fast and efficient. In addition, using a credit card offers you another ally, your credit card company, if you're not completely satisfied with the transaction.

  If you're determined to pay by credit card and the seller doesn't offer this option, you can pay through an escrow company. The escrow service converts your credit card purchase into money for the seller. However, before you can do this, the seller has to agree to use the service, and you'll be paying a fee for this service. We have more on escrow companies later in this chapter.

  Sometimes sellers use a friend's company to run credit card payments for eBay auctions. Don't be surprised if you buy a vintage Tonka bulldozer and your credit card is billed from Holly's Hair-o-Rama!

- ✔ **Money order:** Our second-favorite method of payment and the most popular on eBay is the money order. Sellers love money orders because they don't have to wait for a check to clear.

  Money orders are the same as cash. As soon as the seller gets your money order, there is no reason to wait to send the item. You can buy money orders at banks, supermarkets, convenience stores and your local post office. Average cost is about a dollar. If you're purchasing an item that's being shipped internationally, you can pay with an International Money Order from the U.S. Post Office, which costs about three dollars. International buyers may purchase a Western Union money order; www.westernunion.com provides locations in different cities around the world. The United Kingdom alone, has hundreds of Western Union agents ready to receive your payment.

  If you're new to eBay or have a low feedback rating, don't be surprised if the seller says you can only pay by money order. Many sellers are hesitant to accept more risky payments from people with no track record on eBay.

✔ **Personal or cashier's check:** Paying by check is convenient, but has its drawbacks. Most sellers won't ship you the goods until after the check clears, which means a lag time as long as a couple of weeks. If a seller takes personal checks, it usually says in the item's description how long the check will be held before the item gets shipped. Unfortunately, that means that while the seller is waiting for your check to clear, your merchandise is collecting dust in a box somewhere. This is no fun for you or for the seller. Cashier's checks are available at your bank, but often cost many times more than a money order. It's not worth the extra money — buy more eBay items instead!

Before you send that check, make sure you have enough money to cover your purchase. A bouncing check can earn you negative feedback — too many will bounce you off eBay.

The good news about checks is that you can track whether they've been cashed or not. Personal checks leave a "paper trail" you can follow if there's a problem later.

✔ **C.O.D.:** No, we're not talking about codfish, we're talking about *Cash on Delivery.* As a buyer, you may like the idea that you only have to pay for an item if it shows up. But paying C.O.D. has two problems:

• You have to have the money on hand — the exact amount. When was the last time any of us had exact change for anything?

• Even if you have exact change, if you're not around when the item's delivered, you're out of luck.

If you miss Mr. C.O.D., the shipment heads back to Bolivia, or Oblivion, or wherever it came from, never to be seen again. And what do you get? A lot of angry e-mails, and maybe some bad feedback. No wonder sellers rarely use this option.

Most business on eBay is conducted in U.S. dollars. If you happen to buy an item from an international seller, you may need to convert American dollars into another currency. eBay has a currency converter. Go to the Buyer Guide section in the Help page, and click "International Trading." Then click Buy Globally. Click Currency . You have your choice of two converters. We suggest you try them both to compare.

Or you can go directly from your browser to the converters at www.xe.net/ucc and www.oanda.com/converter/classic. Or try the Web site www.Bloomberg.com and click on its currency calculator. You can find the exchange rates of world-wide currencies at all of these Web sites.

Never use a form of payment that doesn't let you keep a paper trail. If a seller asks for cash, quote Nancy Reagan and "Just Say No." Occasionally, we hear of international buyers sending U.S. greenbacks in the mail. But if a seller asks for cash, chances are you may never see the item or your money again. And if a seller asks you to send to a P.O. box, get a phone number. Many legitimate sellers use post office boxes, but so do the bad guys.

Using an escrow service

Even though about half of all sales on eBay are for items that cost $25 or less, occasionally using an escrow service comes in handy — like when you buy a big-ticket item or something expensive and fragile. Sellers will note in their item descriptions if they are willing to accept escrow. If you're nervous about sending a lot of money to someone you don't really know, like a user named Clumsy who only has two feedback comments and is shipping you bone china from Broken Hill, Australia, consider using an escrow company.

Using an escrow company is only worthwhile if the item you're bidding on is expensive, fragile, or going a long distance. If you're spending less than $200 for the item, we recommend that you use eBay's insurance instead.

eBay has a partnership with two escrow services, i-Escrow and TradeSafe. After an auction closes, the buyer sends the payment to the escrow company. After the escrow company receives the money, it e-mails the seller to ship the merchandise. After the buyer receives the item, he or she has an agreed-upon period of time (normally two business days) to look it over and let the escrow service know that all's well. If everything's okay, the escrow service sends the payment to the seller. If the buyer is unhappy with the item, he or she must ship it back to the seller. When the escrow service receives word from the seller that the item has been returned, it returns the payment to the buyer (minus the escrow company's handling fee, equal to 5 percent of the item's selling price).

Before you start an escrow transaction, make sure you and the seller agree on these terms (use e-mail to sort it out). Here are three questions about escrow that you should know the answers to before you bid:

- ✔ Who pays the escrow fee? (Normally, the buyer, though sometimes the buyer and seller split the cost.)
- ✔ How long is the inspection period? (Routinely, two business days after receipt of merchandise.)
- ✔ Who pays for return shipping if the item is rejected? (The buyer, usually.)

To sign up for escrow from any eBay page, step right up:

1. **Click on the Services link on the main navigation bar.**

   You're taken to the Services Overview page.

2. **On the subnavigation bar, click on Buying and Selling.**

   You're taken to the Buying and Selling Tools page.

3. **Click on the Escrow link under the Buyer Tools heading of the Buying and Selling page.**

4. **Fill out the form with your User ID, password, and item number to start use the escrow service.**

5. **Click on the Proceed button.**

   You're taken to Step 2 of the escrow process. Review all the listed information.

6. **Click on the Proceed button.**

   You're taken to Step 3 of the escrow process. Read the terms and conditions, this is the last chance for you to cancel the process. eBay will send the information to i-Escrow, an internet escrow company for processing.

7. **Click on the I Agree button.**

   Your escrow is in the works, and i-Escrow will either call or e-mail you with information regarding the details of this transaction.

Using an escrow service gives you more payment options. Even if the seller doesn't accept credit cards, you can use plastic to pay for an item in an escrow transaction. The escrow company will charge your card and pay the seller for you. Another great feature is that you can also wire money from your bank directly to the escrow service (faster than a speeding bullet?). But if you pay an escrow company by personal check, the transaction will crawl. Escrow companies hold checks for 10 days before they even tell the seller to send you your stuff. Ouch!

If you use a credit card or bank wire, you can do that right from your computer. If you're not comfortable giving your credit card number online, you can print out the escrow company's credit card form and fax it to them.

Rhinestone cowgirl?

Bet you'd look really cool! Vintage '70s Rhinestone Formal Gown. Get ready to tie a yellow ribbon because you could sing behind Tony Orlando in this groovy 100 percent polyester gown by Jack Bryan. Aqua blue with fabulous rhinestone center and streaming bugle beads. All rhinestones and bugle beads appear to be in place, although it's hard to tell if a few are missing. A few small picks in polyester on front hardly noticeable.

The starting bid was $4.99. This dress did not sell! Even today, some folks may find polyester just too scary.

Shipping and insurance costs

Don't let the sale go down with the shipping. Most auction descriptions end with "buyer to pay shipping charges." If the item is not an odd shape, excessively large, or fragile, experienced sellers calculate the shipping based on Priority Mail at the U.S. Post Office, which is the unofficial eBay standard. Expect to pay $3.20 for the first 2 pounds and another 35 cents to pay for tracking the item.

It's also become somewhat routine for the seller to add a dollar or so for packing materials like paper, bubble wrap, tape and such. The cost of these items can run up over time.

You may come across sellers trying to nickel-and-dime their way to a fortune by jacking up the prices on shipping to ridiculous proportions. If you have a question about shipping costs, ask before you bid on the item!

You can double-check on the shipping charges yourself. The most widely used shippers have their own Web sites for calculating charges. See Chapter 10 for details on how to do this. Before bidding on big stuff, like a barber's chair or a sofa, check for something in the item description that says, "Buyer Pays Actual Shipping Charges." When you see that, always e-mail the seller prior to your bid to find out what those shipping charges would be to your home. On larger items, you may need to factor in packing and crating charges. The seller may also suggest a specific shipping company.

As the bumper sticker says, (ahem) *stuff* happens. Sometimes to the stuff you buy. But before you give up and just stuff it, consider insuring it. eBay transactions sometimes involve two types of insurance that may have an impact on your pocketbook:

✔ **Shipping insurance:** Covers your item as it travels through the U.S. Postal Service, or United Parcel Service, Federal Express, or any of the other carriers.

While many sellers offer shipping insurance as an option, others don't bother because if the price of the item is low, they'd rather refund your money and keep you happy than go through all that insurance paperwork. Don't forget that if you want shipping insurance, you pay for it. Chapter 10 is where to look for details on shipping insurance.

✔ **Fraud insurance:** eBay has some nominal insurance against fraud. They have a deal with the world famous insurer Lloyds of London. eBay insurance pays up to $175 (a maximum of $200 minus a $25 deductible). So if you file a $50 claim, you get $25. If you file a $5,000 claim, you still only get $175. All the details of this type of insurance are covered in Chapter 14.

Placing Your Bid

Okay, you've found the perfect item to track (say a classy Elvis Presley wristwatch), and it's in your price range — you're more than interested — you're ready to bid. If this were a live auction, some stodgy-looking guy in a gray suit would see you nod your head and start the bidding at say, $2. Then some woman with a severe hairdo would yank on her ear, and the Elvis watch would jump to $3.

The eBay reality is more like this: You're sitting home in your fuzzy Elvis slippers, sipping coffee in front of the computer; all the other bidders are cruising cyberspace in their pajamas, too. You just can't see 'em. (Be thankful for little favors!)

When you're ready to jump into the eBay fray, you can find the *bidding form* (shown in Figure 6-5) at the bottom of the auction item page or click on the bid-paddle icon at the top of the auction page. The bidding form restates some vital info that's always good to review before you commit yourself:

- ✔ The name of the item
- ✔ The item number
- ✔ The current high bid
- ✔ The bid increment
- ✔ The minimum bid
- ✔ When the auction closes
- ✔ And of course . . . the seller's feedback! (But you knew that.)

To fill out the bidding form page and place a bid, first make sure you're registered (see Chapter 2 for details), and then follow these steps. After you make your first bid on an item, you can instantly get to auctions you're bidding on from your My eBay page. (If you need some tips on how to set up My eBay, see Chapter 5.)

1. **Enter your maximum bid in the box.**

   You see a box where you're asked to enter your bid. The bid needs to be higher than the current minimum bid.

2. **In a Dutch auction, enter the quantity of items that you are bidding on. (If it's not a Dutch auction, the quantity will be always 1.)**

   You don't need to put in the dollar sign — but *do* use a decimal point, unless you really *want* to pay $104.90 instead of $10.49. If you do make a mistake with an incorrect decimal sign, you can retract your bid (see "Retracting your bid" later in this chapter).

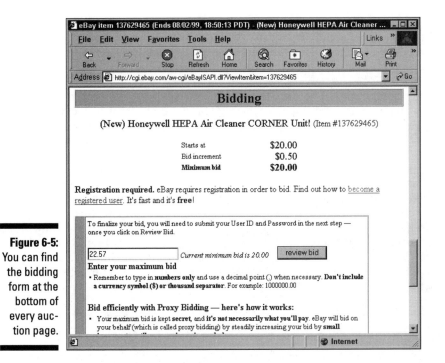

Figure 6-5:
You can find
the bidding
form at the
bottom of
every auc-
tion page.

3. **Click on Review Bid.**

   The Review Bid page loads on your screen, filling it with a wealth of legalese. This is your last chance to change your mind — do you really want the item, and can you really buy it? The bottom line is: If you bid on it and you win, you buy it. eBay really means it.

4. **Type in your User ID and password in the boxes provided.**

5. **If you agree to the terms, click on place bid.**

   Once you agree, the bid confirmation screen appears.

6. **Print out and file a hard copy of your bid.**

   Any time you place a bid, be sure to print out a hard copy and keep it in a file. If any questions or disputes arise later, you have documentation.

Before you get your heart set on winning an item, be sure the auction isn't ending in 20 minutes, because you need a bit of time to track an item and plan your next several moves.

When you first start out on eBay we suggest that you start with a *token bid* — a small bid that won't win you the auction, but which can help you keep tabs on the auction's progress.

Once you make a bid on an item, the item number and title appear at the bottom of your My eBay page, listed under (big surprise) Items I'm Bidding On (shown in Figure 6-6). The Items I'm Bidding On list makes tracking your auction (or auctions, if you're bidding on multiple items) easy.

eBay also sends you an e-mail confirming your bid, and you receive daily confirmations for as long as you're the high bidder on an item. However, eBay's mail server can be slow as a tree-sloth marathon, so don't rely on eBay to keep track of your auctions. After all, this is your money at stake.

Many states consider a bid on an item to be a binding contract. You can save yourself a lot of heartache if you make a promise to yourself — *never bid on an item you don't intend to buy* — and keep to it. Don't make practice bids, assuming that because you're new to eBay you can't win; if you do that, you'll probably win simply because you've left yourself open to Murphy's Law. Therefore, before you go to the Bidding form, be sure you're in this auction for the long haul, and make yourself another promise: *Figure out the maximum you're willing to spend and stick to it.* Read on for doleful accounts of what can happen if you bid idly or get buyer's remorse.

Items I'm Bidding On								See details...
Item	Start	Current	My Max	Quant	Bids	Start	End PDT	Time Left
"Back Street" 1961 vhs Susan Hayward, J.Gavin								
135961748	$9.99	$11.50	n/a	n/a	3	07/23/99	07/30/99, 12:58:28 PDT	0d 19h 44m
TREND FORECASTER BARBIE (NRFB) CC# OK								
137405380	$1.00	$28.57	n/a	n/a	7	07/26/99	07/31/99, 11:34:15 PDT	1d 18h 20m
TREND FORECASTER BARBIE (NRFB) CC# OK								
137405872	$1.00	$21.05	n/a	n/a	9	07/26/99	08/02/99, 11:35:25 PDT	3d 18h 21m
"Hugo Pool" Alyssa Milano movie poster MINT!								
137850553	$1.00	$2.26	n/a	n/a	2	07/27/99	08/03/99, 08:48:05 PDT	4d 15h 34m
Item	Start	Current	My Max	Quant	Bids	Start	End PDT	Time Left
Totals: 4	$12.99	$63.38	-	-	21	-	-	-
Totals: 3	$11.99	$34.81		-	14	-	-	-

Figure 6-6: Keep track of items you're bidding on right from your My eBay page.

Strategies to Help You Outsmart the Competition

Your two cents does matter — at least on eBay. Here's why: Many eBay members tend to round off their bids to the nearest dollar figure. Some choose nice, familiar coin increments like 25, 50, or 75 cents. But the most successful bidders on eBay have found that adding two or three cents to a routine bid can mean the difference between winning and losing. So we recommend that you make your bids in oddish figures like $15.02 or $45.27 as an inexpensive way to edge out your competition. For the first time ever, your two cents may actually pay off!

That's just one of our many strategies to get you ahead of the rest of the bidding pack without paying more than you should. ***Note:*** The strategies in this section are for bidders who are tracking an item over the course of a week or so, so be sure you have time to track the item and plan your next moves. If you find an item you're interested in, but the auction's ending within the next couple of days, we recommend that you skip the current auction (but write down the item name and number for later, so you can look for similar items). Also, get a few auctions under your belt before you throw yourself into the middle of a bidding war.

Dutch-auction strategy

Dutch auctions (auctions in which the seller has multiple items for sale, explained in greater detail in Chapter 1) are funky. Yes, that's a technical term that means that Dutch-auction strategy is a little different. After all, each winner pays the same amount for the item, and Dutch auctions don't have a super-secret reserve price.

But *winning* a Dutch auction isn't all that different from winning other auctions. Therefore, wait until the closing minutes of the auction to bid — and then follow our sage advice for optimum success.

Here are the key things to remember about a Dutch auction:

- ✔ The seller must sell all the items at the *lowest winning price* at the end of the auction, no matter what.
- ✔ Winners are based on the *highest* bids received. If you up the ante, you could win the auction and only pay the *lowest winning price,* which may be lower than your bid.

Confused yet? Say the minimum bid for each of ten Elvis watches is $10 and 20 people bid at $10, each person bidding for one watch. The first ten bidders win the watch. But suppose you come along at the end of the auction and bid $15 as the 21st bidder. You get a watch (as do the first nine people who bid $10), *and* you get the watch for the lowest successful bid — which is $10! Get it?

So here are some things to keep in mind about Dutch auctions:

- ✔ **Know where you stand in the pecking order.** You can see a list of high bidders (and their bids) on the auction page, so you always know where you stand in the pecking order.
- ✔ **Avoid being the lowest or the highest high bidder.** The highest bidder is sure to win, so the usual bidding strategy is to knock out the lowest high bidder. The lowest high bidder is said to be *on the bubble,* and on the verge of losing the auction by a couple of pennies. To avoid being the bidder on the bubble, keep your bid just above the second-lowest winning bid.

✔ **If you want to buy more than one of an item up for auction, make sure you have that number of successful high bids as the auction draws to a close.** Huh? you ask. Remember, winners are based on the *highest* bids. If you're in a Dutch auction for 10 items and place five $15 bids, nothing guarantees you'll win five of the item. Nine other people who want the item could bid $20 apiece. They each win a watch at 15 bucks, and you end up with only one watch. (At least you'd still pay only $15 for it.)

Most bidding on eBay goes on during East Coast work time and early evening hours. This gives you a leg up if you live out West. Night-owl bidders will find after 11:00 p.m. Pacific time, about 2:00 a.m. Eastern time, there are lots of bargains to be had. And believe it or not, there are lots of auctions that end in the wee hours of the morning. Other good times for bargains are weekends, when people aren't sitting around at their computers bidding. Holidays are also great for bargains, especially Thanksgiving. While everyone's in the living room digesting and arguing about what to watch on TV, fire up eBay and be thankful for the great bargains you can win.

Bidding to the max: Proxy bidding

When you make a *maximum bid* on the Bidding form, you actually make several small bids –again and–again until the bidding reaches where you told it to stop. For example, if the current bid is up to $19.99 and you put in a maximum of $45.02, then your bid automatically increases incrementally so that you're ahead of the competition — at least until your maximum bid is exceeded by someone else's. Basically, you bid by *proxy,* allowing your bid to rise incrementally in response to other bidders' bids.

No one else knows you're bidding by proxy; and no one knows how high your maximum bid is. And the best part is that you can be out having a life of your own while the proxy bid happens automatically. (Now if only we had *beds* that made themselves, we'd really be on to something!)

Buyers and sellers have no control over the increments (appropriately called *bid increments*) that eBay sets. The bid increment is the amount of money by which a bid is raised — and eBay's system can work in mysterious ways. The current maximum bid can jump up a nickel or a quarter or even an Andrew Jackson, but there is a method to the madness, even though you may not think so. eBay uses a *bid-increment formula,* which uses the current high bid to determine how much to increase the bid increment. For example:

✔ A five-quart bottle of cold creme has a current high bid of $14.95. The bid increment is 50 cents — meaning that if you bid by proxy, your proxy will bid $15.45.

✔ But a five-ounce can of top-notch caviar has a high bid of $200. The bid increment is $2.50. If you choose to bid by proxy, your proxy will bid $202.50.

Table 6-1 shows you what kind of magic happens when you put the proxy system and a bid-increment formula together in the same cyber-room.

Table 6-1			Proxy Bidding and Bid Increments	
Current Bid	**Bid Increment**	**Minimum Bid**	**eBay Auctioneer**	**Bidders**
$2.50	$.025	$2.75	"Do I hear $2.75?"	Joe Bidder tells his proxy that his maximum bid is $8. He's the current high bidder at $2.75.
$2.75	$.025	$3	"Do I hear $3?"	You tell your proxy your maximum bid is $25 and take a nice, relaxing bath while your proxy calls out your $3 bid, making you the current high bidder.
$3	$.025	$3.25	"I hear $3 from the proxy. Do I hear $3.25?"	Joe Bidder's proxy bids $3.25, and while Joe bidder is walking his dog he becomes the high bidder.

A heated bidding war ensues between Joe Bidder's proxy and your proxy while the two of you go on with your lives. The bid increment inches from 25 cents to 50 cents as the current high bid increases.

$7.50	$.50	$8	"Do I hear $8?"	Joe Bidder's proxy calls out $8, his final offer.
$8	$.50	$8.50	"The bid is at $8. Do I hear $8.50?"	Your proxy calls out $8.50 on your behalf, and having outbid your opponent, you win the auction.

Bidding strategies eBay doesn't talk about

Here's a list of Do's and Don'ts that can help you win your item. Of course, some of them are eBay-endorsed, but we had to get you to notice what we had to say somehow!

✔ **Don't bid early and high.** Bidding early and high shows that you have a clear interest in the item. It also shows that you are a rookie, apt to make mistakes. If you bid early and high, you may spark interest in the item and get people wondering whether maybe "RookieGal" knows a little something they don't know. Then they may start placing bids, which, in turn gets others interested.

Of course, a higher bid does mean more bucks for the sellers and healthy cut for the middleman. No big mystery that many sellers recommend it. In fact, when you sell an item, you may want to encourage it too. (Sauce for the goose . . .)

✔ **Do place an early bid and watch your auction.** If you're interested in an item and you have the time to watch it for from beginning to end, we say that the best strategy is to wait. If you don't have the time, then go ahead — put in your maximum bid early, and cross your fingers!

✔ **Don't freak out if you find yourself in a bidding war.** Don't keel over if, at the split-second you're convinced that you're the high bidder with your $45.02, someone beats you out at $45.50.

You can increase your maximum bid to $46, but if your bidding foe also has a maximum of $46, the tie goes to the person who put in the highest bid first. The early bird catches the item. In plain English, if you aren't the early bird, you lose.

✔ **Do check the item's bid history.** If you find yourself in a bidding war and want an item badly enough, check the bid history and identify your fiercest competitor, and then refer to the section earlier in this chapter, "Get to know the high bidder," for a pre-auction briefing.

To get a pretty exact picture of your opponent's bidding habits, make special note of the times of day when he or she has bid on other auctions. You can adjust your bidding times accordingly. Don't forget to check the bidder's feedback profile.

✔ **Do think twice before trying to outsmart your competition.** If you have reason to think your competition won't follow through with the sale, your instinct may be to *not* outbid your competition. This is a risky move.

✔ **Do remember that most deals go through without a problem.** The overwhelming majority of deals on eBay are closed with no trouble — which means that if the auction you're bidding in is typical and you come in second place, you've lost.

However, if the winning bidder backs out of the auction, the seller *could* (but isn't obligated to) come to the second highest bidder and offer to sell the item at the second bidder's price. Most sellers are understanding if you say no, but most buyers are happy to get a second chance at an item they really wanted. And sellers are thrilled to unload something they would have been stuck with if nobody bought it.

Time Is Money: Strategy by the Clock

There are different bidding strategies depending on how much time is left in an auction. By paying attention to the clock, you can learn about your competition, beat them out, and end up paying less for your item.

Most auctions on eBay run for a week; the auction item page always lists how much time is left. However, sellers can run auctions for as short as three days or as long as ten days. During the end-of-year holiday season, auctions can run as long as two weeks. So synchronize your computer clock with eBay's master time and become the most precise eBay bidder around. If you think we're being slightly Type-A in our recommendation, check out the section, "Using the beat-the-clock strategy," later in this chapter.

To synchronize your clock, make sure that you're logged on to the Internet and can easily access the eBay Web site. Then follow these steps:

1. **Go into your computer's control panel, and double click on the icon that represents your system's date and time functions.**

2. **Go to an eBay subcategory page (such as Antiques: General) by clicking on a main category on the Home page, then any subcategory heading.**

   On the subcategory page you see the Check eBay Official Time link.

3. **Click on the Check eBay Official Time link.**

4. **Check your computer's time against eBay's current time.**

5. **To synchronize the minutes on your system clock with the eBay official time, first click on the minutes in your system clock, and then click the Reload button on your browser.**

6. **Type in the minutes displayed on the eBay subcategory page as soon as the newly reloaded eBay page appears.**

7. **Repeat Steps 5 and 6 to synchronize your system's seconds display with eBay's.**

   This process takes a little practice, but it could mean the difference between winning and losing an auction.

You don't need to worry about the hour display unless you don't mind your system clock displaying Pacific time.

Using the lounging-around strategy

Sometimes the best strategy at the beginning of an auction is to do nothing at all. That's right, relax, take your shoes off, and loaf. Go ahead. You may want to make a token bid, or a low maximum, or just bookmark the page on your browser and check back tomorrow. We take this attitude through the first six days of a week-long auction we want to bid on, and it works pretty well for us. Of course, we check in every day just to keep tabs on the items in our My eBay page, and we revise our strategy as time goes by.

We recommend that if you see an item that you absolutely must have, watch it for a while and plan and revise your maximum bid as the auction goes on.

As you check back each day, take a look at the other bids and the high bidder. Is someone starting up a bidding war? Look at the time that the competition is bidding and note patterns. Maybe at noon Eastern time? During lunch? If you know what time your major competition is bidding, then when the time is right, you can safely bid after he or she does (preferably when your foe is stuck in rush-hour traffic).

If you play the wait-and-see method, then you can decide if you really want to up your bid or wait around for the item to show up again sometime. You may decide you really don't want the item after all. Or you may feel no rush because many sellers who offer multiple items put them up one at a time.

If you think the item you're interested in may become popular in the future, you could be sniffing out a possible trend. Follow your instinct (and spin through Chapter 12 for more about identifying auction trends). Note, however, that eBay takes a dim view of e-mailing a seller to ask whether he or she will have additional items for sale privately after the auction ends — in fact, committing such a faux pas can get you suspended from eBay.

Using the beat-the-clock strategy

You should rev up your bidding strategy during the final 24 hours of an auction — and decide, once and for all, whether you really *have to* have the item you've been eyeing. Maybe you put in a maximum bid of $45.02 earlier in the week. Now's the time to decide whether you're willing to go as high as $50.02.

No one wants to spend the day in front of the computer (ask almost anyone who does). You can camp out by the refrigerator, or at your desk, or wherever you want to be. Just stick a Post-It note where you're likely to see it, reminding you of the exact time the auction ends. You can also use one of the automatic bidding software programs we tell you about in Chapter 19 to bid for you if you know you'll miss the end of an auction.

The bottom line is: Keep tabs on the running time. Don't forget to adjust your clock if you live outside the Pacific time zone and to take daylight-savings time into account (some states don't use it, and the time difference can work to your advantage). You might want to keep one special clock that always shows eBay time — of course, that would mean you're getting pretty serious about your bids . . . .

In the last half hour

With a half-hour left before the auction becomes ancient history, head for the computer and dig in for the last battle of the bidding war. We recommend that you log on to eBay about 15 to 20 minutes before the auction ends. The last thing you want to have happen is to get caught in Internet gridlock and not get access to the Web site.

With 20 minutes remaining, go to the auction page and use your browser to bookmark the item so you can get to it in a hurry. If you're not sure how to create a bookmark, we recommend that you experiment with your browser or ask an Internet-savvy friend how to do it *before* the last 15 minutes of your auction.

With 15 minutes to go, if there's a lot of action on your auction, hit Reload or Refresh every 30 seconds to get the most current info on how many people are bidding.

Sniping to the finish: The final minutes

The rapid-fire, final flurry of bidding is called *sniping*. Sniping is the fine art of waiting until the very last seconds of an eBay auction and then outbidding the current high bidder just in time. Of course, you've got to expect that the current high bidder is probably sniping back.

With a hot item (like some long-ago-retired Beanie Baby, we recommend that you open a second window on your browser (by pressing the Ctrl key and the N key together), keeping one open for bidding and the other open for constant reloading during the closing two minutes. With the countdown at 60 seconds or less, make your final bid. Then keep reloading or refreshing your screen as fast as you can and watch the time tick towards the end of the auction.

eBay doesn't like sniping because some folks consider the practice unseemly and uncivilized — as when dozens of parents used to mob the department store clerks to get to the handful of Cabbage Patch dolls that were just delivered. (Come to think of it, whatever happened to *those* collectibles?) Of course, sometimes a little uncivilized behavior can be a hoot.

We say that sniping is an addictive fun part of life on eBay. And it's a blast. So our unbiased recommendation is that you try sniping. You're likely to benefit from the results — and enjoy your eBay experience even more — especially if you're an adrenaline junkie.

Here's a list of things to keep in mind when you get ready to place your last bid:

- ✔ Know how high you're willing to go.
- ✔ Know how fast (or slow) your computer is.
- ✔ If you know there's a lot of competition, figure out your highest bid to the penny. You should have already researched the item and know its value at this point. Raise your bid only to the level where you're sure you're getting a good return on your investment, and don't go overboard. Certainly if the item has some emotional value to you and you just have to have it, bid as high as you want. But remember, you'll have to pay the piper later. You win it, you own it!
- ✔ Remember, this is a game, and sometimes it's a game of chance, so don't lose heart if you lose the auction.

Although sellers love sniping because it drives up prices and bidders love it because it's fun, a sniper can ruin a week's careful work on auction strategy. The most skillful snipers sneak in a bid so close to the end of the auction that there is no chance for you to counter-bid, which means you lose. Losing too often, especially to the same sniper, can be a drag.

If your computer is slower than state-of-the-art and you want do some sniping, make your final bid two minutes before the auction and adjust the amount of the bid as high as you feel comfortable so you can beat out the competition.

If you can make the highest bid with just 20 seconds left, you most likely will win. The eBay computer may be slow processing a bid with only a second or two left, so your bid might be the last one it records. Figure 6-7 shows the bidding history for a rare copy of a Princeton University yearbook with David Duchovny's photo in it. Talk about a sniping war!

The story of the Snipe sisters

Cory and Bonnie are sisters and avid eBay buyers. Bonnie collects vases. She had her eye on a Fenton Dragon Flies Ruby Verdena vase, but the auction closed while she was at work and didn't have access to a computer. Knowing that, her sister Cory decided to snipe for it. With 37 seconds to go, she inserted the high bid on behalf of her sister. Bang, she was high bidder at $63. But, with 17 seconds left, another bidder sniped back and raised the price to $73. It was, of course, her sister Bonnie. Bonnie got the vase, and they both got a good laugh.

AUCTION ANECDOTE

The auction to-the-death, two-front battle plan

If you get way far into eBay, sniping may become an everyday adrenaline rush for you, and you can increase your odds of success at the last second by viewing the auction you really want to win on *two* separate browser windows — one to reload and watch the action, and the other to bid with.

In the first browser, click the Refresh or Reload button every few seconds to keep you up to date on where the bidding stands; use the second browser to prepare your final bid. If you've got a slow computer, place your bid with about 45 seconds to go. If you have a very fast computer, do it in the last 20 seconds. Some people with nerves of steel wait until T-minus-15 seconds-and-counting to hit Confirm on the bid page.

You don't have to have a second browser to be an expert sniper, but if you want to try sniping with two browsers and you're new to Internet technology, offer to snipe a bid on your technically savvy friend's favorite eBay item if he or she can set you up with two browsers. That gets 'em every time.

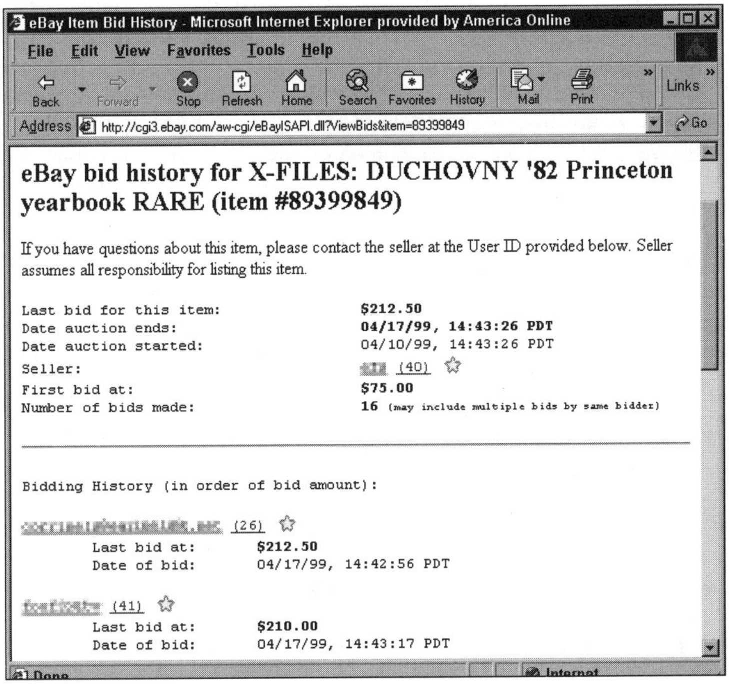

Figure 6-7:
This auction ended at 14:43:26 PDT. Even though the bid of $210.00 was placed just seconds before the auction's end, someone else won the auction with a slightly higher bid.

eBay Item Bid History - Microsoft Internet Explorer provided by America Online

File   Edit   View   Favorites   Tools   Help

Back   Forward   Stop   Refresh   Home   Search   Favorites   History   Mail   Print   Links

Address http://cgi3.ebay.com/aw-cgi/eBayISAPI.dll?ViewBids&item=89399849

eBay bid history for X-FILES: DUCHOVNY '82 Princeton yearbook RARE (item #89399849)

If you have questions about this item, please contact the seller at the User ID provided below. Seller assumes all responsibility for listing this item.

```
Last bid for this item:         $212.50
Date auction ends:              04/17/99, 14:43:26 PDT
Date auction started:           04/10/99, 14:43:26 PDT
Seller:                         ▪▪▪ (40)
First bid at:                   $75.00
Number of bids made:            16 (may include multiple bids by same bidder)
```

Bidding History (in order of bid amount):

```
▪▪▪▪▪▪▪▪▪▪▪▪▪.▪▪▪ (26)
        Last bid at:    $212.50
        Date of bid:    04/17/99, 14:42:56 PDT

▪▪▪▪▪▪▪ (41)
        Last bid at:    $210.00
        Date of bid:    04/17/99, 14:43:17 PDT
```

Done   Internet

Remember that this is supposed to be fun, so don't lose perspective. If you can't afford an item, don't get caught up in a bidding war. Then the only person who wins is the seller. If you're losing sleep, barking at your cat, or biting your nails over any item, it's time to rethink what you're doing. Shopping on eBay is like being on a long line in a busy department store. If it's taking too much of your life, or an item costs too much, be willing to walk away, or log off, and live to bid (or shop) another day.

The Agony (?) of Buyer's Remorse

Maybe you're used to going into a shopping mall and purchasing something that you're not sure you like. What's the worst that could happen? You end up back at the mall, receipt in hand, returning the item. Not so on eBay. Even if you realize you already have a purple feather boa in your closet that's just like the one you won yesterday on eBay, deciding that you don't want to go through with a transaction *is* a big deal. Not only can it earn you some nasty feedback, it can also give you the reputation of a deadbeat.

It would be a shame to float around eBay with the equivalent of a scarlet *D for Deadbeat* above your User ID. Okay, not literally! eBay uses a kinder term — *non-paying bidder* — but for many members, it boils down to much the same thing. If you won an auction and had to back out of your obligation as the winner — even through no fault of your own — you need some info that can keep you in good (well, okay, *better*) standing. Look no farther; you've found it.

Retracting your bid

Remember, many states consider your bid a binding contract, just like any other contract. You can't retract your bid unless some outstandingly unusual circumstances apply:

- ✔ If your bid was clearly a typographical error (you submitted a bid for $4,567.00 when you really meant $45.67), you may retract your bid.

  You won't get any sympathy if you try to retract a $18.25 bid by saying you "meant to" bid $15.25, so review your bid before you send it.

- ✔ If the seller has substantially changed the description of an item after you placed a bid, (the description of the item changes from "can of tennis balls" to "a tennis ball") you may retract your bid.

If you simply must retract a bid, try to do so before the auction ends — and have a good reason for your retraction. eBay users are understanding, up to a point. If you have a good explanation, you should come out of the situation all right. Retracting a bid on the basis of a lame excuse ("I changed my mind") is a classic way to get negative feedback.

So you admit you've made a mistake. Here's how to retract a bid while the auction's still going on:

1. **Click on the Services link on the main navigation bar.**

2. **Click on the buying and selling link on the subnavigation bar.**

3. **Scroll down to Buyer Tools and click on Retract a Bid.**

   The Retracting Bid page appears.

4. **Read the legalese and scroll down the page. Type in your User ID, password, the item number of the auction you're retracting your bid from, and an explanation (in 80 characters or less) in the windows provided.**

   Take a second to review what you've written because once a bid is retracted it cannot be reinstated.

5. **Click on the Retract Bid button.**

   You will receive a confirmation of your bid retraction via e-mail. Keep a copy of it until the auction is completed.

The seller may send you an e-mail to ask for a more lengthy explanation of your retraction, especially if the item was a hot seller that received a lot of bids. You may also get e-mails from other bidders. Keep your replies courteous. Once you retract one bid on an item, all your lower bids on that item are also retracted, and your retraction goes into the bidding history — another good reason to have a really good reason for the retraction.

If you feel something was unfair about the bidding process on an auction, send an e-mail to eBay support@ebay.com. Or if the auction is in progress and time is of the essence, fill out a support Q & A question form at pages.ebay.com/help/basic/main-support.html.

Avoiding deadbeat (non-paying bidder) status

Some bidders are more like kidders — they bid even though they have no intention of buying a thing — but they don't last long on eBay because of all the negative feedback they get. In fact, when honest eBay members spot these ne'er-do-wells, they often post the deadbeats' User IDs on eBay's message boards. Some eBay members have created entire Web sites to warn others about dealing with the deadbeats . . . ahem . . . *non-paying bidders* (civilized-but-chilly, isn't it?). Of course, around chat boards (and on eBay-land in general) they're still called *deadbeats.* That'll probably never change.

Exceptions to the deadbeat (er, sorry, *non-paying bidder*) rule may include the following human mishaps:

- ✔ A death in the family.
- ✔ Computer failure.
- ✔ A huge misunderstanding. If you accidentally sent your payment without any indication of what auction it was for, the seller might think you're a deadbeat because efforts to contact you were in vain and/or you didn't know what you were buying.

If you have a good reason to call off your purchase, make sure eBay knows about it. Figure 6-8 shows you the Non-paying Bidder Appeal form.

Here's how to plead your case from just about any eBay page:

1. **Click on the Help link on the main navigation bar.**

   You're taken to the Help Overview page.

2. **Click on the Community Standards link.**

   You're taken to the community standards page.

3. **Scroll down to the If something goes wrong heading and click on the How to Appeal a Non-paying Bidder Warning link.**

   You're taken to the Non-paying Bidder Appeal page, where you can read eBay's policy and instructions on how to make an appeal.

4. **Scroll down the page and click on the This Form link.**

   You're taken to the Non-paying Bidder Appeal Form page.

5. **On the Non-paying Bidder Appeal Form page, fill in your e-mail address.**

6. **In the message box, write the reasons for your appeal and also include the following information:**

   - The transaction number for the item

   - Your User ID

   - Any supporting information you have to plead your case

7. **Review the information you've given. If you have to change anything you've written, click on the Clear All Data button and start over.**

8. **Click on the Send Inquiry button.**

   All done. Now sit back and cross your fingers.

There is no guarantee that your appeal will be accepted. eBay will contact you after an investigation and let you know whether your appeal was successful.

eBay has a message for non-paying bidders: The policy is *four strikes and you're out.* After the first two complaints about a non-paying (deadbeat) bidder, eBay gives the bad guy or gal a warning. After the third offense, the non-paying (deadbeat! deadbeat!) bidder gets a 30-day suspension. If there is a fourth offense, the (ahem) non-paying bidder is suspended from eBay for good and becomes a *NARU* (Not A Registered User). Nobody's tarred and feathered, but you probably won't see hide nor hair of him or her again on eBay.

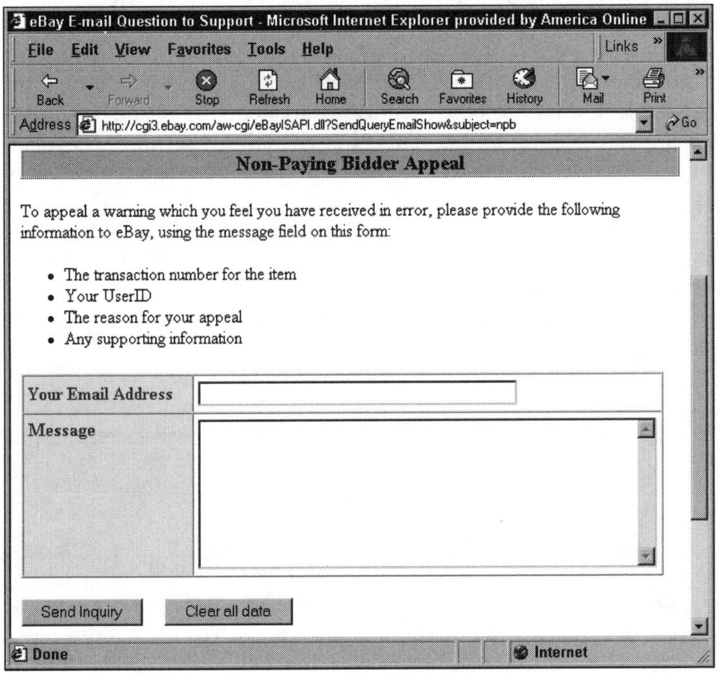

Figure 6-8:
You may succeed at appealing a deadbeat warning if you include good information on this form.

After the Auction: Side Deals?

Losing an auction can be disappointing, but being a loser doesn't mean you're banished to drive a Pinto and wear high-water pants for the rest of your life. You *can* purchase the item of your dreams by trying to make a side deal away from the gaze of eBay's watchful eyes. Side deals do occur in spite of eBay's prohibition against them. It's risky, though.

Buyer's remorse *can* pay off

Sometimes buyer's remorse does pay off! We know one eBay buyer who got a serious case of remorse after winning an auction. She decided to do the right thing and pay for the item even though she didn't want it. After receiving the item, she turned around and *sold* it on eBay for triple what she paid. If you really don't want the item, think like a seller — see whether you can turn a horrible mistake into a profitable venture. For more information on the benefits of selling, have a look at Chapter 8.

If a bidder is outbid on an item that he or she really wants or if the auction's reserve price wasn't met, the bidder may send an e-mail to the seller and see if the seller is willing to make another deal. Maybe the seller has another, similar item or is willing to sell the item directly rather than run a whole new auction.

Make absolutely certain you trust the person with whom you are dealing. Not only will eBay *not* help you if you enter into a deal outside of eBay and it goes south, but eBay *also* strictly prohibits this activity and can suspend you if you are reported for making a side deal.

Final act

Our friend Jack collects autographed final scripts from hit television sitcoms. So when the curtain fell on *Seinfeld,* he had to have a script. Not surprisingly, he found one on eBay with a final price tag that was way out of his league. But he knew that by placing a bid, someone else with a signed script to sell might see his name and try to make a deal. And he was right.

After the auction closed he received e-mail from a guy who worked on the final show and had a script signed by all the actors. He offered it to Jack for $1,000 less than the final auction price on eBay.

Because Jack knows that eBay won't do anything for him if a side deal goes bad, he treads carefully and follows these rules before he even thinks about making a deal:

✔ He checks the seller's feedback.

✔ He only makes side deals with sellers from his local area so that he can go and see the merchandise.

Jack even screened the final episode of *Seinfeld* to see if the seller's name was on the credits before he went to see the script. He made the deal then and there . . . fade to black.

Chapter 7

After You Win the Auction

The thrill of the chase is over, and you've won your first eBay auction. Congratulations — now what do you do? You have to follow up on your victory and keep a sharp eye on what you're doing. The post-auction process can be loaded with pitfalls and potential headaches if you don't watch out. Remember, sometimes money, like a full moon, does strange things to people.

In this chapter, you can get a handle on what's in store for you after you win the auction. We clue you in on what the seller's supposed to do to make the transaction go smoothly, and show you how to grab hold of your responsibilities as a buyer. Although no one could ever accuse us of being as proper as Miss Manners (we like to eat with our elbows on the table!), we give you info here about following proper post-auction etiquette, including the best way to get organized, communicate with the seller professionally, and send your payment without hazards. We also brief you on how to handle an imperfect transaction.

eBay Calling: You're a Winner

The Items I'm Bidding On section of your My eBay page highlights the titles of auctions you've won and indicates the amount of your winning bid. If you think you may have won the auction and don't want to wait around for eBay to contact you, check out this section for yourself and find out — are you a winner?

Throughout the bidding process, items that you're winning will appear in green on your My eBay page. If you've been outbid, the item will appear in red.

After the auction ends, there's no marching band, no visit from Ed McMahon and his camera crew, and no oversize check to duck behind. In fact, you're more likely to find out from the seller that you've won the auction or from the Items I'm Bidding On section of your My eBay page than you are to hear it right away from eBay. eBay tries to get its *End of Auction* e-mails (EOAs) out pronto, but sometimes there's a bit of lag time. For a look at all the contact information in the End of Auction e-mail, see Figure 7-1.

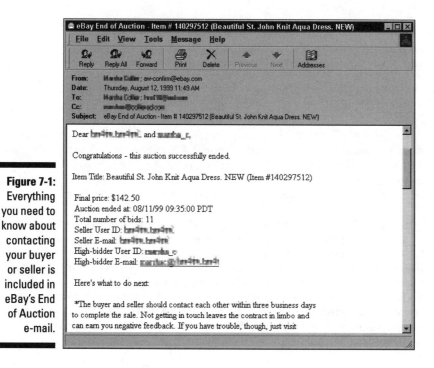

Figure 7-1:
Everything you need to know about contacting your buyer or seller is included in eBay's End of Auction e-mail.

To view the auction page, of the item you won, click on the auction item line on your My eBay page, and the auction page instantly appears.

Getting Your Paperwork Together

Yeah, we know that PCs are supposed to create a paperless society — but cars were supposed to fly by 2000 A.D., too. Maybe it's just as well that some predictions don't come true (think of the way some people drive). Paper still has its uses; printing out hard copies of your auction records can help you keep your transactions straight.

Your auction page shows the amount of your winning bid, the item's description, and other relevant information. The second you find out you've won the auction, print out *two* copies of the auction page. Keep one copy for your files; send the second copy to the seller when you send your payment — it's not only efficient, it's polite.

eBay only displays auctions for 30 days after they end, so don't put off printing out that final auction page.

Many sellers have multiple auctions going at the same time, so the more organized you are, the more likely you will be to receive the correct item (and positive feedback) from the seller. Here's a list of the items you should keep in your auction file — and we do mean an actual manila folder here:

- ✔ A printed copy of your EOA from eBay. Don't delete the EOA e-mail! At least not until you print a copy and keep it for your records. You may need to refer to the EOA e-mail later, and there's no way to get another copy.

- ✔ Printed copies of all e-mail correspondence between you and the seller, especially e-mail that details payment and shipping arrangements.

- ✔ Two printed copies of the final auction page.

Sellers can edit and update their auctions even while they're in progress, and keep your eyes peeled for changes in the auction as you monitor it and place your bids. If there are major changes in the item, you are within your rights to withdraw your bid. (See Chapter 6 for more on the bidding process.)

Getting Contact Information

The eBay rules and regulations say that buyers and sellers must contact each other by e-mail within three business days of the auction's end. So, if an item closes on a Saturday, you have until Wednesday before you have to make contact.

Sellers running multiple auctions may take a little longer to get in touch with you. While eBay rules do say three business days, eBay members are an understanding group of folks if it takes a day or two more.

Most sellers contact auction winners promptly because they want to complete the transaction and get paid. Few buyers or sellers wait for the official eBay EOA to contact each other. In fact, you have several ways to find contact information:

✔ Click on the Ask Seller a Question link on the auction page, which takes you to the User ID History and E-mail Address Request Form in the Find Members section.

✔ Click on the Site Map link, located in the top right corner of every eBay page, and then click on the Search for Members link.

✔ Click on the Search link on the main navigation bar, and then click on the Find Members link of the submenu.

All three of these options take you to Hawaii. Okay, they take you to the Find Members page, shown in Figure 7-2, but we *wish* they would take us to Hawaii.

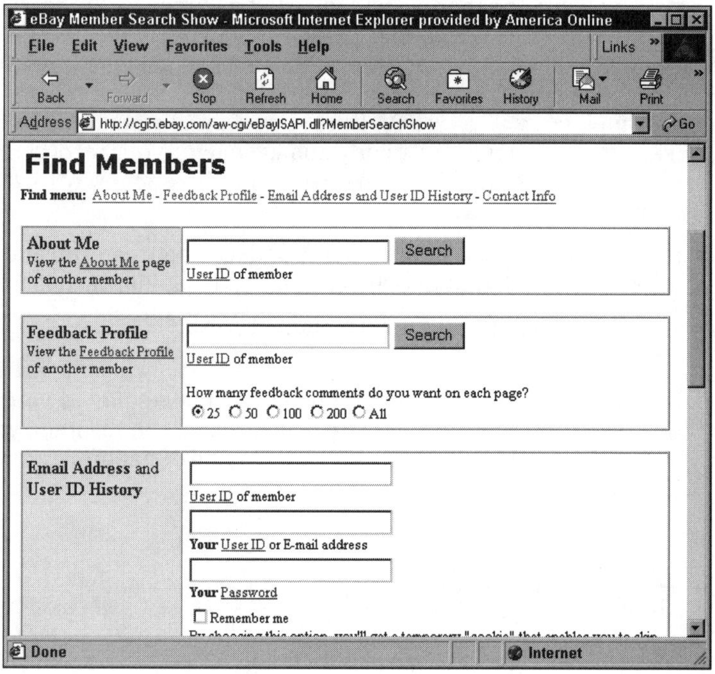

Figure 7-2:
To find contact information about a member, go to the Find Members page.

Within the first three business days after an auction, limit yourself to requesting the seller's e-mail address by filling out the User ID History and E-mail Address window on the Find Members page (refer to Figure 7-2) and then click on the Submit button. The seller's User ID History and e-mail address, shown in Figure 7-3, immediately appear.

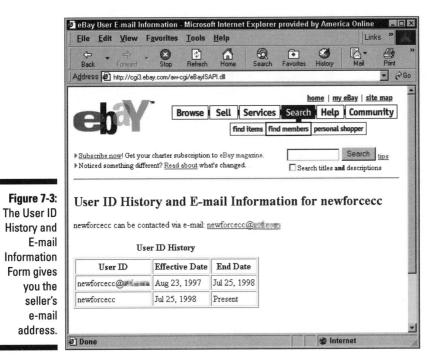

Figure 7-3:
The User ID
History and
E-mail
Information
Form gives
you the
seller's
e-mail
address.

So, What's Your Number?

If you don't hear from the seller after three business days and you've already tried sending an e-mail, you need to get more contact information. Remember back when you registered and eBay asked for a phone number? eBay keeps this information for times like this.

To get an eBay member's phone number, go back to the Find Members page and fill out the contact information window (shown in Figure 7-4) by entering the seller's User ID, as well as your User ID and password, and then clicking on the Submit button.

If all the information is correct, you automatically see a request-confirmation page, and eBay automatically generates an e-mail to both you and the other user, as shown in Figure 7-5.

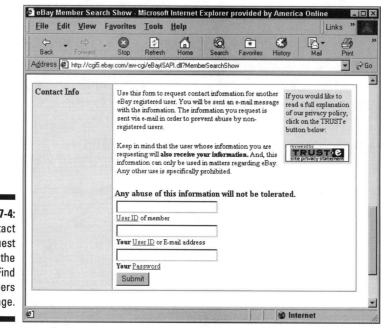

Figure 7-4:
The Contact
Info Request
Form on the
Find
Members
page.

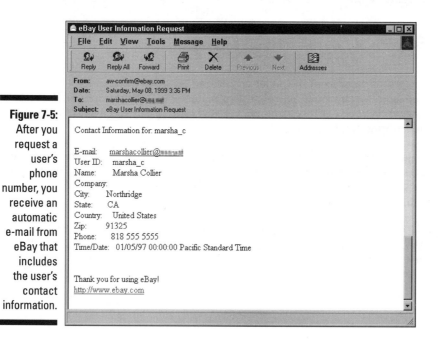

Figure 7-5:
After you
request a
user's
phone
number, you
receive an
automatic
e-mail from
eBay that
includes
the user's
contact
information.

eBay's e-mail includes the seller's User ID, name, company, city, state, and country of residence, as well as the seller's phone number and date of initial registration. eBay sends this same information about you to the user you want to get in touch with.

Often, sellers jump to attention when they receive this e-mail from eBay and get the ball rolling to complete the transaction.

eBay doesn't tolerate any abuses of its contact system. Make sure you only use this resource to communicate with another user about a specific transaction. If you abuse the contact system, eBay can investigate you and kick you off the site. To find out more about eBay's approach to patrolling the system, jump to Chapter 13.

If the seller doesn't contact you in *three business days,* you may have to do some nudging to complete the transaction. See "Keeping in Touch: Dealing with an AWOL Seller," later in this chapter (and have a look at Chapter 11).

Talking Turkey: Communicating with the Seller

Top-notch sellers know that communication is the absolute key to a successful transaction, and they do everything they can to set a positive tone for the entire process with speedy and courteous e-mails.

Here's what a good e-mail from a professional eBay seller should include:

- ✔ Confirmation of the winning price.
- ✔ The address for sending payment or a phone number for credit card processing.
- ✔ Shipping and insurance options. See Chapter 10 for more information on shipping and postal insurance.
- ✔ A review of the shipping price (the fee you pay).
- ✔ Confirmation of escrow (if offered in the auction).
- ✔ The date the item will be shipped.

When you read the seller's e-mail, make sure

- ✔ To compare the terms the seller's laid out in his or her e-mail with the terms laid out on the auction page.
- ✔ That the form of payment and where it should be sent are clear to you.

When you e-mail the seller a reply, you should

✔ Let the seller know what form of payment you're using. For more on payment options, see Chapter 6.

✔ Include your address, your name, and your User ID (if it's different from your e-mail address).

✔ Include the item's title and item number so that the seller knows exactly what you are referring to and can get your item ready to ship as soon as the payment arrives.

✔ Include your phone number if you plan to pay with a credit card. If there's a problem with the credit-card number you've given, the seller can contact you promptly to let you know.

✔ Request that the seller e-mail you any shipping information, such as tracking numbers and an approximate arrival date.

The e-mail you receive from the seller after the auction's over should be a confirmation of the options laid out on the auction item page. If there are significant differences between what the seller's saying now and what you see on your print out of the auction item page, address them immediately with the seller before you proceed with the transaction. For more on clarifying payment options during the bidding process, see Chapter 6.

Sending Out the Payment Promptly and Securely

So how many times have you heard the saying, "The check's in the mail"? Yeah, we heard it about a thousand times too. If you're on the selling end of a transaction, hearing this from the buyer but not getting the money is frustrating and very bad form. It also leads to bad feedback for the buyer.

Being the good buyer that you are (you're here finding out how to do the right thing, right?), naturally you'll get your payment out pronto.

Most sellers expect to get paid within ten business days after the close of the auction. While this timeline isn't mandatory, it makes good sense to let the seller know payment is on the way.

Send your payment promptly. If you have to delay payment for any reason (you have to go out of town, you ran out of checks, you broke your leg), let the seller know as soon as possible. Most sellers are understanding if you send them a kind and honest e-mail. Let the seller know what's up and give them a date by which the money can be expected and then meet that deadline. If the wait is unreasonably long, the seller has every right to offer the item to the next highest bidder or cancel the auction. In that case, you can expect to get some bad feedback.

Here are some tips on how to make sure your payment reaches the seller promptly and safely:

✔ **Double-check your check.** If you are paying by check, have your name and address printed on the check. For privacy and safety reasons, *never* put your driver's license number or Social Security number on your check. On the flip side, a check without a printed name or address sends up a big red flag to sellers that the check might not clear. Sellers are also wary of a check with a very low number (such as check #101).

✔ The number one pet peeve of most eBay sellers is that they get a payment but don't know what it's for. Sellers often complain that buyers send checks without any auction information. Always write the item title, item number, and your User ID on a check or money order.

✔ If you're paying with a credit card and you want to give the seller the number over the telephone, make sure to request the seller's phone number in your reply to the seller's initial e-mail and explain why you want it. Also ask when a good time to call is.

✔ If you can't get the seller by phone, you can safely e-mail your credit card information over the course of several e-mails, each with four numbers from your credit card. Stagger your e-mails so that they're about 20 minutes apart, and don't forget to let the seller know what kind of credit card you're using. Also, give the card's expiration date. We've been doing credit card transactions this way for years and so far we've had no hackers bugging us.

Buyers routinely send out payments without name, address, or a clue as to what it was that was purchased. No matter how you pay, be sure to include a copy of the eBay confirmation letter or a printout of the item description, or a copy of the e-mail the seller sent you. If you pay with a credit card via e-mail or over the phone, you should still send this info through the mail just to be on the safe side. eBay's Emergency Contact Board is filled with sellers begging their buyers to contact them. If you think you may be one of those missing buyers, have a look at Chapter 15 to find out more about the Emergency Contact Board and other helpful bulletin boards.

An order of fries with a menu on the side

One seller offered an old menu from Howard Johnson's, estimating its era as the 1950s from the cars pictured on the cover — and the prices (fried clams were $1.25)! Also included was a separate menu card that listed fresh seafoods and had a liquor menu (with Pieman logo) on the back — plus a list of locations in the New York City area. Except for a couple of staple holes at the top of the front cover (maybe evidence of daily specials past), the menu was in very good condition. The starting bid was $5; it sold for $64!

(Wonder what they want for fried clams in New York these days . . .)

Keeping in Touch: Dealing with an AWOL Seller

The eBay community, like local towns and cities, is not without its problems. With the millions of transactions that go on every week, transactional difficulties do pop up now and then.

The most common problem is the AWOL seller — the kind of person who pesters you for payment and then disappears. Just as you're expected to hustle and get your payment off to the seller within a week, the seller has an obligation to notify you within a week of receiving your payment with an e-mail that says the item has left and will be on your doorstep by a certain day. If you sent the money and you haven't heard a peep in awhile, don't jump the gun and assume the person's trying to cheat you, but be smart and proactive.

Before you contact the seller to find out what's taking so long, make sure the delay isn't *your* fault. See if the check you wrote has cleared or call your credit card company to see if your transaction's gone through. Maybe the seller hasn't responded because he or she is still waiting to get paid. And if you haven't already done so, double-check to see that you've printed all the documentation of the auction.

Follow this week-by-week approach if you've already paid for the item but you haven't heard from the seller:

- **Week one, the gentle nudge approach:** Remind the seller with an e-mail about the auction item, its number, and the closing date. "Perhaps this slipped your mind and got lost in the shuffle of your other auctions" is a good way to broach the subject. Chances are good that you'll get an apologetic e-mail about some family emergency, or last-minute business trip. You'll find that the old saying, "You can attract a lot more bees with honey than with vinegar," works great on eBay.

- **Week two, the civil but firm approach:** Send an e-mail again. Be civil, but firm. Set a date for when you expect to be contacted.

  Meanwhile, tap into some of eBay's resources. See the section, "Getting Contact Information" in this chapter to find out how to get an eBay user's phone number. Once you have this information, you can send a follow-up letter or make direct contact and set a deadline for some sort of action.

- **Week three, take action:** If you still haven't heard from the seller, sail over to SafeHarbor and file a complaint. Explain in detail what has transpired. eBay will launch its own internal investigation. See Chapter 14 to find out more about filing complaints and using other tools to resolve problems.

All's well that ends well, but watch it

When an autographed NBC Sports jacket was put up for auction during a segment on the *Today Show* (proceeds going to the Toys for Tots charity), the bidding heated up to fast and furious right after the show aired. Within hours, the bidding for this leather jacket went over $100,000. Nobody was more amazed than the folks at eBay and NBC. With hundreds of bids coming through the system for the jacket, eBay staffers scrambled to verify each bid. The bidding war escalated to $102,000. The high bidder then had a serious case of remorse when he realized he'd have to dip into his life savings to pay for the jacket. He'd been swept up in the moment; rather than clean him out, eBay let him off the hook. Over the next few days, eBay was able to verify the winning bid of $11,400. Fewer zeros, but it was still a pretty penny — and a wonderful donation to Toys for Tots!

You Get the Item (Uh-Oh! What's This?)

The vast majority of eBay transactions go without a hitch. You win, you send your money, you get the item, you check it out, you're happy. If that's the case — a happy result for your auction — then skip this section and go leave some positive feedback for the seller!

On the other hand, if you're not happy with the item you've received, the seller may have some 'splaining to do. E-mail or call the seller immediately and politely ask for an explanation if the item isn't as described. Some indications of a foul-up are pretty obvious:

- ✔ The item's color, shape, or size doesn't match the description.
- ✔ The item's scratched, broken, or dented.
- ✔ You won an Elvis Presley tee-shirt and received a poster instead.

TIP

A snag in the transaction is annoying, but don't get steamed right away. Contact the seller and see if you can work things out. Keep the conversation civilized. Most sellers want a clean track record and good feedback, so they'll respond to your concerns and make things right. Assume the best about the seller's honesty, unless you have a real reason to suspect foul play. Remember, you take some risks whenever you buy something that you can't touch. If the item has a slight problem that you can live with, leave it alone, and don't go to all the trouble of leaving negative feedback about an otherwise pleasant, honest eBay seller.

Of course, while we can give you advice on what you *deserve* from a seller, you're the one who has to live with the item. If you and the seller can't come to a compromise and you really think you deserve a refund, ask for one.

If you paid the post office to insure the item and it arrives at your home pretty well pulverized, call the seller and then locate the insurance stamp or paper tag attached to the package. This tag is your proof of insurance. Then take the whole mangled shebang back to the post office and talk to the good folks there about filing a claim. Check out Chapter 10 for more tips on how to deal with a shipping catastrophe.

Jump over to Chapter 14 to find out how to file your eBay insurance claim.

Don't Forget the Feedback

Good sellers should be rewarded — and potential buyers should be informed. That's why no eBay transaction is complete until the buyer fills out the feedback form. Here are some handy hints on what kind of feedback to leave for a seller. (For more info on leaving feedback, see Chapter 4.)

✔ Remember that sometimes no one's really at fault when transactions get fouled up; communication meltdowns can happen to anyone.

✔ Give the seller the benefit of the doubt. If the transaction could have been a nightmare but the seller really tried to make it right and meet you halfway, that's an easy call — leave positive feedback.

✔ Whenever possible, reward someone who seems honest or tried to fix a bad situation.

✔ If the seller worked at a snail's pace but you eventually got your item and you're thrilled with it, you may want to leave positive feedback with a caveat. Something like *Item as described, good seller but very slow to deliver* sends the right feedback message (in this case, accurate and neutral).

✔ If the seller worked at a snail's pace, did adequate packaging and the item was kinda-sorta what you thought, you might want to leave neutral feedback; it wasn't bad enough for negative, but didn't deserve praise. For example: *Really slow to deliver, didn't say item condition was good not excellent but did deliver.* Wishy-washy is okay as a response to so-so; at least the next buyer will know to ask very specific questions.

✔ Never write negative feedback in the heat of the moment and never make it personal. Do expect a response, but don't get into a negative feedback war. Life's interesting enough without taking on extra hassles.

"The Accidental Deadbeat" might be an intriguing title for a movie someday, but being a deadbeat isn't much fun in real life. See Chapter 6 for more details on buyer's remorse and retracting a bid *before* the end of an auction.

Part III

Are You Selling What They're Buying?

The 5th Wave   By Rich Tennant

@RICHTENNANT

"Frankly, I'm not sure this is the way to enhance your eBay auction item page."

In this part . . .

A lot of different factors are at work when a seller makes a nice profit on an item he or she has put up for sale.

If you're new to selling, you can find out all the benefits of selling and be pointed in the right direction to find items that could make you a tidy profit. In fact, you may be sitting on profits in your own home. eBay has its rules, though, so when you're assessing an item's value to prepare for your auction, you should probably check to see that the item isn't prohibited from being sold on the eBay site.

We walk you through the required paperwork you need to fill out to sell your item, and we show you how to close the deal and ship the item without any hassles. But even though we're good, we can't stop problems from occurring, which is why we walk you through every conceivable mishap. We also have a chapter for those eBay newbies out there who know that a picture's worth a thousand words. That's right — if you really want to make money on eBay, then you can't miss our advanced strategies.

Chapter 8

Selling in Your Bedroom Slippers for Fun and Profit

. . . .

In This Chapter

▶ Discovering the benefits of selling

▶ Looking for inventory in your own backyard

▶ Knowing what to sell, when to sell, and how much to ask

▶ Staying out of trouble — what you can't sell on eBay

▶ Paying the piper with eBay fees

▶ Keeping the taxman happy (or at least friendly)

. . . .

So you're ready to sell stuff on eBay but you're not quite sure what to put up for auction, huh? Take a look around. Your inventory is in front of you, or down in the basement, or even over at the mall or your local discount store. Finding items to sell can be as easy as opening up your closet and as challenging as acquiring antiques overseas. Either way, establishing yourself as an eBay seller isn't that difficult when you know the ropes.

In this chapter, we show you how to look for items under your own roof, figure out what they're worth, and turn them into instant cash. But before you pick your house clean (we know eBay is habit-forming but keep a *few* things for yourself!), read up on the eBay rules of the road — like how to sell, when to sell, and what *not* to sell. If you're interested in finding out how to set up your auction page, get acquainted with Chapter 9; if you want to read up on advanced selling strategies, Chapter 12 is where to find them.

Why Should You Sell Stuff on eBay?

Whether you need to clear out 35 years of odd and wacky knick-knacks cluttering your basement or you seriously want to earn extra money, the benefits of selling on eBay are as diverse as the people doing the selling.

For us, the biggest plus to selling on eBay is wheeling and dealing from our homes in pajamas and fuzzy slippers (every day is casual Friday in our book!). But no matter where you conduct your business or how you dress, lots of more important big-time rewards exist for selling on eBay. You can

- Start a business for little or no money. (Call it do-it-yourself e-commerce.)

- Get a taste of running a business. ("Please tell Donald Trump I'll call him back!")

- Clear out your household clutter. ("Oh, so *that's* what the garage looks like empty!")

- Make as much money as you are willing to work for. ("We did great last month — let's go to Maui.")

- Learn about your items while selling. ("I thought Chippendales were dancers, not furniture.")

- Teach your kids life lessons. ("Remember, always buy low, sell high!")

- Have fun wheeling and dealing. ("Nah, let's go to Maui another time, I wanna run some more auctions this week.")

Most people starting a business have to worry about rounding up investment capital (start-up money they may lose), building inventory (buying stuff to sell), and finding a selling location like a booth at a swap meet or even a small store. Today, even a little Mom-and-Pop start-up operation requires a major investment. eBay's helped to level the playing field a bit; everybody can get an equal chance to start a small business with just a little money. Anyone who wants to take a stab at doing business can get started with just enough money to cover the Insertion Fee.

Life lessons learned on eBay

If you have kids, get them involved with your eBay selling. They'll learn real life lessons they can't learn in school. Give them a feel for meeting deadlines and fulfilling promises. Get them writing e-mails (if they aren't already). eBay is a great place to learn basic economics and how to handle money. We know somebody who even teaches her children about geography by using eBay. Every time she completes a transaction, she marks the city in which the buyer lives by placing a pin on a huge map of the United States.

Get creative and make eBay a profitable learning experience too! Remember, however, that eBay doesn't let anyone under the age of 18 register, buy, or sell — so make sure you're in charge of handling all transactions. Your kids can help out, but they need to be under your supervision at all times.

Start your budding business empire with just one item. Put the item up for auction, get it sold, collect the payment, and ship it out. Or, to paraphrase instructions from shampoo bottles, "Sell, ship, repeat."

Get a few transactions under your belt. See how you like the responsibilities of marketing, collecting money, shipping, and customer service. Grow a bit more and then brush up on Chapter 12 to find out about spotting trends, acquiring inventory, and marketing your items for maximum profit. In no time you'll be making items disappear faster than David Copperfield (though you may have a little trouble with the Statue of Liberty — how'd he *do* that, anyway?).

Mi Casa, Mi Cash-a: Finding Stuff to Sell

Got an attic groaning with the weight of years of unwanted tchotchkes? Closets bulging with long-abandoned sporting equipment? A garage so crammed that you can't even park a matchbox car inside? You are not alone! Clearing out the clutter is a pretty common reason for joining eBay!

Finding merchandise to sell on eBay is as easy as opening up a closet and as tough as climbing up to the attic. Just about anything you bought and stashed away (because you didn't want it, forgot about it, or it didn't fit), is fair game. Think about all those really awful birthday and holiday presents (hey, it was the thought that counted — and the giver may have forgotten about them, too). Now you have a place you can try to unload them (they could even make somebody happy)!

In your closet, find what's just hanging around:

- ✔ Clothing that no longer fits. (Do you really want to keep it around in case it fits again?)

- ✔ Clothing that's out of date. (You wouldn't be caught dead in it, but others may think your old clothes are *retro cool!*)

- ✔ Shoes and boots you wore once and put away. They're not your style, but they're almost brand new. (Cowboy boots are big sellers, pardner.)

- ✔ Kids' clothes. (Kids outgrow things fast. Use profits from the old items to buy new clothes they can grow into. Now, that's recycling!)

And consider what's parked in your basement, garage, or attic:

- ✔ Old radios, stereo and video equipment, 8-track systems. (Watch these items fly out of your house, especially the 8-tracks — believe it or not, people love 'em!)

- Books you finished reading long ago, and don't want to read again. Look on the copyright page at the beginning of your old hardcover books by famous authors. (Some of these earn big money on eBay.)

- Leftovers from an abandoned hobby. (Who knew that building miniature dollhouses was so much work?)

- Unwanted gifts. Have a decade's worth of birthday, graduation, or holiday gifts collecting dust? Put them up on eBay and hope Grandma or Grandpa doesn't bid on them because they think you need another mustache spoon!

Saleable stuff may even be lounging around in your living room or bedroom:

- Home décor you want to change. Lamps, chairs, rugs (especially if they're antiques) sell quickly. If you think an item is valuable but you're not sure, get it appraised first.

- Exercise equipment. If you're like us, you bought this stuff with every intention of getting in shape, but now all that's building up is dust. Get some exercise carrying Stair-Masters, treadmills, Nordic Tracks — even Suzanne Somers's famous Thigh-Master — to the post office after you've sold them on eBay!

- Records, videotapes, and laser discs. Sell them after you upgraded to new audio and video formats like DVD or DAT (Digital Audio Tape). A lot of people out there would like to get their hands on old movies and albums. (Think Betamax is dead? You may be surprised.)

- Autographs. Did you forget about that old 8 x 10 autographed picture of Lucille Ball you got in the 1970s? Put it up for auction and it could bring in around $100. All types of autographs — sports figures, celebrities, world leaders — are very popular on eBay. A word of caution though: A lot of fakes are on the market, so make sure what you're selling (or buying) is the real thing.

Don't overlook selling your items as a collection. If you have piles of stamps, coins, or even a run of magazines that you saved as a kid, organize 'em by specific topic or date and call the whole shebang a collection.

Sometimes you may want to get rid of something you don't know anything about. Before selling that contraption that's been sitting in your basement for ages, do your homework. Hit the library, look over any magazines you can find about the item, see if other eBay sellers are offering something similar. Go to the eBay chat boards and get advice from collectors. In short, make sure you know all about the item and have a ballpark idea of its value before you put it up for auction.

The Tiger Beat goes on!

Selling these magazines as a set, this seller scored a pretty nice profit:

3 Tiger Beat Mags 1972 David Cassidy Donny Osmond. Here's a lot of three issues of the excellent teen mag Tiger Beat (8"x11", 76 pages) from the tail end of the Bobby Sherman era, January, February and March, 1972. Bobby is still featured in all three, but starting with the February issue, his photo is no longer on the cover. The mags contain dreamy color pinups of David Cassidy, Donny Osmond, and The Osmonds. All three mags are fully intact and in very good condition, although there's a little yellowing of the inside pages due to age. Winning bidder pays $4.50 shipping and handling.

The starting price for this collection was $8.00. The selling price was $23.50.

Know When to Sell

Warning . . . warning . . . we're about to hit you with some clichés: *Timing is everything, Sell what you know and know when to sell. Buy low and sell high.* Okay, we're done. Ouch! Clichés may be painful to hear over and over again, but they do contain nuggets of good information. (Maybe they're well known for a reason?)

Experienced eBay sellers know that when planning an auction, timing is *almost* everything. You don't want to be caught with 200 Cabbage Patch Kids during a run on Furbies, and Superman action figures are good sellers — *unless* a new Batman movie is coming out.

Some items — such as good antiques, rugs, baseball cards, and sports cars — are timeless. But timing still counts. Don't put your rare antique paper-cutter up for auction if someone else is selling one at the same time. We guarantee that will cut into your profits.

Timing is hardly an exact science. Rather, timing is a little bit of common sense, a dash of marketing, and a fair amount of information-gathering. Do a little research among your friends. What are they interested in? Would they buy your item? Use eBay itself as a research tool. Search to see whether anyone's making money on the same type of item. If people are crazed for some fad item (say, Beanie Babies) and you have a bunch, *yesterday* was the time to sell. (In other words, if you want your money out of 'em, get crackin'!)

Snapping up profits

Way back in 1980, when Pac-Man ruled, our friend Ric decided to try his hand at photography. Hoping to be the next Ansel Adams or to at least snap something in focus, he bought a 1/4 Kowa 66, one of those cameras you hold in front of your belt buckle while you look down into the viewfinder. Soon after he bought the camera, Ric's focus shifted. The camera sat in its box, instructions and all, for over 15 years until he threw a garage sale.

Ric and his wife didn't know much about his Kowa, but they knew that it was worth something. When he got an offer of $80 for it at the garage sale, his wife whispered, "eBay!" in his ear, and he turned the offer down.

Ric and his wife posted the camera on eBay with the little information they had about its size and color, and the couple was flooded with questions and information about the camera from knowledgeable bidders. One bidder said that the silver-toned lens made it more valuable. Another gave them the camera's history.

Ric and his wife added each new bit of information to their description and watched as the bids increased with their every addition — until that unused camera went for more than $400 in a flurry of last-minute sniping! These days, when Ric posts an auction, he always asks for additional information and adds it to the auction page.

If the eBay market is already flooded with dozens of an item and no one is making money on them, you can afford to wait before you plan your auction.

Know Thy Stuff

At least that's what Socrates would have said if he'd been an eBay seller. Haven't had to do a homework assignment in a while? Time to dust off those old skills! Before selling your merchandise, do some digging to find out as much as you can about it.

Getting the goods on your goods

Here are some ideas to help you flesh out your knowledge of what you have to sell.

- **Hit the books.** Check your local library for books about the item. Study price guides and collector magazines.

- **Go surfin'.** Conduct a Web search and look for info on the item on other auction sites. If you find a print magazine that strikes your fancy, check to see whether the magazine is available on the Web by typing the title of the magazine into your Web browser's search window. (For detailed information on using search engines to conduct a more thorough online search, check out Chapter 5.)

✔ **When the going gets tough, go shopping.** Browse local stores that specialize in your item. Price it at several locations.

When you understand what the demand for your product is (whether it's a collectible or a commodity) and how much you can realistically ask for it, you're on the right track to a successful auction.

✔ **Call in the pros.** Need a quick way to find the value of an item you want to sell? Call a dealer or a collector and say you want to *buy* one. A merchant who smells a sale will give you a current selling price.

✔ **eBay to the rescue.** eBay offers some guidance for your research on its category pages. One source eBay offers is Inside Scoop, where you can get background articles on all kinds of items. (For a look at Inside Scoop, see Chapter 5.) Another source, Front Page, shown in Figure 8-1, offers timely collecting advice. Finally, eBay has category-specific chat rooms, where you can read what other collectors are writing about items in a particular category. Figure 8-2 shows you what the Category-Specific Chat Rooms page looks like.

Figure 8-1:
Find out more about the items you're selling by reading Front Page.

Toy Shop 1998 Readers' Awards - Microsoft Internet Explorer provided by America Online

File   Edit   View   Favorites   Tools   Help   Links

Back   Forward   Stop   Refresh   Home   Search   Favorites   History   Mail   Print

Address http://pages.ebay.com/community/library/catindex-toys-shop.html

Toys & Bean Bag Plush

Toy Shop 1998 Readers' Awards:
Readers Pick Their Faves of 1998; Beanies, Barbie Among Top Vote Getter

It was an enviable task, indeed.

Try to narrow down a year's worth of toys to select the few most deserving of honor. Most worthy of mention.

That was the task put to *Toy Shop* readers several months ago when we debuted our Readers' Awards. We thought there would be a lot of interest. We were right.

Thanks to the healthy response of readers, we were able to tally the winners in 17 categories. We present those winners now.

The winning companies will be sent certificates of honor. **Toy Shop** editor Sharon Korbeck and associate editor Merry

front page

Beans for Balkans
Toy Shop 1998 Readers' Awards
The Ultimate Soldier
Others Challenge Ty
Making Action Figures
Beanie Authenticity
Safe, Not Sorry
Fifty Years of Frisbee
What a Drag
Collecting Board Games
Toy Shop's Top 40
Help the Homeless
Bug's Life

Click here to bid on Sally Winey bears

Done   Internet

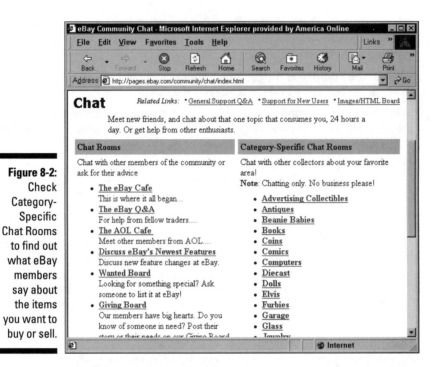

Figure 8-2:
Check
Category-
Specific
Chat Rooms
to find out
what eBay
members
say about
the items
you want to
buy or sell.

To get to those Inside Scoop, Front Page, and Category-Specific chat-room pages from the eBay Home page, follow these steps:

1. **Click on any one of the Community links on the navigation bar found on every eBay page.**

    You're taken to the Community overview page.

2. **Click on the Chat link on the subnavigation bar to get to all of eBay's chat rooms and message boards, or click on the Library link to get the Inside Scoop or Front Page of a specific category.**

Collectors still use published price guides when they put a value on an item. With so much fast-moving e-commerce on the Internet, price guides often lag behind the markets they cover. Take their prices with a grain of salt.

For information on how items are graded and valued by professional collectors, jump back to Chapter 5, where we discuss grading your items.

Be certain you know what you have — not only what it is and what it's for, but *whether it's genuine*. Make sure it *is* the real McCoy. You are responsible for your item's authenticity; counterfits and knock-offs are not welcome on eBay. In addition, manufacturers are keeping an eye out on eBay for counterfeit and stolen goods, and may tip off law enforcement.

If you're having trouble finding out information about an item you want to sell, try finding information on a related subject. For example, say you have an old lamp that your mother swears is Art Deco, but you've struck out when you've looked for info on lamps. Try looking for info on the Art Deco period — you may just find the tidbit you want that way.

Spy versus spy: Comparison selling

Back in the old days, successful retailers like Gimbel and Macy spied on each other to figure out ways to get a leg up on the competition. Today, in the bustling world of e-commerce, the spying continues, and dipping into the intrigue of surveiling the competition is as easy as clicking your mouse.

Assessing an item's value using price guides

The following material comes from Lee Bernstein and is also available on the eBay Web site. The opinions offered here are not eBay's, and eBay doesn't validate or endorse their accuracy. You can visit Lee Bernstein's Web site at www.elee.com.

Call it collectible-mania, but hundreds of books on collectibles and their values are out there, written by knowledgeable and responsible experts who go to great lengths to give their readers the finest information possible. The prices quoted in these books are known as *book price,* or *secondary market price,* which is different from the *fair market value* (the price an item is legitimately expected to sell for).

Book price and fair market value are not always the same; they may vary according to geographic region and who is selling the piece. A dealer, for example, can command a higher price than a consumer.

Price guides, however useful they may be, don't show final price, bargaining price, or even whether an item sold at book price *at all.* Instead they offer collectors a ballpark price — and

even a good approximation is still approximate. The true value of an item can only be assessed when two or more bidders compete. A desirable piece may go higher or lower than expected, depending on the number of bids.

Book price doesn't always show you what to expect if the item is in less-than-excellent condition. Whether buying or selling, you have to calculate the item's price based on its actual condition.

Values fluctuate, so by the time you get a book, the value it shows for an item may already be out of date.

Smart sellers seldom expect to get book price for their items. How close they get to it depends on how much a buyer is actually willing to pay.

The prices quoted in most collectors' books are intended to be flexible reference points to help guide shoppers. Check the guidelines that you'll find at the beginning of every good collecting book; they lay out how the author has determined the prices you see listed.

Let's say you finally have to admit that you're the biggest *X-Files* fan ever. Maybe you collect *X-Files* stuff — posters from the movie, lunchboxes, that sort of thing. *Lunchboxes?* That piece of tin that holds your lunchtime vittles may very well fetch a nice sum of money. To find out for sure, you can do some research on eBay. To find out the current market price for an *X-Files* lunchbox, you can conduct a Completed Search on the Search page and find out exactly how many *X-Files* lunchboxes have been on the auction block in the last month. You can also find out their selling prices and how many bids the lunchboxes received by the time the auction was over. See Figure 8-3 for what the results page looks like; Chapter 5 offers specific info on conducting a Completed Search from the Search page.

Sometimes sellers make errors when they write item titles. In the case of our *X-Files* lunchbox, we suggest that you conduct a second Completed Search, only this time try typing in **X-Files lunch box** (putting a space between *lunch* and *box*). Sure enough, when we tried this tactic, we found a fourth listing for an *X-Files Lunch Box,* which sold for $46.50 and received 23 bids. Also, if you type **X-File** (without the *s*) you may find only a fraction of the items you could find by typing the correct *X-Files* title.

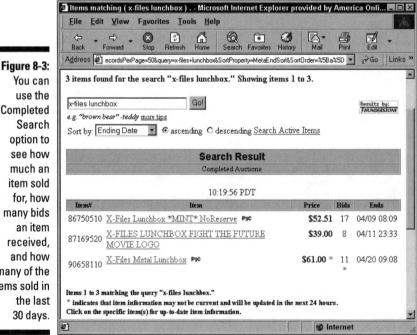

Figure 8-3: You can use the Completed Search option to see how much an item sold for, how many bids an item received, and how many of the items sold in the last 30 days.

Always search for the same item with different word variations. This is about the only time "creative" spelling can actually help you.

At the time of our search, an *X-Files* lunchbox was a popular item. Here's how we know that:

- Only four had sold within the 30 days before our search — which means people hang on to them and sell them high.
- Each lunchbox we found received a good number of bids, and the average selling price was around $50.

Although your search results may vary, you can get a ballpark value of an item using this search method and get a good idea what price to set when you prepare to set up your auction. Table 8-1 shows you the stats on our *X-Files* search.

Table 8-1	Completed *X-Files* Lunchbox Auctions
Selling Price	*Number of Bids*
$52.51	17
$39.00	8
$61.00	11
$46.50	23

Look at the individual auction item pages for each item that your Completed Search turns up — that way, you can confirm that the items (lunchboxes, for example) are identical to the one you want to sell. When you do your research, factor in your item's actual condition. Read the individual item descriptions — if your item's in better condition, expect (and ask) more money for it; if your item is in worse condition, expect (and ask) less. Also, note the categories the items are listed under — they may give you a clue about where eBay members are looking for items just like yours.

If you want to be extremely thorough in your comparison selling, go to one or two of eBay's competing auction sites to see whether the results of your eBay search mesh with what's going elsewhere. If you find that there are no items like yours for sale anywhere else online and you're pretty sure people are looking for what you have, you may just find yourself in Fat City.

Don't forget to factor in the history of an item when you assess its value. Getting an idea of what people are watching, listening to, and collecting can help you assess trends and figure out what's hot. For more about using trend-spotting skills to sniff out potential profits, take a gander at Chapter 12.

Know What You Can (and Can't) Sell

The majority of auctions found on eBay are aboveboard. But sometimes eBay finds out about auctions that are either illegal (in the eyes of the state or federal government) or prohibited by eBay's rules and regulations. In either case, eBay steps in, calls a foul, and makes the auction invalid.

eBay doesn't have rules and regulations just for the heck of it. They want to keep you educated so you won't unwittingly bid on—or sell—an item that has been misrepresented. They also want you to know what's okay and what's prohibited so that if you run across an auction that looks fishy, you'll help out your fellow eBay members by reporting it. And they want you to know that getting your auction shut down is the least of your worries — you can be suspended if you knowingly list items that are prohibited. And we won't even talk about criminal prosecution.

Officially, the biggest no-no's on eBay are

- ✔ Items that are prohibited from being bought, sold, or owned in the state of California.

- ✔ Items that infringe on a third party's ownership of a trademark, copyright, logo, or any other form of intellectual property.

- ✔ The unofficial third type of item is anything that could make eBay liable.

The items that you absolutely *cannot* sell on eBay fit into *all three* categories. Those items can be legally ambiguous at best, not to mention potentially risky and all kinds of sticky. To find a detailed description of which items are prohibited on the eBay Web site:

1. **Click on the Help link on the main navigation bar at the top of all eBay pages.**

   The subnavigation bar appears while you are simultaneously taken to the friendly Help Overview page.

2. **Click on the Community Standards link on the subnavigation bar.**

   You can find all the answers you need under the Policies and Conduct heading of the Community Standards page.

You can also click on the Site Map, go to the Help heading, and click on the Prohibited and Infringing Items link.

Sometimes an item is okay to own, but not to sell. Other times the item is prohibited from being *sold and possessed.* To complicate matters even more, some items may be legal in one part of the United States but not in others. Or an item may be illegal in the United States but legal in other countries.

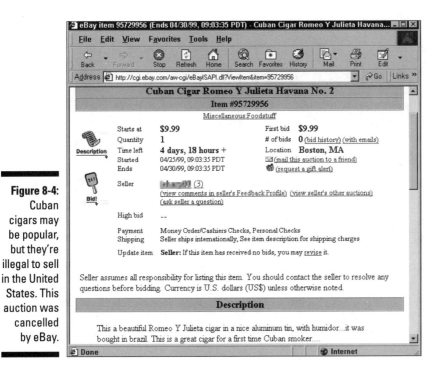

Figure 8-4:
Cuban
cigars may
be popular,
but they're
illegal to sell
in the United
States. This
auction was
cancelled
by eBay.

Because eBay's base of operations is in California, United States law is enforced — even if both buyer and seller are from other countries. Cuban cigars, for example, are legal to buy and sell in Canada, but even if the buyer *and* the seller are from Canada, eBay says "no permiso" and shuts down auctions of Havanas fast. Figure 8-4 shows an auction that was shut down soon after we found it.

Even though possessing (and selling) many of the items in the following list is legal in the United States and elsewhere, you are absolutely, positively *prohibited* from buying and selling the following on eBay:

✔ **Firearms of all types,** as well as firearms accessories, including antique, collectible, sport or hunting guns, air guns, BB guns, silencers, converters, kits for creating guns, gunpowder, high-capacity ammunition magazines (receptacles designed to feed ten rounds or more into a gun, not the publications you might read about ammo), and armor-piercing bullets. You can't even sell a gun that doesn't work.

You *can* buy and sell *single* bullets, shells, and even antique bombs and musketballs, *as long as they have nothing explosive in them.*

✔ **Military weapons** like bazookas, grenades, and mortars.

All for one and none for musket balls!

Who woulda thunk that this item didn't go flying off the shelf?

It was a large-caliber 17th- or 18th-century musket ball, found in England with other early

artifacts. Although, these large-size calibers were getting hard to find — and the starting price was $3 — the item did not sell.

✔ Stop in the name of the law if you're thinking about buying or selling **police and other law enforcement badges and IDs,** including actual United States federal badges or imitation badges. In fact, selling just about any U.S. government badge can get you in hot water.

You also can't own or sell those agencies' identification cards, credential cases, or those really cool jackets they use in raids. Selling a copy or reproduction of any of these items is prohibited, too, because these items are copyrighted. (See the section on infringing items in this chapter.)

If you find a badge that's legal to sell and own, you need to provide a letter of authorization from the agency. The same letter of authorization is required for fake badges, such as reproductions or movie props.

✔ If you've had it with Buster, your pet ferret, don't look to eBay for help in finding him a new home. **Pets and wildlife,** including animal parts from endangered species, are prohibited on the eBay site. You can't sell stuffed spotted owls or rhino-horn love potions, either. If you're in the animal business, *any* animal business, eBay is not the place for you.

You can get a list of endangered species from the U.S. Fish and Wildlife Service at `www.fws.gov/r9endspp/lsppinfo.html`. (And if you have an exotic pet who needs a new home, you can probably find Web sites devoted to the species. Buster, for example, is in luck; several ferret clubs have Web sites and would be happy to help find him a new home.)

✔ **Child pornography** is strictly prohibited on eBay, but you can sell other forms of pornography here. See the section later in this chapter about questionable items.

✔ Stay away from **forged items.** Autographs from celebrities and sports figures are big business — and a big opportunity for forgers. Selling a forgery is a criminal act. The state of New York is taking the lead on this issue, investigating at least two dozen suspected forgery cases linked with online auctions.

If you're in the market for an autograph, don't even consider bidding on one unless it comes with a *Certificate of Authenticity* (COA). Reputable sellers offer COAs as a means of ensuring that what you see is exactly what you get. Many sellers take authenticity so seriously that they give buyers the right to a full refund if any doubt about authenticity crops up. Figure 8-5 shows a COA from an auction on eBay.

If you're selling an autograph or other item that may benefit from authentication, you can find links to many authentication services right on eBay. Check out Chapter 14 for more information.

Don't assume that just because an item has a COA that the item is authentic. Unfortunately, COAs can be forged, too. Be sure to check the authenticity of the authenticator; a good place to start is the feedback area. If they have many happy customers, you may be okay to "go-a" with their "co-a." Say that five times fast!

Figure 8-5: When bidding on an item with a COA, make sure the seller is reputable (hint, hint, check for feedback).

✔ **Items that infringe on someone else's copyright or trademark.** See the section on infringing items, coming up shortly in this chapter.

✔ **Stolen items.** Need we say more? (Seems obvious, but you'd be surprised.) If what you're selling came to you by way of a "five-finger discount," or "fell off a truck" or is "hot," do not sell it on eBay.

Infringing items

In school, if you copied someone's work, you were busted for plagiarism. Even if you've been out of school for a while, you can get busted for copying someone else's work. Profiting from a copy of someone else's legally owned *intellectual property* is an *infringement* violation. Infringement, also known as *piracy,* is the encroachment on another person's legal ownership rights on an item, trademark, or copyright. eBay prohibits the selling of infringing items on its site.

All the legal mumbo-jumbo, translated to English, comes down to this: Profiting from someone else's idea, original work, or patented invention is very, very bad and can get you in hot water.

Here's a checklist of no-no items commonly found at the center of infringement violations:

- ✔ Selling music that's been recorded from an original compact disc, cassette tape, or record.

- ✔ Selling movies that have been recorded from an original DVD, Laser Disc, or commercial VHS tape.

- ✔ Selling television shows that have been recorded off the air, off cable, or from a satellite service.

Selling a used original CD, tape, commercial VHS movie cassette, DVD, or CD-ROM is perfectly legal. Some television shows have sold episodes on tape; you can sell those originals as well. If you're tempted to sell a personal copy that you made of an original, you are committing an infringing violation.

- ✔ Software and computer games that have been copied from CD-ROMs or disks (and that includes hard disks — anybody's).

- ✔ Counterfeit items (also called *knock-offs*), such as clothes and jewelry, that have been produced, copied, or imitated without the permission of the manufacturer. (Bart Simpson knock-off T-shirts abounded in the early '90s.)

If you pick up a brand-name item dirt-cheap from a discount store, you can check and see whether it's counterfeit by taking a look at the label — if something isn't quite right, the item is probably a knock-off.

But take heart, media buffs — here are some promotional items that you probably *can* sell on eBay:

- ✔ **Movie press kits.** Distributed by movie studios, they usually contain production notes, bios of the cast, and production stills.

Although the promotional materials sent out by movie studios, book publishers, and recording studios are technically "for publicity purposes only" and not for resale, some owners of these shows turn a blind eye to this kind of infringement violation. Others decidedly don't. Always check with producers or licensors of a promo item to see how they feel about your selling the item on eBay.

✔ **Clothing.** Human billboards are walking around everywhere publicizing movies or products on hats, T-shirts, jackets, even underwear! If the item was put out by the company, it's okay to sell. If the item is a counterfeit, however, it could be violating trademark or copyright laws. You are responsible for checking it out before selling.

✔ **Gifts.** Companies are finding ways to plaster logos and movie titles on everything in sight these days — cups, lunchboxes, paperweights, posters, all are fair game. And all can go up for sale on eBay.

Trademark and copyright protection doesn't just cover software, music and movies. Clothing, toys, sunglasses, and books are among the items covered by law. This book, for example, is copyrighted, and the eBay name is covered by a trademark and used with permission. So if you want to introduce a friend to the joys of eBay, don't photocopy this book — buy another one!

Intellectual property owners actively defend their rights and, along with the help from average eBay users, continually tip eBay off to fraudulent and infringing auctions. Rights owners can use eBay's Verified Rights Owner (VeRO) program, as well as law-enforcement agencies. We give you more on the VeRO program later in this chapter.

Know-the-laws-where-you-live items

Because some items are prohibited in one place and not another, eBay lists a few items that you can trade; however, these items are restricted and regulated. As a member of eBay, you're responsible for knowing the restrictions in your area as well as on the eBay Web site.

✔ **Wine and alcohol:** Selling wine and alcohol on eBay — and anywhere else, for that matter — is tricky business. For starters, you have no business in this business unless you're at least 21. eBay is currently reviewing its policy on alcholic beverages, so keep yourself informed if this kind of auction interests you.

Every state has its own laws about shipping alcohol and wine. Some states require licenses to transport it; some limit the amount you can ship. You're responsible for knowing what your state laws are (and expected to conduct your auctions accordingly).

You can find all the contact names, numbers, and links you need to keep your wine-shipping business on the good side of the law at `www.wine institute.org/shipwine` or check with the Alcoholic Beverage Control agency of your state. The ABC's telephone number is listed in the government section of your local phone book.

✔ **Erotica:** Some forms of pornography are allowed on eBay. To see what eBay allows and what it prohibits, refer to the eBay Community standards link we discussed earlier in this chapter.

One thing that's definitely illegal, wrong, and criminal is child pornography. If someone reports that you're selling child pornography, eBay forwards your registration information to law enforcement for criminal prosecution.

Okay, so you're looking at a thingamajig you pulled out of the attic and you suspect it might be saleable. How do you figure out whether it's okay to sell on eBay? Glad you asked. That's up next.

Verboten auctions

The folks at eBay didn't just fall off the turnip truck. eBay staffers have seen just about every scam to get around paying fees or following policy guidelines. Chances are good that if you try one of these, you'll get caught. eBay cancels the auction and credits you for the listing fee. Do it once, shame on you! Do it a lot and you're out of eBay!

✔ **Raffles and prizes.** You need to *sell* something in your auction, not offer tickets or chances for a giveaway.

✔ **Want ads.** If you want something, make a posting on the Wanted Board — don't try to pass an ad off as an auction. We explain in Chapter 14.

✔ **Advertisements.** An eBay auction is not the place to make a sales pitch (other than attractive copy describing your item, that is). Some eBay bad guys list an auction name and then use the auction to send bidders to some other auction or Web site.

✔ **Bait-and-switch.** A variation on the ugly old sales technique of pretending to sell what you're not really selling. Some eBay users who are selling an unfamiliar brand of item try to snag bidders by putting a more familiar brand in the title. For instance, writing *Beanie Baby — not really, but a lot like it!* is a fake-out. eBay calls it *keyword spamming*. We call it lousy.

✔ **Choice auctions.** These are like Dutch auctions gone crazy. Normally sellers can offer only one item per auction in a regular auction and multiples of the same item in a Dutch auction. Choice auctions offer a mishmash of multiple items. They don't work because bidders don't really know what they've bought until the auction is over.

✔ **Mixing apples with oranges.** This gambit tries to attract more bidders to view an item by putting it in a high-traffic category where it doesn't belong. Forget it. eBay will move it for you if necessary, but it's more considerate to keep that rutabaga recipe book *away* from the list of automotive repair manuals.

Hot property busted

In 1961, a young jockey named John Sellers won his first Kentucky Derby on a horse named Carry Back. He was so emotional about the victory that he was crying as he crossed the finish line. Seventeen years later, someone broke into his California home and stole his priceless trophy. But today, more than two decades after it was stolen, it's back in his possession — thanks to an observant eBay member. The prized trophy was put up for auction in 1999 by a seller who had bought it legitimately. An eBay member who knows the history of the trophy saw it was for sale and alerted the seller. The seller stopped the auction immediately, contacted the former jockey, and personally returned the trophy to him. Now, that's a great finish!

✔ **Catalogues.** "Buy my catalogue so you buy more stuff from me!" Uh-huh. We don't know why anyone would put a *bid* on a catalogue (unless it's a Sears-Roebuck antique). If it's only a booklet that shows off all the cool junk you're selling, it's illegal to offer as an auction item.

Reporting a Problem Auction

You probably don't think that eBay can monitor millions of auctions on a daily basis. You're right, they can't. They rely on eBay members like you to let them know when a shady auction is afoot. If you ever smell something fishy, for goodness sakes, report it to eBay. Sometimes eBay takes a few days to cancel an auction, but rest assured, eBay invests a lot of time protecting its users from fraudulent auctions.

If you see an auction that just doesn't look right, you should report the auction to `ctywatch@ebay.com` (don't forget the auction number in your e-mail).

You can also go to the Community Watch forum:

```
pages.ebay.com/services/safeharbor/report-infringing.html
```

If eBay agrees with you that your intellectual property is being infringed, they invalidate the auction, and the seller is informed by e-mail that the auction "is not authorized." The high bidders in the auction are also notified and warned that they may be breaking the law if they continue the transaction.

eBay understands that sometimes people don't know that they're selling infringing items, but it draws a hard line on repeat offenders. Not only does eBay shut down, but repeat offenders of this ilk are suspended. Also, eBay cooperates with the proper authorities on behalf of its VeRO program members.

Your very special friend, VeRO

If you own intellectual property that you think is being infringed upon on the eBay site, eBay has a program called the Verified Rights Owner (VeRO) Program. Owners of trademarked or copyrighted items and logos, as well as other forms of intellectual property, can become members of this program for free.

You can find out more about the VeRO program by clicking on the Help link of the main navigation bar. Click on the Community Standards link of the subnavigation bar, and then click on the VeRO link under the Policies and Conduct heading of the Community Standards Overview page. Download the form, fill it out, and fax it to eBay, and you're on your way to protecting your intellectual property from being auctioned to the highest bidder. Remember, only you can stop the infringement madness.

eBay doesn't personally prosecute its users; nor would eBay want such a huge responsibility. However, eBay does have a stake in protecting its honest users and acts as an intermediary between honest eBay users and law-enforcement agencies.

If eBay deems your auction invalid because the item doesn't meet eBay's policy's and guidelines, you can find out why by e-mailing ended@eBay.com. Be sure to include the auction item number in the e-mail.

eBay Fees? What eBay Fees? Oops . . .

The Cliché Police are going to raid us sooner or later, but here's one we're poking a few holes in this time around — *You gotta spend it to make it.* This old-time business chestnut means you need to invest a fair amount of money before you can turn a profit. Although the principle still holds true in the real world (at least most of the time), on eBay you don't have to spend *much* to run your business. This is one reason eBay has become one of the most successful e-commerce companies on the Internet and a darling of Wall Street. eBay keeps fees low and volume high — and with over 250,000 items going up for auction every day, that's where they make their money — volume.

eBay charges three types of fees for conducting auctions:

- ✔ Insertion Fees (from $.25 to $2.00)
- ✔ Final Value Fees (a percentage of the sales price)
- ✔ Optional Fees (which vary)

The Feds are online, too

The U.S. government uses two laws on the books to go after eBay outlaws. One is the Federal Trade Commission (FTC) Act, which prohibits deceptive or misleading transactions in commerce. The other is the Mail or Telephone Order Merchandise Rule, which requires sellers to ship merchandise in a timely manner or offer to refund a consumer's money. The FTC is in charge of pursuing these violations. If you have a question about federal laws, you can find a lot of information online. For example, we found these two Web sites that keep fairly current lists of U.S. law and federal codes.

`www4.law.cornell.edu/uscode`

Speaking of the Feds, have a look ahead in this chapter at our friendly advice on reporting your profits to the *very* friendly IRS.

Insertion Fee

For starters, eBay charges a small fee that you pay when you list your auction. Think of the Insertion Fee as the cost of taking out a really cheap ad in a newspaper. But in this case, your ad (auction) will be seen by millions of people around the world. (Hold your horses — we explain how to start auctions in Chapter 9.)

The Insertion Fee is calculated on a sliding scale that's based on the minimum bid (your starting price) or on the Reserve Price of your item. (Later in this chapter, we explain how the Reserve Price affects what you eventually have to pay.) See Table 8-2 for eBay's Insertion Fee structure.

Table 8-2:	Insertion Fee Charges
If Your Minimum Bid Is:	*The Insertion Fee Is:*
$.01 to $9.99	$.25
$10.00 to $24.99	$.50
$25.00 to $49.99	$1.00
$50.00 to $(gazillions)	$2.00

If you're running a Reserve Price auction (explained in detail in Chapter 9), eBay bases its Insertion Fee on the Reserve Price and not on the Minimum Bid. (The *Reserve Price* is the secret lowest price that you're willing to sell your item for.) eBay also charges a fee to run a Reserve Price auction.

Selling houses and cars on eBay

If you have the urge to put your castle or old Betsy up for sale, you can give eBay a shot. Houses and cars crop up for auction on eBay with some frequency — and to sweeten the pot, they even came up with a pricing structure to make the transaction more cost-effective for sellers.

For vehicles — including cars, classic cars, trucks, and RVs — eBay charges an Insertion Fee of $25, no matter what your minimum bid is. Instead of calculating the Final Value Fee by percentages, you just pay an additional $25. So for

50 bucks you can say good-bye to that old set of wheels.

If you sell your house, check the listing policy on the Community Standards page. Normally, you just have to pay an Insertion Fee of $50 and there's no Final Value Fee at all. For $50 you can sell your entire house, and you don't even have to ship it to the buyer (thank heaven for small favors). Now let's see, how much would it cost to sell a house with a car in the garage? Hmm, that'll run you a grand total of a hundred bucks. Now that's what we call the ultimate garage sale!

Here's a little snapshot of how Reserve Price affects your Insertion Fee. If you set a Minimum Bid of $1 for a gold Rolex watch (say *what?*) but your Reserve Price is $5,000 (that's more like it), you'll be charged a $2 Insertion Fee based on the $5,000 Reserve Price.

In a Dutch auction (explained in Chapter 9), the Insertion Fee is based on the Minimum Bid — as in a regular auction — but then eBay multiplies it by the number of items you list. So if you set a minimum bid of $1 for 300 glow-in-the-dark refrigerator magnets, it costs you a $75 Insertion Fee for listing. (If you sell them all, no problem; you'd make $225.)

So what does the Insertion Fee buy you on eBay?

- ✔ A really snazzy-looking auction page of your item for millions of eBay members to see, admire, and breathlessly respond to. (Well, we can hope.)

- ✔ Easy access to your auction (buyers can find it quickly with eBay's search engine). See Chapter 5 for details.

- ✔ The use of eBay services, such as the SafeHarbor Program, that somewhat ease your auction experience. (Chapter 14 tells you how to use SafeHarbor during and after your auctions.)

Final Value Fees

If you follow the movie business, you hear about some big A-list stars who take a relatively small fee for making a film but negotiate a big percentage of the gross profits. This is known as a "back-end" deal — in effect, a commission based on how much the movie brings in. eBay does the same thing, taking a small Insertion Fee when you list your item, and then a commission on the "back-end" when you sell your item. This commission is called the *Final Value Fee,* and is based on the final selling price of your item.

In real life, when you pay sales commissions on a big purchase like a house, you usually pay a fixed percentage. eBay's Final Value Fee structure is different, set up as a three-tiered system. See Table 8-3 for Final Value Fee charges.

Table 8-3	Final Value Fees
If Your Item Sells between	*You Pay a Final Value Fee of*
$.01 to $25.00	5 percent of the selling price
$25.01 to $1,000.00	5 percent on the first $25, plus 2.5 percent on selling prices of $25 to $1,000
$1,000 and up	5 percent on the first $25, plus 2.5 percent on selling prices of $25.01 to $1,000, plus another 1.25 percent on selling prices over $1,000

After your sale is over, eBay automatically (and within an hour of the auction close) calculates the appropriate fee and debits your account. Check out Chapter 4 for more information on keeping track of your eBay account.

So how do all these percentages translate to actual dollar amounts? Take a look at Table 8-4. We calculated the Final Value Fee on some sample selling prices.

Table 8-4	Sample Prices and Commissions	
Closing Bid Price	*Percentage*	*What You Owe eBay*
$10	5 percent of $10	$.50
$256	5 percent of $25 plus 2.5 percent of $231	$7.01
$1,284	5 percent of $25 plus 2.5 percent of $974.99 plus 1.5 percent of $974.99 of $248	$29.17
$1,000,000	5 percent of $25 plus 2.5 percent of $974.99 plus 1.5 percent of $999,000	$12,413.12 (ouch!)

Because of the sliding percentages, the higher the final selling price, the lower the commission eBay charges. Math can be a beautiful thing. For proof, look at Figure 8-6.

Figure 8-6:
Your cost is $99.95 to get your auction top billing using eBay's Featured Auctions option.

As a hint of things to come, Table 8-5 lists the eBay auction options and what they'll cost you:

Table 8-5	eBay Optional Fees
Option	*Fee*
Boldface Title	$2.00
Featured Auction	$99.95
Featured in Category	$14.95
Great Gift Icon	$1.00
The Gallery	$.25 and $19.95 (Featured Auction in Gallery)

Error in your favor — collect 56 bucks

Here's an auction item that's worth *more* than its weight in gold. The description told the tale:

20 Dollar US Paper Money Error from 1950 series. Federal Reserve note in almost uncirculated condition. Cutting error in bottom left corner. If you win auction you will be notified in three business days. Buyer pays $5 shipping and handling. Seller will wait ten bank working days for personal checks to clear. Item will be sent 2-3 days upon funds clearing.

The starting bid was $40, and it sold on eBay for $56.

Keep current on your cash flow

When you've done all the legwork needed to make some money, do some eye-work to keep track of your results. The best place keep watch on your eBay accounting is on your My eBay page, a great place to stay organized while you're conducting all your eBay business. We describe all the functions of the page in Chapter 4.

Here's a checklist of what to watch out for after the auction closes:

- ✔ **Keep an eye on how much you are spending to place items up for auction on eBay.** If you have automatic credit card billing, you don't want any nasty surprises, and you don't want to find out that you spent more money to set up your auction than you received selling it.

- ✔ **If you decide to turn your eBay selling into a business, keep track of your expenses for your taxes.** (We explain Uncle Sam's tax position on eBay later in this chapter — next, in fact. Stay tuned.)

- ✔ **Make sure you get refunds and credits when they're due.**

- ✔ **Double-check your figures to make certain eBay hasn't made mistakes.** If you have any questions about the accounting, let eBay know.

Find an error or something that isn't quite right with your account? E-mail your questions to billing@ebay.com.

Optional fees

You won't have to pay a license fee and destination charge, but setting up your auction can be like buying a car — eBay has all sorts of options to jazz up your auction! (Sorry, they're fresh out of two-tone metallic paint — but how about a nice a pair of fuzzy dice for your mirror?) We explain how all these bells, whistles, and white sidewalls dress up your auction in Chapter 9. In the meantime, Figure 8-6 shows you what a Featured Auction on eBay looks like.

Uncle Sam Wants You — to Pay Your Taxes! (Oops . . .)

What would a chapter about money be without taxes? As Ben Franklin knew (and we've all found out since his time), you can't escape death and taxes. (Hey, it's not a cliché, it's traditional wisdom!) Whether in cyberspace or face-to-face life, never forget that Uncle Sam is *always* your business partner.

If you live outside the United States, check the tax laws in that country so you don't end up with a real headache down the road.

Two wild rumors about federal taxes

We've heard some rumors about not having to pay taxes on eBay profits. If you hear any variation on this theme, smile politely and don't believe a word of it.

Here are two of the more popular (and seriously mistaken) tax notions running around the eBay community these days:

Rumor #1: No taxes on e-commerce?

One story claims that "there will be no taxes on e-commerce sales (sales conducted online) for three years." No one ever seems to know when those three years start or end.

(Right. As if Uncle Sam would pass up such an opportunity. Get real.)

Now the facts about Rumor #1

Congress recently passed the Internet Tax Freedom Act. It states that until October 2001 Congress and state legislatures can't institute *new* taxes on Internet transactions. Congress wants to give states, and even other nations, time to sort out how cyber-commerce is working. If you're betting that some custom-tailored taxation will magically appear after October 2001, we sure won't bet against you.

How Rumor #1 applies to you

You won't have to worry about paying any *new* taxes the government may or may not think up for Internet transactions *until* late 2001. *This has nothing to do with current taxes*, like income taxes on profits. Those you have to pay. Now.

Rumor #2: Are garage sales and such exempt?

"eBay is like a garage sale, and you don't have to pay taxes on garage sales."

(Uh-huh. And the calories in ice cream don't count if you eat it out of the carton. Who comes up with this stuff anyway?)

Now the facts about Rumor #2

This notion is just an urban (or shall we say, *suburban*) legend — somebody's wishful thinking that's become folklore. If you make money on a garage sale, you have to declare it as income — just like anything else you make money on. Most people never make any money on garage sales because they usually sell things for far less than they bought them for — and often the exact opposite is true of an eBay transaction.

Even if you lose money, you may have to prove it to the government, especially if you're running a small business. You might want to have a heart-to-heart with your accountant if you're unsure. Our best advice: If it might look bad in an audit if you *don't* declare it, consider that a big hint.

How Rumor # 2 applies to you

To get the reliable word, we checked with the IRS's brand new e-commerce office. How new were they? They were still waiting for office furniture. (No kidding!) They told us that even if you make as little as a buck on any eBay sale — after all your expenses (the cost of the item, eBay fees, shipping charges) — you still have to declare it as income on your federal tax return.

Even though you may be hearing a lot these days about the "new and friendly" IRS, it's still their job to collect taxes; how friendly are they likely to be if you mess with them? Will they track you down if you don't report your eBay profits? Who knows? But we think that failing to report your profits is a dangerous and illegal roll of the dice. To keep your eBay activities above-board and fun, pay up (grinning while you do it is optional). The IRS is still getting up to speed on e-commerce, but who's to say they won't pick a few eBay users out to audit, just to let people know they're looking?

The IRS says that if you're making a profit on eBay, *any* profit, declare it on your taxes. If you "forget," you could face the same penalties that land on any other failure to report income. Those penalties range from interest charged on the money you owe to criminal prosecution for fraud.

If you're already a business owner with an employer identification number and you're selling on eBay, you already know a lot about paying taxes — but it never hurts to refresh your knowledge as the tax code continues to mutate. Use your Schedule D the same way you do with any other income.

If you have questions about eBay sales and your taxes, check with your personal accountant, call the IRS Help Line at 1-800-829-1040, or visit the IRS Web site at www.irs.ustreas.gov. And be friendly.

State taxes

Yes, it's true — not only is Uncle Sam in Washington, D.C., looking for his slice of your eBay profits, your state government may be hankering to join the feast.

If you have a good accountant, give that esteemed individual a call. Accountants actually do more than just process your income tax returns once a year; they can help you avoid major pitfalls even before April 15!

Here's how to find out what your responsibilities are in your home state:

- ✔ You may need to collect and pay state taxes only if you sell to someone in your state.
- ✔ You can get tax information on line at this Web site:

  www.kentis.com/siteseeker/taxusst.html

- ✔ The site has links to tax information for all 50 states.
- ✔ Call your state tax office and let the good folks there explain what the requirements are. They're listed in the Government section of your phone book.

As with offline transactions, knowledge is power. The more you know about buying and selling on eBay before you actually start doing it, the more savvy the impression you make — and the more satisfying your experience. Now you can get down to the nitty-gritty and start creating your auction item page.

Chapter 9

Filling in the Blanks: Cyber Paperwork for the Savvy Seller

. . . .

In This Chapter

▶ Getting ready to set up your auction

▶ Choosing your item category

▶ Writing your item description

▶ Setting up your options

▶ Making changes after your auction has started

. . . .

*A*re you ready to make some money? Yes? (Call it an inspired guess.) You're on the threshold of adding your items to the hundreds of thousands that go up for auction on eBay every day. Some are so hot that the sellers quadruple their investments. Others, unfortunately, are so stone-cold they don't even register a single bid. (Hey, eBay doesn't offer any guarantees, but as with the lottery, you gotta be in it to win it!)

In this chapter, we explain all the facets of the Sell Your Item page — the page you fill out to get your auction going on eBay. We give you some advice that can increase your odds of making money, and we show you the best way to position your item so buyers can see it and bid on it. We also show you how to modify, extend, or end your auction whenever you need to.

Getting Ready to List Your Item

After you decide what you want to sell, find out as much as you can about it — and conduct a little market research — you should have a good idea of the item's popularity and value. To get this info, check out Chapter 8.

Before you list your item, make sure you've got these bases covered:

- ✔ **The specific category under which you want the item listed.** Ask your friends where they'd look for such an item, and remember the categories you saw most frequently when you conducted your market research. Think about item information that should be in the item description.

- ✔ **What you want to say in your auction item description.** Jot down your ideas. We know all about writer's block — if you're daunted by the Sell Your Item page but struggle through it anyway, then you've already done the *hard* work before you even begin.

- ✔ **Whether you want to attach a picture to your description via a Uniform Resource Locator (URL).** Pictures help sell items, but you don't have to do this (and this information won't be on the test, but if you want to know more, see Chapter 12).

- ✔ **The price at which you think you can sell the item.** Be as realistic as you can. (That's where the market research comes in.)

Examining the Sell Your Item Page

Figure 9-1 shows you the Sell Your Item page, which is where your auction is born. Filling out your auction paperwork requires a couple of minutes of clicking, typing, and answering all kinds of questions. The good news is that when you're done, your auction is up and running and (hopefully) starting to earn you money.

Before you begin, you have to be a registered eBay user. If you still need to register, go to Chapter 2 and fill out the preliminary cyber paperwork. Then you're ready to set up your auction.

To find eBay's Sell Your Item page from the eBay Home page, click on the Sell link on the navigation bar at the top of the page and you're whisked there immediately.

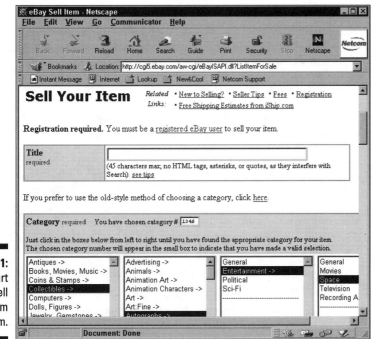

Figure 9-1:
The top part
of the Sell
Your Item
form.

You can also start your auction from your My eBay page:

1. Scroll down to the Items I'm Selling heading.

2. Click on the Add an Item link.

You're taken to the Sell Your Item page. Here's the info you're asked to fill out as it appears on the Sell Your Item page. Each of the items is discussed in detail later in this chapter:

- **Title:** The name of your item (required).

- **Category:** The category that best describes your item (required).

- **Description:** What you want to tell eBay buyers about your item (required).

- **Picture URL:** The Web address of any pictures you want to add (optional). See Chapter 12 for more about using images in your auction.

- **The Gallery:** Add your item's picture to eBay's photo gallery. This option is now available for items in every category. eBay charges $.25 extra to add the item to the gallery and $19.95 to make your item a featured auction in the Gallery (optional).

- **Gallery Image URL:** The Web address of the JPG image you want to place in the Gallery (optional). See Chapter 12.

- **Boldface Title:** A selling option to make your item listing stand out. eBay charges $2 extra for this feature (optional).

- **Featured Auction:** You can place your auction in a premium viewing section. eBay charges $99.95 extra for this feature (optional).

- **Featured in Category:** You can have your auction appear at the top of the category in which you list it. eBay charges $14.95 extra for this feature (optional).

- **Great Gift Icon:** You can have a special gift icon placed next to your item title letting eBay members know it's a great gift idea. eBay charges $1 extra for this feature (optional).

Of course, if you're discreetly trying to find a different home for that birthday power tie that looks like an accident in a Chuck E. Cheese's, you might want to skip the Great Gift icon.

- **Item Location:** The region, ZIP code, and country from which the item will be shipped (required).

- **Method(s) of Payment/Shipping Terms:** How you want to be paid, who pays for shipping, and where in the world you're willing to ship to (required).

You may want to consider whether you want to be in the international shipping business. Buyers usually pick up the tab, but you have to deal with post office paperwork (they want to know what's leaving the country in that nicely packaged box). If time is money, you may want to skip it entirely — or at least have all the forms filled out *before* you get in line at the post office. But, remember if you don't ship internationally, you're blocking out a bunch of bidders.

- **Quantity:** The number of items you're offering in this auction — always 1 unless you plan to run a Dutch auction (required).

- **Minimum Bid:** The starting price you set (required).

- **Duration:** The number of days you want the auction to run (required).

- **Reserve Price:** The secret price you set that must be met before this item can be sold (optional). eBay charges you a fee for this feature.

- **Private Auction:** You can keep the identity of all bidders secret with this option (optional).

- **Your User ID and password** (required).

Filling in the Required Blanks

Yes, the Sell Your Item page looks daunting, but filling out its 22 sections doesn't take as long as you may think. Some of the questions you're asked aren't things you even have to think about — just click on an answer and off you go, unless you forgot your password again! Other questions ask you to type in information. Don't sweat a thing, we have all the answers you need right here. You can find info on all the required stuff, and later in this chapter, we talk about optional stuff.

Item title info

After you fill in your User ID and password, eBay wants to get down the nitty-gritty — what the heck to call that thing you're trying to sell. Think of your item title as a great newspaper headline.

Give the most essential information right away. You want to grab the eye of the reader who's just browsing, and you want to be clear and descriptive enough to get noticed by eBay's search engine. You only have room for 45 characters in your title, including spaces. First impressions count, and being cute isn't nearly as important as being clear and concise.

Tell it like it is. If you're selling a Persian rug, then that's exactly how you should start your title. If you're selling a Beanie Baby, then say so. Got an antique fire hose? Lay that out. Figure 9-2 shows examples of good titles.

Figure 9-2:
These item titles are effective because they're clear, accurate, and easy on the eyes.

Beautiful Summer Sophisticate Barbie-NRFB
Item #129449952

~ NEW Small Line MAYCO C-30HD Concrete Pump ~
Item #128822430

BLAIR WITCH PROJECT Original B 27x40 POSTER
Item #139285073

Here are some ideas to help you write your item title:

✔ Use the most common name for the item.

✔ If the item is rare or hard to find, mention that.

> ✔ Mention the item's condition, and mention whether it's new or old.
>
> ✔ Mention the item's special qualities, like its style, model, or edition.
>
> ✔ Avoid fancy punctuation or unusual characters, such as $, hyphens, L@@K, because they just clutter up the title and buyers rarely search for them.

Don't put any *HTML tags* in your title! (HTML stands for HyperText Markup Language, which in plain English means that it's the special code you use to create Web pages.) A computer can get very upset and behave weirdly if it finds code where no code is supposed to be — and tries to execute it. (Let's not even go there.) If you want to know more about designing Web pages and using HTML tags, ask a friend who's into that sort of thing or have a look at *HTML 4 For Dummies,* by Ed Tittel and Stephen Nelson James, published by (who else?) IDG Books Worldwide, Inc.

Ordinarily, we don't throw out French phrases just for the fun of it. But where making a profit is an issue, we definitely have to agree with the French that picking or not picking *le mot juste* can mean the difference between having potential bidders merely *see* your auction and having an all-out bidding war on your hands. Read on for tips on picking the best words to let your auction item shine.

Look for a phrase that pays

Here's a crash course in eBay lingo that can help bring you up to speed on attracting buyers to your auction. The following words are used frequently in eBay auctions, and they can do wonders to jump-start your title:

✔ Hard-to-find

✔ Rare

✔ Very rare

✔ Unusual

✔ One of a kind

✔ Vintage

✔ Collectible

✔ Pristine

✔ Old

✔ Very old

✔ Unique

✔ Primitive

✔ Well-loved

✔ Slightly used

Don't use words and phrases like this unless they're true. If you found an arrowhead in the backyard and you're not sure how old it is, *don't* call it "primitive" or "rare." Murphy's Law practically guarantees that the *one* arrowhead expert in a three-state area will come calling and want to know all about it. Then what'll you say?

There's a whole science (called *grading*) to figuring out the value of a collectible. You're ahead of the game if you have a pretty good idea of what most eBay members *mean by that.* Do your homework before you assign a grade to your item — for example, is it something people *really* collect, or something you wish they *would* collect? If you need more information on what these grades actually mean, Chapter 5 provides a translation.

eBay lingo at a glance

Common grading terms and the phrases in the preceding section aren't the only marketing standards you have at your eBay disposal. As eBay has grown, so has the lingo that members use as short cuts to describe their merchandise.

Table 9-1 gives you a handy list of common abbreviations and phrases used to describe items. (Hint: *Mint* means "might as well be brand new," not "cool chocolate treat attached.")

Table 9-1	A Quick List of eBay Abbreviations	
eBay Code	*What It Abbreviates*	*What It Means*
MIB	Mint In Box	The item's in the original box, in great shape, and just the way you'd expect to find it in a store.
MIMB	Mint in Mint Box	The box has never been opened and looks like it just left the factory.
MOC	Mint On Card	The item's mounted on its original display card, attached with the original fastenings, in store-new condition.
NRFB	Never Removed From Box	Just what it says, as in, *bought but never opened.*
COA	Certificate Of Authenticity	Documentation that vouches for the genuineness of an item, such as an autograph or painting.

(continued)

Table 9-1 *(continued)* A Quick List of eBay Abbreviations

eBay Code	What It Abbreviates	What It Means
MWBMT	Mint With Both Mint Tags	Refers to stuffed animals, which have a *hang tag* (usually paper or card) and a *tush tag* (that's what they call the sewn-on tag — really) in perfect condition with no bends or tears.
OEM	Original Equipment Manufacture	You're selling the item and all the equipment that originally came with it, but you don't have the original box, owner's manual, or instructions.
NR	No Reserve Price	A *reserve price* is a secret price you can set when you begin your auction. If bids don't meet the reserve, you don't have to sell. Many buyers don't like reserve prices because they don't think that they can get a bargain. If you're not listing a reserve for your item, let bidders know.
HTF	Hard To Find	Out of print, only a few ever made, or people grabbed up all there were. (Doesn't mean you spent a week looking for it in the attic.)

Normally you can rely on eBay slang to get your point across, but make sure you mean it and that you're using it accurately. Don't label something MIB (Mint In Box) when it looks like it's been Mashed In Box by a meat grinder. (Of course, you might not want to use the MIB abbreviation anyway if you're selling *Men in Black* memorabilia.)

For a complete list of eBay lingo, go to this book's handy Appendix for detailed definitions — and review the grading section in Chapter 5.

More title tips

If you write an unintelligible title, people won't spot it. Imagine going to a supermarket and asking someone to show you where *the stringy stuff that you boil* is instead of asking for *spaghetti*. You might end up with mung bean sprouts — delicious to some, but hardly what you had in mind.

Check and recheck your spelling. Buyers use the eBay search engine to find merchandise; if the name of your item is spelled wrong, the search engine can't find it. Poor spelling and incomprehensible grammar also reflect badly on you. If you're in competition with another seller, the buyer is likelier to trust the seller *hoo nose gud speling.*

If you've finished writing your item title and you have spaces left over, fight the urge to dress it up with lots of exclamation points and asterisks — no matter how gung-ho you are about your item, the eBay search engine might overlook your item if the title is encrusted with meaningless **** and ! ! ! ! symbols. Potential buyers might never see your title — and if they did, they could get annoyed at the virtual shrillness and ignore it anyway!!!!!!! (See what we mean?)

Another distracting habit is overdoing capital letters. To buyers, seeing everything in caps is LIKE A CRAZED SALESMAN SCREAMING AT THEM TO BUY NOW! All that "shouting" is rude and tough on the eyes. Use capitalization SPARINGLY, just to finesse a point. For that matter, you might want to restrict your use of capital letters to words and phrases that really need them (say, _IBM computer_ or _NFL helmet_).

Choosing a category

Choosing your item category is an important decision. eBay gives you almost 2,000 categories and subcategories, offering you this wealth of choices in a handy point-and-click way. If you're unfamiliar with the types of items you can actually _find_ in those categories, however, you might want to pore over Chapter 3 before you choose one to describe _your_ item. Figure 9-3 shows you the category listings on the Sell Your Item page.

Figure 9-3:
With all the categories to choose from, take the time to pick the one that best fits your item.

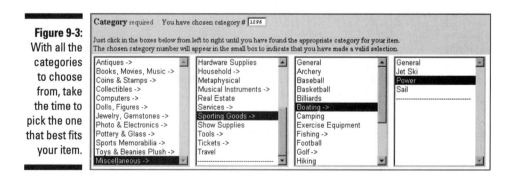

To select a category, here's the drill:

1. **Click on one of the main categories.**

    You see a list of subcategories.

2. **Select the most appropriate subcategory.**

3. **Continue selecting subcategories until you have narrowed down your item listing as much as possible.**

You know when you've come to the last subcategory when you don't see any more right-pointing arrows on the category list.

Most bidders scan for specific items in subcategories. For example, if you're selling a Bakelite fruit pin, don't just list it under Jewelry, keep narrowing down your choices — in this case, you can put it in Jewelry: Costume: Bakelite. We guarantee that the real Bakelite jewelry collectors out there know where to look to find the jewelry they love. eBay makes it easy to narrow down the category of your item — just keep clicking until you hit the end of the line.

If you've chosen to list an item, bid on an item, or even just browse in the Adult/Erotica category, you need to follow separate, specific guidelines because it contains graphic nudity or sexual content that could offend some members. You must

- ✔ Be at least 18 years of age.

- ✔ Have a valid credit card.

- ✔ Complete a waiver stating that you're voluntarily choosing to access adults-only materials. For more on how to do this (and a handy primer on privacy issues), see Chapter 13.

If you have Adult/Erotica items you'd like to sell in a private auction, study up on the section later in this chapter that details the Private Auction option.

Writing your description

Once you hook potential bidders with your title, reel 'em in with a fabulous description. Don't think Hemingway here, think infomercial (the classier the better). Figure 9-4 shows the description section of the Sell Your Item page. All you have to do is click in the box and start typing.

Listing baubles on eBay

Most people love jewelry, but selling it on eBay can be tricky. Strict laws and regulations govern the use of what seem to be common terms. For instance, when you call your item *gold,* you'd better mean 24-karat solid gold. Anything less is not accurate, according to industry standards. Know the difference between Natural and Laboratory-produced, as well as the difference between Vermeil, Gold Plated, and Gold Flashed. For help, click on the Inside Scoop link of eBay's Jewelry Category. For more information on jewelry-selling guidelines, log on to the Federal Trade Commission's Web site: www.ftc.gov. The FTC sets the industry standards; know them before you put your gems up for auction.

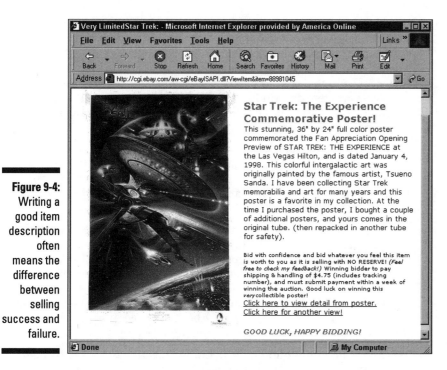

Figure 9-4:
Writing a
good item
description
often
means the
difference
between
selling
success and
failure.

Here's a list of suggestions for writing an item description:

✔ **Accentuate the positive.** Give the buyer a reason to buy your item. Be excited about your product. List all the phenomenal reasons your product is special. Mention anything and everything that makes it worth bidding on. Unlike the title, you can use as much space as you want. Even if you use a photo, be precise in your description — how big is it, what color, what kind of fabric, what's the design? Refer to this chapter's "Item title info" section, as well as Table 9-1, for ideas on what to emphasize and how to word your description.

✔ **Include the negative.** Don't hide the truth of your item's condition. Trying to conceal flaws costs you in the long run — you'll get tagged with bad feedback. If the item has a scratch, a nick, a dent, a crack, a ding, a tear, a rip, missing pieces, replacement parts, faded color, dirty smudges or a bad smell (especially if cleaning might damage the item), mention it in the description. If your item has been overhauled, rebuilt, repainted or hot-rodded (say, a "Pentium computer" that was a 386 till you put in the new motherboard), say so. You don't want the buyer to send back your merchandise because you weren't truthful about imperfections or modifications.

✔ **Be precise about all the logistical details of the post-auction transaction.** Even though you're not required to list any special S&H (shipping and handling) or payment requirements in your item description, the majority of eBay users do. Try to figure out what it would cost to ship in the United States and add that to your description. If you offer shipping insurance, add it to your item description. You want everything out in the open before the bidding starts. Once the terms are out there, a bidder can ask for changes and you can take 'em or leave 'em.

✔ **Promote your other auctions.** The pros always do a little cross-promotion — and it works. When Jane Pauley on *Dateline NBC* tells you to stay tuned for the morning news, she's trying to prevent you from turning to the competition. So, if you're selling Furbies and Beanie Babies, say something like, "Check out my Tabasco the Bull Beanie Baby Auction."

✔ **While you're at it, promote yourself too.** As you accumulate positive feedback, tell potential bidders about your terrific track record. Add statements like, "I'm great to deal with, check out my feedback section." If bidders are trying to decide among a few similar auctions, prove you're a top-notch seller to tip the scales more in your favor. You can even take it a step further by linking your auction page to your personal Web page (if you have one) or your About Me page. (Chapter 12 gives you some tips on how to make your auction seen by a wider audience.)

✔ **Wish your potential bidders well.** Communication is the key to a good transaction, and you can set the tone for your auction and post-auction exchanges by including some simple phrases that show your friendly side. Always end your description by wishing bidders good luck, invite potential bidders to e-mail you with questions, and offer the option of providing additional photos of the item if you have them.

Occasionally sellers offer an item as a *pre-sell* — an item that the seller doesn't yet have in stock but expects to. Common examples of pre-sells include merchandise connected to movies, such as action figures and movie posters. If you're offering this kind of item, make sure you spell out all the details in the description. Don't forget to include the actual shipping date. We have found that putting an item up for sale without actually *having it in hand* is a practice fraught with risk. The item you are expecting may not arrive in time or arrive damaged. We've heard of one too many sellers who had to go out and purchase an item at retail for a buyer to preserve their feedback when caught in this position.

The same way a store can hang a sign in its door that says *No shirt, no shoes, no service,* so can eBay members refuse to do business with certain members. You have the right to be selective (within reason and the law, of course) about whom you want as a prospective buyer for your item. You should limit your restrictions to phrases like *No Negative Feedback bidders* or *Will not sell to bidders who have no feedback.* It's your auction, and you can protect your investment any way you want, but you can't discriminate or break any state or federal laws in your description.

Filling out the item location

eBay wants you to list the general area in which you live and the country you live in (and if you live in the United States, your ZIP code). The idea behind telling the bidder where you live is to give him or her a heads-up on what kind of shipping charges to expect. Don't be esoteric (listing where you live as *The Here and Now* isn't a whole lot of help) — but don't go crazy with cross-streets, landmarks, or degrees of latitude. Listing the city you live in is usually enough, but don't forget your ZIP code. (Bidders do not ever see your ZIP code, but eBay uses it for regional sites.)

If you live in a big area — say, suburban Los Angeles (who, us?), which sprawls on for miles — you may think about narrowing down your region a little. You may find a bidder who lives close to you, which could swing your auction. If a bidder has a choice between something shipped cross-country or delivered cross-town, he or she may be willing to bid higher for the cross-town sale just to save money and time on shipping. We suggest that if you do a face-to-face transaction, do it in a public place.

Some eBay users trying to cash in on regional searches (the Los Angeles area, for example) put in their home state but use the popular 90210 ZIP code so they can be listed in the regional category as well.

On the flip side, when you list the country you live in, bear in mind that you may receive some international bids. If you live in the United States, you're likely to receive bids from Canada, Uncle Sam's biggest trading partner. See Chapter 10 to find out how currency matters might have an impact on your sale.

Listing the payment methods you'll accept

Yeah, sure, eBay's loads of fun, but the bottom line to selling is the phrase *show me the money!* You make the call on what you're willing to take as money from the high bidder of your auction. Just click on the payment options eBay offers that you like. They are:

- ✔ **Money orders/cashier's check.** The safest method of payment is a money order or cashier's check. It's the closest thing you can get to cash. As a seller, you want to get paid with as little risk as possible.

- ✔ **C.O.D. (Collect on Delivery).** We think that this option is the least attractive for both buyers and sellers. The buyer has to be home with the cash ready to go on the day that the package arrives. Odds are that on the day the item's delivered, your buyer is taking his or her sick pet goldfish to the vet for a gill-cleaning. Then the item ends up back at your door, and you have no sale.

✔ **See item description.** This option is selected for you by default. We think you should always state in your item description how you want to be paid. Why? Because there's no good reason not to.

Standard practice is to restate and fully explain payment and shipping terms in your item description, but you don't *have* to.

✔ **Personal check.** An extremely popular option, comes with a risk: The check could bounce higher than a lob at Wimbledon. If you accept personal checks, explain in your item description how long you plan to wait for the check to clear before sending the merchandise. The average hold is about five business days. Some sellers wait as long as two weeks.

Cut down on the risk of bad checks by reading the bidder's feedback when the auction's underway. Be wary of accepting checks from people with negative comments. (We explain all about feedback in Chapter 4.)

eBay is trying to take some of the mystery and foreboding out of accepting checks with their ID Verify program, which allows *Equifax,* a gigantic check-verification company, to run credit checks and present eBay members with a clean bill of health. (For more on ID Verify, see Chapter 14.)

Don't go overboard with the rules and regulations about your auction. An auction description filled with three-quarters of a page of rules will scare away potential bidders. Just the facts, ma'am (or sir), just the facts.

Never ship an item until you're certain the check has cleared.

✔ **Online escrow.** An escrow service acts as a referee, a neutral third party. Unless you're selling an expensive item, however, it's overkill to offer escrow. Usually, the buyer pays for this service. Escrow companies charge 5 percent of the sale price. On big-ticket items, it may give some bidders an added sense of security.

If you do offer escrow, the winning bidder should inform you right after the auction that he or she intends to use escrow. You can find more on escrow in Chapter 6.

Sometimes a buyer asks for escrow even if it's not in the item description. Work out those details before the auction closes. If the sale hinges on escrow, you may want to agree to it — but know what you're agreeing to.

✔ **Other.** If you're offering payment options that are not listed here, select this option. Some buyers (mostly international) like to pay in cash, but we think this is way too risky and never ever deal in cash. If there is a problem — for either buyer or seller — there's no evidence that payment was made or received. Avoid it!

✔ **Credit cards (Visa, MasterCard, American Express, Discover).** Unless you already have access to credit and charge card processing, you're not going to be offering this option. It's generally offered by dealers or members with very good friends willing to share credit card processing capabilities. A couple of companies offer to process credit cards for you for a price. Skip it. You'll only be losing some of your hard-earned eBay money. Some sellers using credit card services try attaching an additional fee to the final payment. However, that's against the law in California, home of eBay — and therefore against eBay rules. So forget about it.

Most sellers offer buyers several ways to pay. You can choose as many as you want. When the auction page appears, your choices are noted at the top of the listing. Listing several payment options makes you look like a flexible, easygoing professional.

Setting shipping terms

Ahoy, matey! Hoist the bid! Okay, not quite. Before you run it up the mast, select your shipping options. You've got these:

- ✔ **Ship To Home Country Only.** Once again, this is selected by default; it means you only ship domestically.

- ✔ **Will Ship Internationally.** The world is your oyster! But make sure you can afford it.

eBay has lots of good international users, so you may want to consider selling your items around the world. If you do, be sure to clearly state in the description all extra shipping costs and customs charges. See Chapter 10 for more information on how to ship to customers abroad.

You're also asked who you want to pay for shipping. Choose an option:

- ✔ **Seller Pays.** You're picking up the shipping tab.

- ✔ **Buyer Pays Actual Shipping Cost.** You let the buyer know *exactly* how much the item costs to ship, and the buyer picks up the tab.

- ✔ **Buyer Pays Fixed Amount.** You state a fixed shipping price in your item description; the buyer agrees to include this amount in the payment for the item.

- ✔ **See Item Description.** This is another option selected by default; we see no reason not to explain your terms in the item description.

We recommend choosing the Buyer Pays Fixed Amount option. Check out Chapter 10 to get more information on each of these options.

Listing the number of items for sale

Unless you're planning on holding a Dutch auction, the number of items is always 1. This means you're holding a traditional auction. If you need to change the quantity number from 1, just type the number in the box.

A matching set of cufflinks is considered one item, as is the complete 37-volume set of *The Smith Family Ancestry and Genealogical History since 1270*. If you have more than one of the same item, we suggest that you sell them one at a time.

Whether you list your items individually in auctions or together in a Dutch auction, eBay won't allow you to list the same item in more than seven auctions at one time.

Setting a minimum bid — how low can you go?

eBay requires you to set a *minimum bid,* the lowest bid allowed in an auction. What do a baseball autographed by JFK, a used walkie-talkie, and a Jaguar sports car have in common? They all started with a $1 minimum bid. You may be surprised to see stuff worth tens of thousands of dollars starting at just a buck. These sellers haven't lost their minds. Neither are they worried someone could be tooling down the highway in a $100,000 sports car for the price of a burger.

Setting an incredibly low minimum (just type it in the box *without* the dollar sign but *with* the decimal point) is a subtle strategy that gives you more bang for your buck. You can use a low minimum bid to attract more bidders, who will drive up the price to the item's real value, especially if, after doing your research, you know that the item is particularly hot. If you are worried about the outcome of the final bid, you can protect your item by using a *reserve.* Then you won't have to sell your item for a bargain basement price because your *reserve price* — the price the bidding needs to reach before the item can be sold — protects your investment. The best advice is set a reserve price that is the lowest amount you will take for your item, then set a minimum bid that is ridiculously low. Use a reserve only when absolutely necessary, as many bidders may pass up a reserve auction. If you want to know more about setting a reserve price, skip ahead in this chapter.

eBay's Reserve Price auction policy is always evolving. Currently, eBay charges a fee to set a reserve, and more changes are on the horizon. Check the Announcement Board for updates.

Starting with a low minimum is also good for your pocketbook. eBay charges the seller an insertion or placement fee — based on your opening bid. If you keep your opening bid low, you get to keep some more of your money. (See Chapter 8 for more about eBay fees.)

The more bids you get, the more people want to bid on your item because they think the item is hot. eBay actually designates every item that has 31 bids or more a Hot item and attaches a Hot icon to that auction. The item is also listed in the Hot category. A designated Hot item draws bidders the way a magnet attracts paper clips.

Going Dutch

If you've got five Dennis Rodman Wedding Dolls, 37 Breathalyzers, or 2,000 Beanie Babies, and you want to sell them all at once to as many bidders as possible, sell them in a Dutch auction. Dutch auctions are mainly used by dealers and businesses who want to move lots of items fast.

eBay has requirements for starting a Dutch auction. You have to be an eBay member at least 60 days with a feedback rating of ten or higher. Click on the Dutch auction link for more information on how to conduct this type of auction, and check out Chapter 1 for more info on how a Dutch auction works. If you're interested in bidding on a Dutch auction, take a look at Chapter 6.

Learn the ropes before you try the low-minimum-bid strategy. Before you set any minimum bid, do your homework and make some savvy marketing decisions. If your auction isn't going as you hoped, you *could* end up selling your Grandma Ethel's Ming vase for a dollar. Once you set your minimum bid, you can't change it, so don't be hasty. Think about your strategy.

When putting in your minimum bid, type in only the numbers and a decimal point. Don't use dollar signs ($) or cents signs (¢).

Setting your auction time

How long do you want to run your auction? eBay gives you a choice — 3, 5, 7, or 10 days. Just click on the number you want in the box. During the peak gift-giving season, eBay sometimes lets auctions run for two weeks.

Our auction length strategy depends on the time of year and the item we're selling, and we have great success. If you've got an item that you think will sell pretty well, run a seven-day auction so bidders have time to check it out before they decide to bid. (We almost always run 7-day auctions.) However, if you know you've got a red-hot item that's going to fly off the shelves — like a rare Beanie Baby or a hard-to-get Furby — choose a 3-day auction. Eager bidders tend to bid higher and more often to beat out their competition if the item's hot and going fast.

No matter how many days you choose to run your auction, it ends at exactly the same time of day as it starts. A seven-day auction that starts on Thursday at 9:03:02 a.m., ends the following Thursday at 9:03:02 a.m.

Although we know the folks at eBay are pretty laid-back, they do run on military time. That means they use a 24-hour clock that's set to Pacific Coast time. So, 3:30 in the afternoon is 15:30, and one minute after midnight is 00:01. Questions about time conversions? Checkout our Cheat Sheet. At ease.

Find eBay's official time on any subcategory page. For example, Antiques: Prints or Collectibles:Comic Books. There's also a Check eBay official time link on the subcategory page that takes you to a nifty-looking map with the actual time in different parts of the country.

Once a week, eBay conducts a mandatory outage for database maintenance, which means that they close up shop on Fridays from midnight to 4 a.m. Pacific Time (that's 3 a.m. to 7 a.m. Eastern Time). Never post an auction right after this outage. eBay regulars won't be around to bid on it.

With auctions running 24 hours a day, seven days a week, you should know when the most bidders will be around to take a gander at your wares. Here are some times to think about:

✔ **Saturday/Sunday:** Always run an auction over a weekend — people log on and off of eBay all day.

Never start or end your auction on a Saturday or Sunday. That may seem strange, but bidders are busy having lives on weekends, and their schedules are unpredictable. Some eager bidders may log on and place a maximum bid on your auction, but if they have something better to do on a Saturday or Sunday, you can bet they'll do it instead of sitting at a computer making a last-minute flurry of competitive bids.

✔ **Holiday weekends:** If a holiday weekend's coming up around the time you're setting up your auction, run your auction through the weekend.

Don't end an auction on the last day of a three-day holiday. People in the mood to shop are generally at department stores collecting bargains. If eBay members aren't shopping, they're out enjoying an extra day off.

✔ **Time of day:** The best time of day to start and end your auction is during eBay's peak hours of operation, 5 p.m. to 9 p.m. Pacific Time, right after work on the West Coast.

Unless you're an insomniac or a vampire and want to sell to werewolves, don't let your auctions close in the middle of the night. There aren't enough bidders around to cause any last-minute bidding that would bump up the price.

Your secret safety net — reserve price

Here's a little secret. The reason sellers list big-ticket items like Ferraris, grand pianos, and high-tech computer equipment with a starting bid of $1 is because they're protected from losing money with a *reserve price*. Reserve price is the lowest price that must be met before the item can be sold (and is not required by eBay, but can protect you). eBay charges an additional fee for this offer that varies depending on how high your reserve is.

For example, say you list a first edition book of John Steinbeck's *The Grapes of Wrath*. You set the starting price at $1, and you set a reserve price of $80. That means that people can start bidding at $1, and if at the end of the auction the book hasn't reached the $80 reserve, you don't have to sell the book.

As with everything in life, there's an upside and a downside to using a reserve price for your auctions. Choosy bidders and bargain-hunters blast past reserve-price auctions because they see a reserve price as a sign that proclaims *No bargains here!* Many bidders figure they can get a better deal on the same item with an auction that proudly declares *NR* in its description. (NR means "no reserve.") As an enticement to those bidders, you see lots of NR listings in auction titles.

On lower-priced items, we suggest that you set a higher minimum bid and set no reserve. Otherwise, if you're not sure about the market, set a low minimum bid, but set a high reserve to protect yourself.

If bids don't reach a set reserve price, some sellers e-mail the highest bidder and offer the item at what the seller thinks is a fair price. Two caveats:

- ✔ eBay can suspend the seller *and* the buyer if the side deal is reported to SafeHarbor.
- ✔ The bidder has the right to turn the seller down (of course).

You can't use a reserve price in a Dutch auction. And reserve-price auctions aren't eligible to have their goods placed in the Hot Items category.

eBay Options: Ballyhoo on the Cheap

Although eBay's display options aren't quite as effective as a three-story neon sign in Times Square, they do bring greater attention to your auction. And unlike the sign in Times Square, most of these attention-grabbers won't break the bank. Here are the options:

- ✔ **Boldface title.** eBay Fee: $2. Bold type does catch your attention, but don't bother using it on items that'll bring in less than $20. Do use it if you're in hot competition with other similar items and you want yours to stand out.

- ✔ **Featured Auction.** eBay Fee: $99.95. As with expensive real estate, you pay a premium for "location, location, location." The $99.95 puts your auction on the Featured Auction page — and it occasionally appears smack in the middle of the eBay Home page, as well as on the main Categories auction page and on the individual category pages of the featured items (kinda hard to miss). Figure 9-5 shows the Featured Auctions on eBay's Home page.

Featured Auctions

Figure 9-5:
High traffic
on eBay's
Home page
means high
visibility for
Featured
Auctions.

Bidders do browse the Featured Auctions to see what's there — just as you might head directly to the "new releases" section of your video store — but because the vast majority of auctions found on eBay are under $25, the average seller doesn't use the Featured Auctions option.

✔ **Featured in Category.** eBay Fee: $14.95: You want top billing? You can buy it here. This option puts you on the first page of your item category. We like this option for moving special merchandise. Often bidders just scan the top items; if you want to be seen, you gotta be there. Ask yourself: Is it worth $15 to have more people see your item? If yes, then go for it. See Figure 9-6 to observe how items are listed in the Featured in Category listings.

You need a Feedback rating of at least 10 to make it to the Featured Auctions and Featured in Auctions.

✔ **Great Gift.** eBay Fee: $1. A dollar doesn't buy much these days, but here it puts a cute little gift icon next to your auction. eBay says the icon alerts prospective bidders to think about your item as a gift idea. Who knows whether they're right or not, but for a buck it can't hurt — especially around holidays like Mother's Day and Father's Day.

Category Featured Auctions are randomly selected for display on category pages (and every category has one). eBay makes it clear there are no guarantees that a specific auction will appear there.

	eBay Listings: Baseball - Microsoft Internet Explorer provided by America Online			

Address http://listings.ebay.com/aw/listings/endtoday/all/category204/index.html

Featured Auctions in Baseball

Ending Today   = Gallery   = Picture   = Hot!   = New!

Status	Item	Price	Bids	Ends PDT
	MARK MCGWIRE/SAMMY SOSA SIGNED BIGSTICK BAT	$280.00	31	07/30 15:33
	COCHRANE,DICKEY,BERRA SIGNED GLOVE 2 COA'S!	$202.50	8	07/30 18:59
	MARK MCGWIRE/SAMMY SOSA SIGNED NL BASEBALL	$112.50	17	07/30 19:54
	1929 - 31 Sports News, Ruth, Gehrig, L@@K	$50.00	-	07/30 20:34
	GAME USED worn home jersey- 1978 George Brett	$1695.00	1	07/30 21:18
	Ebbets Field signed LITHO/BRICK ++ FREE GIFT	$102.50	14	07/31 05:02
	MARK MCGWIRE SIGNED RAWLINGS BIGSTICK BAT	$157.50	27	07/31 08:50
	MARK McGWIRE & SAMMY SOSA LITHOGRAPH / NR	$49.95	1	07/31 09:10
	Spectacular Mickey Mantle LITHOGRAPH / NR	$49.95	-	07/31 09:16

Done   Internet

Figure 9-6: Items at the top of the Featured in Category listings are very visible to buyers.

I want to be alone: The private auction

You just considered all kinds of options to bring more attention to your auction, now we take a step back to make it more private.

In a private auction, bidders' User IDs are kept under wraps. Sellers usually do this to protect the identities of bidders during auctions for high-priced big-ticket items (say, that restored World War II fighter). Wealthy eBay users may not want the world to know they have the resources to buy expensive items. Private auctions are also held for items from the Adult/Erotica category. (Gee, there's a shocker!)

Bidders and sellers do have access to each other's e-mail address in case questions arise.

Put me in the Gallery

The Gallery is a highly specialized auction area that lets you post pictures to a special photo gallery that's accessible from the listings. Many buyers enjoy browsing the Gallery catalog-style, and it's open to all categories. If you choose to go this route, your item is listed in both the Gallery and in the regular text listings. (We explain how to post your pictures in Chapter 12.)

Checking Your Work and Starting the Auction

When you've filled out all the blanks on the Sell Your Item page and you think you're ready to join the world of e-commerce, follow these steps:

1. **Click on the Review button at the bottom of the Sell Your Item page.**

   You waft to the Verification page (shown in Figure 9-7), the place where you can catch mistakes before your item is listed. The Verification page shows you a condensed version of all your information and tallies up how much eBay is charging you in fees and options to run this auction.

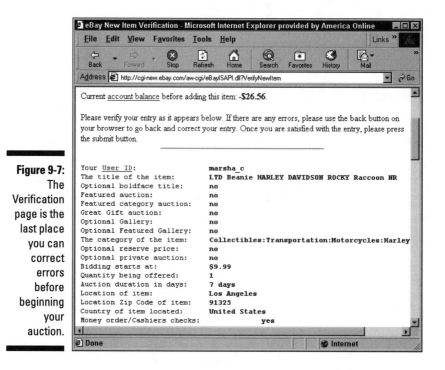

Figure 9-7: The Verification page is the last place you can correct errors before beginning your auction.

You also may find the Verification page helpful as a last-minute chance to get your bearings. If you've chosen a very general category, eBay asks you whether you're certain there isn't a more appropriate category. You can go back to the Sell Your Item page by clicking on the Back button of your browser, make category changes or any other changes and additions, and then head for the Verification page again.

2. **Check for mistakes.**

   Nit-pick for common, careless errors; you won't be sorry. We've seen eBay members make goofs like these:

   - Wrong password

   - Wrong category

   - Spelling errors

   - Grammatical errors

   - Missing information on shipping, handling, and insurance

   - Missing information on how long a seller plans to hold a personal check before depositing or cashing it

3. **When you're sure everything's accurate and you're happy with your item listing, click on the Submit My Listing button.**

   An Auction Confirmation page pops up from eBay. At that precise moment, your auction begins.

Print out the Auction Confirmation page and hold on to it for future reference. You also get a confirmation of your auction e-mailed to you within 24 hours. Print that out and hang on to it as well; it's handy if anybody involved in the auction has questions later.

Your auction appears in its category listing within about two hours from when you receive the Auction Confirmation page. If you want to see your auction right away and check for bids, your Auction Confirmation page provides a link for the purpose; click on it and you're there. You can also keep track of your auctions by using the My eBay page. (To find out how, see Chapter 4.)

All auction pages come with this friendly warning:

Seller assumes all responsibility for listing this item. You should contact the seller to resolve any questions before bidding.

Some eBay veterans just gloss over this warning after they've been wheeling and dealing for a while, but it's an important rule to remember. Whether you're buying or selling, you are responsible for your own actions.

For the first 24 hours after your auction is underway, eBay stamps it with a funky sunburst icon next to the listing. Just a little reminder for buyers to come have a look at the latest items on auction.

Mid-Course Corrections: Fixing Current Auctions

If you make a mistake filling out the Sell Your Item page — but don't notice it until after the auction's up and running — don't sweat it. Pencils have erasers, and eBay allows revisions.

Here's what you can change about your auction before bids have been placed:

- ✔ The title of your auction
- ✔ The item category
- ✔ The item description
- ✔ The URL address of the picture you're including with your auction
- ✔ Accepted payment methods, payment terms, and shipping terms

When you revise an auction, eBay puts a little disclaimer on your auction page that reads: Seller revised this item before the first bid. (Think of it as automatic common courtesy.) To revise an auction before bids have been received:

1. **Go to the auction page and click on the Revise link.**

   If the item hasn't received any bids, a message appears on your screen to indicate that you may update the item.

   You're taken to the Update Item Information Request Form page, where the Item number of your auction and your User ID are already entered on the form.

2. **Type your password and click on the Submit button.**

   You're taken to the Update Your Item Information page.

3. **Make changes to the item information and then click on the Verify button at the bottom of the page when you're finished.**

   A summary of your newly revised auction page appears on your screen.

4. **If you're happy with your revisions, click on the Update button.**

   If not, click on the Back button of your browser and redo the Update Your Information page.

You're taken to your newly revised auction item page, where you see a disclaimer from eBay that says you've revised the auction before the first bid.

If your auction is up and running and already receiving bids, you can still make some slight modifications to it. Newly added information is clearly separated from the original text and pictures. In addition, eBay puts a time stamp on the additional info in case questions from early bidders crop up later.

After your item receives bids, eBay allows you to

✔ **Change your item category:** If you think your auction isn't doing well because you listed it in the wrong category, change it. No moving vans or packing is required, you can find a new home for your item faster than you can say "Century 21"!

✔ **Add to your item's description:** If you feel you were at a loss for words in writing up your item's description or the item is not selling as well as you'd expect, go ahead and make all the additions you want — but whatever you put there the first time around stays in the description as well. If a lot of potential bidders keep asking the same questions about your item, that's a clue that you should add that information to your item description.

To change your item's category from the eBay Home page after the item's received bids:

1. **First click on the Services link on the navigation bar, and then click on Buying and Selling Tools on the subnavigation bar.**

   You're taken to the Services overview page.

2. **Click on the Change my item's category link.**

   You're taken to the Changing My Item's Category page.

3. **First type in your User ID, password, and the Item number for the auction item you want to modify, and then select the item's new category.**

4. **Click on the Change Category button.**

   Your auction appears in its new listings in about an hour.

You've discovered that the Apollo 11 cookie jar you thought was a reproduction is really an original? Better change that description before you sell it. To change your item's description from the eBay Home page, follow these steps:

1. **First click on the Services link on the navigation bar, and then click on Buying and Selling Tools on the subnavigation bar.**

   You're taken to the Services overview page.

2. **Click on the Add to My Item's Description link.**

   You're taken to the Adding To My Item Description page.

3. **First type in your User ID, password, and the Item number of the item you want to add to, and then add any text you want to add to your item's description.**

4. **Click the Review button to see the additional information attached to your previous description.**

5. **If you like the changes, click on the Add To Description button.**

   A message appears on your screen, bearing the glad tidings that your addition has been recorded.

Don't let an oversight grow into a failure to communicate — and don't ignore iffy communication till the auction is over. Correct any inaccuracies now to avoid problems later on.

Always check your e-mail to see whether bidders have questions about your item. If a bidder wants to know about flaws, be truthful and courteous when returning e-mails. As you get more familiar with eBay (and with writing auction descriptions), the number of e-mail questions will decrease. If you enjoy good customer service in your day-to-day shopping, here's your chance to give some back.

Chapter 10

Going, Going, Gone:
Closing the Deal

In This Chapter:

▶ Staying organized

▶ Communicating with the buyer

▶ Packing and sending the item

*T*he auction's over, and you have a winning bidder who (you hope) is eager to send you money. Sounds perfect, doesn't it? It is if you watch your step, keep on top of things, and communicate like a professional.

In this chapter, we help you figure out how to stay organized by showing you what documents you need to keep and for how long. We also give you tips and etiquette on communicating with the buyer so that you're most likely to come out with positive feedback. We also show you how to pack your item, assess costs, and make sure the item reaches the buyer when you say it will (oh, yeah — in one piece).

Bookkeeping and Staying Organized

Though we don't recommend lining your nest with every scrap from every auction you run, you can safely keep some documents without mutating into a giant pack rat. We think you should print and file these essentials:

> ✔ **The auction page as it appeared when the auction closed.** This page gives you a record of the item name and number, the bidding history, every bidder's User ID, and a lot of other useful information. The page also includes the auction item description (and any revisions you've made to it) — very handy if the buyer argues that an item's disintegrating before his eyes and you honestly believe it's just *well-loved*.

You may think you don't need this information because you can always look it up, but here practicality rears its head: eBay trashes completed auctions after 30 days (hey, nothing lasts forever). Print your auction page *before* you forget about it; file it where you know you can find it; *then* forget about it.

- **The End of Auction (EOA) e-mail you receive from eBay that notifies you that the auction is over.** If you lose this e-mail, you can't get it back because eBay doesn't keep it.

- **E-mail between you and the buyer.** In the virtual world, e-mail is as close to having a face-to-face conversation as most people get. Your e-mail correspondence is a living record of all the things you discuss with the buyer to complete the transaction. Even if you're selling just a couple of items a month on eBay, keep track of who's paid up and who owes you money. And more importantly, if the buyer says, "I told you I'd be out of town," you can look through your e-mail and say, "Nope, it doesn't show up here." or "You're right! How was Timbuktu? Is the check on the way?" (Or something more polite.) Be sure to keep that e-mail with the headers and date on it so that you can't be accused of (ahem) creative writing.

- **Any bank statements you receive that reflect a payment that doesn't clear.** Keep anything related to payments, especially payments that didn't go through. That way if a buyer says he's sure he sent you a check, you can say, "Yes sir, Mr. X, you did send me a check, and it was made of the finest rubber." (Or something kinder. Especially if you want that payment.)

- **Any insurance or escrow forms that you have.**

- **Refund requests you make.** If you make a request to eBay for a refund from an auction that doesn't go through, hold on to it until the process is completed.

- **Receipts for items that you buy for the sole purpose of selling them on eBay.** This will come in handy as a reference so that you can see if you're making a profit. It can also be helpful at tax time.

When it comes to printouts of e-mails and documents about transactions, we say that as soon as you get your positive feedback, you can dump them. If you get negative feedback, hang on to your documentation a little longer (say, until you're sure the issues it raises are resolved and everyone's satisfied). If selling on eBay becomes a fairly regular source of income, save all receipts for items you've purchased to sell; for tax purposes, that's inventory.

Once a month, we conduct a By Seller search on ourselves so that we can print out all the information we want on the bid histories of our most recent auctions.

Tales from the formerly Type-A

We have to confess. We used to keep all our paperwork — auctions, e-mails, the works. Now we keep the letters and receipts sent to us until we know a transaction is completed. Then they go wafting off to Recycle Heaven so that we can still find a flat surface in the house.

These days we stay on top of our eBay finances with auction-management software that helps

us keep track of who has paid us and who hasn't. These programs also help us figure out our expenses, profits, and other financial calculations, almost painlessly. They also help jazz up the look of auctions. Ah, progress. Check out Chapter 19 for suggestions on what to buy.

Someday the Internal Revenue Service (or government agency in your area) may come knocking on your door. Scary, but true. Like hurricanes and asteroid strikes, audits happen. Any accountant worth his or her salt will tell you that the best way to handle the possibility of an audit is to be prepared for the worst — even if every single eBay transaction you conduct runs smooth as silk and you've kept your nose sparkling clean. See Chapter 8 for more tax information.

If you sell specialized items, you can keep track of trends and who your frequent buyers are by saving all your paperwork. This prudent habit becomes an excellent marketing strategy if you discover that a segment of eBay users faithfully bids on your auctions. (An *audience*. Imagine.)

Talking to Buyers: The ABCs of Good Communication

You've heard it countless times — *talk is cheap*. Compared to what? Granted, empty promises are a dime a dozen, but honest-to-goodness talk and efficient e-mail are worth their weight in gold and good feedback — especially on eBay. Sometimes *not* talking is costly.

We say that a smooth exchange of money and merchandise really starts with you (the seller). Your first e-mail, soon after the auction is over, sets the entire transaction in motion and helps set the tone for that transaction. If all goes well, no more than two weeks should elapse between getting paid and sending the item.

After the close of the auction, print out a copy of both the auction page that indicates the winning bidder's final closing price and e-mail address page. Keep it handy.

Take a proactive approach and start the ball rolling yourself. We suggest contacting the buyer even *before* you get eBay's EOA. Here's how to get the buyer's e-mail address:

1. **Start on the main auction page of the item that you sold.**
2. **On the auction page, click on the winning bidder's User ID.**

   This takes you to the User ID History and Email Address Request Form.

3. **Type in your User ID, type your password, and check the little *Remember me* box. Click on the Submit button.**

Choosing the Remember me feature puts a temporary *cookie* (a computer file that makes it easier to get around a Web site) in your computer so that you'll automatically get the e-mail addresses of eBay users without going through this process again. The cookie will be erased after you finish the current online session. For more tasty info on cookies, see Chapter 13.

You now see the User ID History and E-mail Information for (the user's name)'s page. It tells you some needed information:

- The person's e-mail address
- The person's User ID (or multiple User IDs if the person did any name changes in the past)
- The date the User ID became effective
- The end date of the User ID (if this person had others in the past)

4. **Print this information and put it in a place where you can find it again.**

Thank you! I mean it!

What do all the successful big-name department stores have in common? Yes, great prices, good merchandise, and nice displays. But with all things being equal, customer service always wins hands-down. One department store in the United States, Nordstrom, has a great reputation in that area; they happily took back a set of snow tires because the customer wasn't happy. No big deal, maybe — until you notice that Nordstrom doesn't even *sell* snow tires!

A friend of ours who owns restaurants calls this level of customer satisfaction the "Wow!" Effect. If customers (no matter what they're buying) say "Wow!" during or after the transaction — admiringly or happily — you've succeeded.

A good rule is to give people the same level of service you'd expect when you're on the buying end.

The best way to start is with an introductory e-mail to your buyer. Congratulate the person on winning the auction; thank the buyer for bidding on your item. Then provide the important details:

- Item name and auction number

- Winning bid amount

- Estimated cost of shipping and packing, (you'll know more exactly when you find out where the buyer lives) as well as any shipping or insurance restrictions (We give pointers on determining shipping and packaging costs later in this chapter.)

- Payment options (check, money order, C.O.D., credit cards)

- How long you will hold a check (usually seven to ten days)

- The shipping timetable

We also recommend that in the first e-mail, you mind a few vital details:

- Ask for the seller's home address (and daytime phone number if you think you need to call); ask whether this is where you should ship the item. If not, ask for the correct shipping address.

- Include your name and the address to which you want the payment sent.

- Remind your buyers to *write the item number* on whatever form of payment they send (you'd be surprised how many buyers forget to give you the item number).

- Include your phone number if you think it will speed up the process.

- Suggest that if all goes well, you'll be happy to leave positive feedback for the buyer. (See Chapter 4 for more on feedback.)

Keep a copy of your buyer's e-mail with a copy of the auction page that shows the winning bid.

Let's keep e-mailing

If you've got a good transaction going (and the majority of them are), the buyer will reply to your e-mail within three business days. Customarily, most replies come the next day. If your buyer has questions regarding anything you asked in your e-mail, you'll get those inquiries now. Most of the time, all you get back is, "Thanks — payment on the way." Hey, that's good enough for us!

If any last-minute details need to be worked out, usually the buyer asks to set up a time to call — or request further instructions about the transaction.

Respond to this communication as soon as possible. If you can't deal with it at the moment, let the buyer know you're working on it and will shoot those answers back ASAP. Never let an e-mail go unanswered.

As soon as you get the hang of sending e-mail, you can actually put in an eBay link that takes the buyer right to the Feedback Forum with just a click of the mouse. We explain how to do that in Chapter 12. Buyers and sellers can also link to the feedback forum from the final auction page by clicking the Leave Feedback.

Shipping without Going Postal

Shipping can be the most time-consuming (and most dreaded) task for eBay sellers. Even if the selling portion of your transaction goes flawlessly, the item has to get to the buyer in one piece. If it doesn't, the deal could be ruined — and so could your reputation.

This section briefs you on shipping etiquette, gives you more details about the main three most popular shipping options (the U.S. Postal Service, United Parcel Service, and Federal Express); and offers tips on how to make sure your package is ready to ride.

The best way to avoid shipping problems is to do your homework beforehand, determine which method is likely to work best, and spell out on your auction page exactly how you intend to ship the item. We always say `Buyer pays actual shipping, handling, and insurance` in our item description, and that's what we charge, although we can make allowances if the buyer wants a specific method of shipment within reason. Here's how we handle the whole process:

1. **After the auction, get the package ready to ship.**

   You don't have to seal the package right away, but you should have it ready to seal — because the two critical factors in shipping are weight and time. The more a package weighs and the faster it has to be delivered, the higher the charge. (We cover packing materials and tips later in this section.) The time to think about packing and shipping is actually *before* you put the item up for auction, that way there are no last-minute surprises while your buyer is waiting impatiently!

2. **Make sure you know what your carrier options are.**

   In the United States, the three main shipping options for most eBay transactions are the U.S. Postal Service, Federal Express, and United Parcel Service. See "Shopping for a shipper" (try saying *that* five times fast) on how you can get rate options from each service, painlessly and online. Compare costs and services.

3. **Before you share the cost estimate with the winner of your auction, make sure you've included all appropriate costs.**

   We recommend that you charge a nominal handling fee ($1 is not out of line) to cover your packing materials, which can add up quickly as you start making multiple transactions. You should also include any insurance costs and any delivery-confirmation costs. See the sidebar "Insuring your peace of mind (and your shipment)" for more information.

   Some eBay scam artists inflate shipping and handling costs to make added profit. Shame on them. Purposely overcharging is tacky, ugly, and so immature. And the buyer often figures it out after one look at the outrageous postage on the box.

   Bidders often e-mail sellers while the auction is still going on to find out how much the shipping cost will be so that they can weigh this cost when they consider their bidding strategies. Figure out what the packed item will weigh, and then give a good guess; the online calculators can help. Be sure to say you're just giving an estimate, and that the final cost will be determined after the auction is over. Optionally, you could tell the bidder how much the item weighs and where you're shipping from (some bidders don't *mind* doing the math).

   Occasionally, shipping calculations can be off-target, and you may not know that until after you take the buyer's money. If the mistake is in your favor and is a biggie, notify the buyer and offer a refund. But if shipping ends up costing you a bit more, take your lumps and pay it. You can always let the buyer know what happened and that you paid the extra cost. Who knows, it may show up on your feedback from the buyer! (Even if it doesn't, spreading goodwill never hurts.)

4. **E-mail the buyer, offering congratulations on winning; reiterate what your shipping choice is and how long you expect it will take.**

   Make sure you're both talking about the same timetable. If the buyer balks at either the price or the shipping time, try working out an option that will make the buyer happy.

5. **Send the package.**

   When should you ship the package? Common courtesy says it should go out as soon as the package and shipping are paid for. If the buyer has held up his or her side of the bargain, you should do the same. Ship that package no more than a week after payment — and if you can't, immediately e-mail the buyer and explain the delay. Also e-mail the buyer as soon as the package is sent, asking for an e-mail to confirm arrival after the item gets there (and putting in a plug for positive feedback).

Send a prompt follow-up e-mail to let the buyer know the item's on the way. In this e-mail, be sure to include when the item was sent, how long it should take to arrive, any special tracking number (if you have one), and a request for a return e-mail confirming arrival after the item gets there. We also include a thank-you note in each package we send out. We appreciate when

Insuring your peace of mind (and your shipment)

Sure, "lost in the mail" is an excuse we've all heard hundreds of times, but despite everyone's best efforts, sometimes things actually do get damaged or misplaced during shipment. The universe is a dangerous place; that's what insurance is for. We usually offer to get insurance from the shipper if the buyer wants to pay for it, and *always* get it on expensive items, one-of-a-kind items, or very fragile items. We spell it out in our item description that the buyer pays for it.

The major shippers all offer insurance that's fairly reasonably priced, so check out their rates at their Web sites. But don't forget to read the details. For example, many items on eBay are sold MIMB (Mint in Mint Box). True, the condition of the original box often has a bearing on the final value of the item inside, but the U.S. Postal Service will only insure whatever is *in* the box. So, if you sold a Malibu Barbie mint in a mint box, USPS will only insure the doll and not the original box. Pack carefully so that your buyer gets what's been paid for. Be mindful that shippers won't make good on insurance claims if they suspect you of causing the damage by doing a lousy job of packing.

We also offer our own type of *self-insurance*. No, we're not pretending we're State Farm or Allstate (though our hands *are* pretty good). Here's what we offer our buyers at no cost to them:

- On lower-priced items, we are willing to refund the buyer's money if the item is lost or damaged.

- On some items we sell, we have a *risk reserve*. That means we have more than one of the item we sold. If the item is lost or destroyed, we can send the backup item as a replacement.

we get one in eBay packages, and it always brings a smile to the recipient's face. It never hurts to take every opportunity to promote goodwill (and future positive feedback!).

More often than not, you do get an e-mail back from the buyer to let you know the item arrived safely. If you don't, it doesn't hurt to send another e-mail (in about a week) to ask whether the item arrived in good condition. It jogs the buyer's memory, and demonstrates your professionalism as a seller. Use this opportunity to gently remind your buyer(s) that you'll be leaving positive feedback for them. Ask whether they're satisfied and don't be bashful about suggesting they do the same for you. Leave positive feedback right away so that you don't forget.

Shopping for a shipper

If only you could transport your item the way they do on *Star Trek* — "Beam up that Beanie, Scotty!" Alas, it's not so. Priority Mail via the U.S. Postal Service is pretty much the eBay standard if you are shipping within the United States and Canada. Many Americans also rely on it to ship internationally as well. Federal Express and United Parcel Service are global alternatives that work well, too.

Whether you're at the post office, UPS, FedEx, (or your doctor's office), be ready, willing, and able to wait in line. We definitely have a "rush hour" at our neighborhood office — everybody's in a rush, so everything moves at a glacial pace. We avoid both the noontime and post-work crunches (easier on the nerves). A good time to ship is around 10:30 a.m., when everyone is still in a good mood. If we have to go in the afternoon, we go about 3:00 p.m., when the clerks are back from their lunch breaks and friendly faces (ours — we always smile!) can take the edge off those brusque lunchtime encounters. And no matter what shipper you use, fill out the shipping forms before you get to the drop-off center. That saves time and frustration.

The U.S. Postal Service

The skinny: The U.S Postal Service is the butt of a lot of unfair jokes and cheap shots, but when it comes right down to it, we think the USPS is still the most efficient and inexpensive way to ship items — eBay or otherwise. They also supply free boxes, labels, and tape for Priority and Express Mail packages. Here are some of ways eBay members get their items from here to there via the USPS:

- ✔ **Priority Mail.** As mentioned earlier, this is the *de facto* standard method of shipping for eBay users. We love the free boxes, and we like the rate. Promised delivery time is two to three days, although we've experienced rare delays of up to a week during peak holiday periods.

  Cost? As of this writing (rates are always subject to change), Priority Mail costs $3.20 for packages up to 2 pounds, and an additional $.90 for each of the next 3 pounds. Over 5 pounds, the charge is calculated according to weight and distance.

- ✔ **Express Mail.** If the item needs to be delivered the next day, use Express Mail. The post office promises delivery no later than noon the following afternoon (even weekends or holidays). And you can get free boxes.

  Cost? Express Mail runs $11.75 for packages 8 ounces and under, $15.75 for packages 8 ounces to 2 pounds, and $2.75 for every pound over 2 (up to 70 pounds).

  The post office will make a special pick-up for Priority Mail and Express Mail. The pick-up costs $8.25, no matter how many separate packages are included. If you have quite a few packages, this is an excellent option to consider, and the extra cost can be covered in your "handling" charge.

- ✔ **First-class mail.** If your item weighs 13 ounces or less, you can use first-class mail, as long as the item is flat like a letter. First class is slightly cheaper than Priority Mail — the first ounce is 33 cents, and every additional ounce is 22 cents. Unfortunately, if the envelope is an unusual size (too big, too small, too oblong), tack on another 11 cents.

iShip, you ship, we all ship!

iShip (www.iship.com) is an online shipping-comparison Web site that allows you to compare the charges from each of four major shipping companies (USPS, FedEx, UPS, and Airborne Express). This handy site is easy to use although sometimes slightly imprecise:

1. In the Price It section on the left side of the iShip Home page, enter your ZIP code (or the ZIP code from the city you'll be sending the package from), the ZIP code of the address you're sending it to, and the weight of the package.

2. Click on the Go button.

   This takes you to a rates and delivery time graphic that shows you the costs of each of

the four major services and when your package will be delivered. Each of the services is represented by a specific color on the graphic: red for Airborne Express, purple for Federal Express, brown for United Parcel Service, and blue for the U.S. Postal Service. Click on any of the color-coded rates in the graphic for more information on that specific service.

We double-checked iShip's listed rates against the USPS, FedEx, and UPS online calculators and found iShip is sometimes slightly off. Even so, this is still a handy tool for getting the big picture of what it costs to send packages around the United States.

✔ **Other options:** The Postal Service offers all sorts of add-ons. We always get the Delivery Confirmation service that you can add to Priority Mail as well as other mailing services. A mere 35 cents buys you the knowledge of when and where your item was delivered. With the parcel's tracking number, you can check on whether the package was delivered (or an attempt was made to deliver it) by calling 1-800-222-1811. If you go online at www.usps.gov/cttgate, you can get a more complete report.

Delivery Confirmation also comes in handy if you're trying to collect insurance if the item was never delivered or if the buyer says it was never delivered. It gives you proof from the Postal Service that the item was sent. (We explain insuring shipments later in this chapter.)

Connecting online: You can get to the USPS Web site (www.usps.gov) directly from the eBay Home page. Just click the Priority Mail link, shown in Figure 10-1. This helpful link gives you an overview of the U.S. Postal Service rates so that you can see all of your options. (Sure beats standing in that endless line! For an explanation of domestic rates, check out this page: www.usps.gov/consumer/domestic.htm.

Even better, the USPS has a page that can help you determine exactly what your item costs to mail (after you've packaged it all up and weighed it, of course). Start at the Domestic Rate Calculator page at `postcalc.usps.gov` and follow the instructions. Rates to send packages from the United States to foreign countries can be found by clicking International Rate Calculator.

United Parcel Service (UPS)

The skinny: The folks in the brown UPS trucks love eBay. The options they offer are pretty varied, with everything from overnight service to the UPS Ground service. We use UPS for items that are heavy (say, antique barbells) or extremely large (such as a 1920s steamer trunk), because UPS ships anything up to 150 pounds in a single box — 80 more pounds than the Postal Service takes. UPS also takes many of the odd-shaped large boxes — such as those for computer equipment — that the Postal Service won't.

UPS makes pick-ups, but you have to know the exact weight of your package so that you can pay after the UPS driver shows up. But, the pickup service is free (our favorite price!).

Connecting online: You can find the UPS Home page at `www.ups.com`. For rates, go to the UPS Home page and click their Quick Cost Calculator, which gives you prices based on ZIP codes and package weights.

One warning: The Quick Cost Calculator prices online are based on what they charge regular and high-volume users. When you get to the counter, the price might be slightly higher than what you find on the Web.

Our favorite link on the UPS site is the transit map that shows a map of the United States and how long it will take to reach any place in the country (based on the originating ZIP code). If you're really thinking of shipping that compact refrigerator to Alaska, you can check out this fun and informative page at `www.ups.com/using/services/servicemaps/servicemaps.html`.

If you use UPS, always buy the Delivery Confirmation option for $1.25. As soon as the package gets to its destination and is signed for, UPS sends you back a confirmation so that you have evidence showing it had been shipped. But what's really cool is the free UPS online tracking. Every package is barcoded, and that code is read everywhere your package stops along its shipping route. You can follow its progress by its package number at the following address: `www.ups.com/tracking/tracking.html#top`.

Federal Express (FedEx)

The skinny: We use FedEx all the time for business in our day jobs, but FedEx seems a little expensive for our eBay shipping. However, if the buyer wants it fast and is willing to pay, we'll send it by FedEx, you bet. We like the online tracking option, and FedEx takes packages over 150 pounds. But fees add up pretty quickly because FedEx offers everything à la carte, so check the rates carefully. FedEx will pick up your package for a $3 charge.

Rough ride

This old U.S. Post Office (Pony Rider) patch was found when I was disposing of my patch collection. This patch is a mint-condition example of the old United States post office Department uniform patch. The patch was used prior to the current U.S. Postal Service eagle's head emblem, and is in the form of the old mail rider on horse back, as seen in use in the Kevin Costner film *The Postman*. This patch *is* an old original, not a movie prop, and even comes with the hard-to-obtain detached Letter Carrier arc tab — so that you actually get two patches! Buyer pays shipping, with USPS money order payment preferred, checks take 10 days to clear.

The starting price was $14.99. It received no bids and did not sell. (Maybe the bidders thought it would be sent via Pony Express?)

We also like FedEx's boxes, which are — like one of our favorite actors (Joe Pesci from *My Cousin Vinnie* and the *Lethal Weapon* movies), small but tough. Thinking of using them for shipping by any other service? Forget it. The FedEx logo is plastered all over every inch of their freebies, and they may get seriously peeved about it.

Connecting online: Find the FedEx home page at www.fedex.com/us where the Rate Finder is conveniently at the bottom of the page.

Getting the right (packing) stuff

You can never think about packing materials too early. You may think you're jumping the gun, but by the law of averages, if you wait until the last minute you won't find the right-size box, approved tape, or the labels you need. Start thinking about shipping even before you sell your item.

But before you pack, give your item the once-over. Here's a checklist of what to consider about your item before you call it a wrap (love that Hollywood lingo!).

✔ **Is your item as you described it?** If the item has been dented or torn somehow, e-mail the winning bidder immediately and come clean. And if you've sold an item along with its original box or container, don't just check the item, make sure the box is in the same good condition as the item inside. Collectors place a high value on original boxes, so make sure the box lives up to what you described in your auction. Pack to protect it as well.

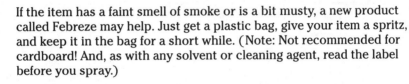

Catch the bus: Shipping with Greyhound

Did you know that the Greyhound bus line not only gives rides across the United States but takes packages as well? We have, on rare occasions, used Greyhound — it's cheap but very slow. To check out Greyhound's rates, go to www.greyhound.com and click on Package Express.

✔ **Is the item dirty, dusty, or does it smell of smoke?** A major complaint from buyers is that the item they received is dirty or smelly, especially from cigarette smoke. Make sure the item is fresh and clean, even if it's used or "vintage." If something is dirty, check to make sure you know how to clean it properly (you want to take the dirt off, not the paint), and then give it a spritz with an appropriate cleaner or just soap and water. If you can't get rid of the smell or the dirt, say so in your item description. Let the buyer decide whether the item is desirable "aromas and all."

If the item has a faint smell of smoke or is a bit musty, a new product called Febreze may help. Just get a plastic bag, give your item a spritz, and keep it in the bag for a short while. (Note: Not recommended for cardboard! And, as with any solvent or cleaning agent, read the label before you spray.)

When the item is ready to go, then you're ready to pack it up. The following sections give you suggestions on what you should consider using and where to find the right stuff.

Packing material: What to use

This may sound obvious, but you'd be surprised: Any list of packing material should start with a box. But you don't want just any box — you want a heavy cardboard type that is larger than the item. If the item is extremely fragile, we suggest you use *two* boxes, with the outer box about 3 inches larger on each side than the inner box that holds the item, to allow for extra padding. And if you still have the original shipping container for such things as electronic equipment, consider using the original, especially if it still has the original foam inserts (they were designed for the purpose, and this way they stay out of the environment a while longer).

As for padding, Table 10-1 compares the most popular types of box filler material.

Table 10-1	Box Filler Materials	
Type	*Pros and Cons*	*Suggestions*
Bubble wrap	**Pros:** Lightweight, clean, cushions well	**Cons:** Cost. Don't go overboard taping the bubble wrap. If the buyer has to battle to get the tape off, the item might go flying and end up damaged. And for crying out loud, don't pop all the little bubbles, okay?
Newspaper (wadded or shredded)	**Pros:** Cheap, cushions	**Cons:** Messy. Seal fairly well. Put your item in a plastic bag to protect it from the ink. We like shredding the newspaper first. It's more manageable and doesn't seem to stain as much as wadded-up paper. We spent about $30 at an office-supply store for a shredder (or find one on eBay for a lot less!).
Cut-up cardboard	**Pros:** Handy, cheap	**Cons:** Transmits some shocks to item, hard to cut up. If you have some old boxes that aren't sturdy enough to pack in, this is a pretty good use for them.
Styrofoam peanuts	**Pros:** Lightweight, absorb shock well, clean	**Cons:** Environmentally unfriendly, annoying. Your item may shift if you don't put enough peanuts in the box, so make sure to fill the box. Also, don't buy these — instead, recycle them from stuff that was shipped to you (trash bags are great for storing them). And *never* use plastic peanuts when packing electronic equipment, because they can create static electricity — and even a little spark can trash a computer chip.
Popped popcorn	**Pros:** Lightweight, environmentally friendly, absorbs shock well, clean (as long as you don't use salt and butter — but you knew that), low in calories (ditto)	**Cons:** Cost, time to pop. You don't want to send it anywhere there might be varmints who like it too. The U.S. Postal Service suggests popcorn. Hey, at least you can eat the leftovers!

Here are a few other items you'll need:

- **Plastic bags.** These protect your item from moisture. We once sent a MIB doll to the Northeast, and the package got caught in a snowstorm. The buyer e-mailed us with words of thanks for the extra plastic bag, which saved the item from being soaked along with the outer box. (Speaking of boxes, if you're sending an item in an original box, bag it!)

  For small items, such as stuffed animals, you should always protect them in a lunch baggie. For slightly larger items, go to the 1-quart or 1-gallon size. Be sure to wrap any paper or cloth products (clothing and linens!) in plastic before you ship.

- **Address labels.** You'll need extras, because it's always a good idea to toss a duplicate address label *inside* the box, with the destination address and a return address, in case the outside label falls off or becomes illegible.

- **2- or 3-inch shipping tape.** Make sure you use a strong shipping tape for the outside of the box. Use nylon-reinforced tape or pressure-sensitive package tape. Remember not to plaster every inch of box with tape; leave space for those "fragile" and "insured" rubber stamps.

- **2-inch clear tape.** For taping the padding around the inside items. We also use a clear strip of tape over the address on the outside of the box so that it won't disappear in the rain.

- **Scissors.** A pair of large, sharp scissors. Having a hobby knife to trim boxes or shred newspaper is also a good idea.

- **Glue gun**. We use one for reconstructing cut-down boxes.

- **Handy liquids.** Three that we like are Goo-Gone (available in the household supply section of most retail stores and a wonder at removing unwanted stickers and price tags); WD40 (the unstick-everything standby that works great on getting stickers off plastic); and Un-Du (the best liquid we've found to take labels off cardboard). If you can't find Un-Du in stores, lighter fluid also does the trick — but be careful handling it and make sure you clean up thoroughly.

- **Black permanent marker**. These are handy for writing addresses and the all-important FRAGILE all over the box. We like the thick Sharpie markers.

If you really plan to become an eBay mover and shaker, consider adding a 5-pound weight scale (for weighing packages) to your shipping department. Why 5 pounds? Because that's the weight/price break for the Postal Service's Priority Mail.

Taking it to the mat

1985 Rare! WWF Hulk Hogan with tee-shirt! One action figure you don't want to miss! Serious collectors can take advantage of this 1985 Hulk Hogan wrestling figure. This is the second Hulk Hogan figure released by LJN Toys. The first was the common one that most collectors have that depicts the Hulkster in yellow tights with no shirt. This more scarce version depicts Hulk with a white Hulkamania T-shirt. This item is sealed in original packaging. The package has very little wear around the corners, otherwise in great condition. Buyer pays shipping. U.S./Canada orders only please.

The opening bid was $10, but the item later sold on eBay for $80.98. How's that for a body slam!

Whatever materials you use, make sure you pack the item well and that you secure the box. Many shippers will contest insurance claims if they feel you did a lousy job of packing. Do all the little things that you'd want done if you were the buyer — using double boxes for really fragile items, wrapping lids separately from containers, and filling hollow breakables with some kind of padding.

Not sure how to pack your item? No problem. Just call a store in your area that deals in that kind of item and ask them how they pack for shipment. They'll probably be glad to offer you a few pointers. Or post a question to seasoned eBay veterans in the chat room for your auction's category. (We introduce you to chat rooms in Chapter 15.)

When it comes to fragile items, dishes, pottery porcelain, china, anything that can chip, crack or smash into a thousand pieces, DOUBLE BOX. The boxes should be about 3 inches different on each side. Make sure there's enough padding so that the interior box is snug. Just give it a big shake. If nothing rattles, ship away!

Packing material: Where to find it

The place to start looking for packing material is the same place you should start looking for things to sell on eBay — your house. Between us, we've done over a thousand eBay transactions and never once paid for a carton. Because we buy most of our stuff from catalogs and online companies (we love e-commerce!), we save all the boxes, bubble wrap, padding, and packing peanuts we get in the mail. Marsha is most proud of the bubble-wrap blanket that covers her car!

Sí, oui, ja, yes! Shipping internationally

Money's good no matter what country it comes from! We don't know why, but lots of people seem to be afraid to ship internationally and list `I don't ship overseas` on the auction page. Of course, sending an item that far away may be a burden if you're selling a car or a street-sweeper (they don't fit in boxes too well), but we've found that sending a package across the Atlantic can be just as easy as shipping across state lines. The only downside: Our shipper of choice, the U.S. Postal Service, does not insure packages going to certain countries (check with your post office to find out which ones; they seem to change with the headlines).

A couple of other timely notes about shipping internationally:

✓ You will need to tell what's inside the package. Be truthful when declaring value on customs forms. Be sure to use descriptions that customs agents can figure out without knowing eBay shorthand terms. For instance, instead of declaring the contents as "MIB Furby," call it a "small stuffed animal toy that talks." Some countries require the buyers to pay special duties and taxes, depending on the item and the value. But that's the buyer's headache.

✓ Wherever you send your package (especially if it's going to a country where English is not the native language), be sure to write legibly. (Imagine getting a package from Russia and having to decipher a label written in the Cyrillic alphabet. 'Nuff said.)

If you recently got a mail-order shipment box that was only used that once — and it's a good, sturdy box with no dents or dings — there's nothing wrong with using it again. Just be sure to cover any old labels so the delivery company doesn't get confused.

Beyond the ol' homestead, here are a couple of other suggestions for places where you can rustle up some packing stuff:

✓ **Check out your local supermarket, department store, or drug store.** You won't be the first person pleading with a store manager for boxes. (Ah, fond memories of moving days past . . .) Stores actually like giving them away because it saves the extra work of compacting them and throwing them away.

We've found that drug stores have a better variety of smaller boxes. And be careful that you don't take dirty boxes with food smells.

✓ **Check out the inside of your local supermarket, department store, or drug store.** Places like K-mart, Wal-Mart, Target, and office supply stores often have good selections of packing supplies.

✔ **Contact shippers like UPS, FedEx and the Postal Service**. They offer all kinds of free supplies as long as you use them to ship things with their service. The Postal Service also will ship free boxes, packing tape, labels, and shipping forms for Express Mail, Priority Mail, and Global Priority Mail to your house. You can order by phone (1-800-222-1811) or online (supplies.usps.gov). A couple of rules for USPS orders:

- Specify the service (Priority Mail, Express Mail, or Global Priority Mail) you're using because the tape, the boxes, and the labels all come with the service name printed all over them, and you can only use it for that specific service.

- Order in bulk. For example, address labels come in rolls of 500 and boxes in packs of 25.

  - The boxes come flat, you have to assemble them. Hey, don't look a gift box in the mouth — they're free!

✔ **Check out other places online.** Many terrific online sites can offer you really good deals. Here are a couple of sites that we recommend:

- Allied Shipping and Packaging Equipment (www.erinet.com/asap)

- Discount Box & The Packaging Store (www.movewithus.com)

- Mylan Enterprises (www.Mylanusa.com)

- Uline Shipping Supplies (www.uline.com)

✔ And of course you can riffle through the auctions on eBay in quest of shipping supplies. Just search for Shipping. You can find some great deals, especially on bubble wrap.

Chapter 11

Troubleshooting Your Auction

· ·

In This Chapter

▶ Dealing with a difficult buyer

▶ Handling other auction mishaps

▶ Ending an auction early

▶ Canceling an auction after it ends

▶ Relisting an item

▶ Getting refunds from eBay

· ·

*T*here's no getting around it: The more transactions you conduct on eBay, the more chances you have of facing some potential pitfalls. In this chapter, we give you pointers on how to handle an obnoxious buyer as if he or she is your new best friend (for a little while anyway). In addition, we explain how to keep an honest misunderstanding from blowing up into an e-mail war. We show you how to handle an auction that's (shall we say) on a road to nowhere, how to get some attention, and if it all goes sour, how to relist and get the money you paid eBay back. We don't think all of what we mention here will happen to you, but the more you know, the better off you'll be.

Dealing with a Buyer Who Doesn't Respond

Most of the time, the post-auction transaction between buyers and sellers goes smoothly. However, if you have difficulty communicating with the winner of your auction, you should know the best way to handle the situation.

You've come to the right place if you want help dealing with a potential non-paying bidder (more commonly known as deadbeat bidders, which is how we refer to them). Of course, you should start with good initial post-auction communications; see Chapter 10. (For more information on how to deal with a fraudulent seller, see Chapter 14.)

Going into nudge mode

Despite our best efforts, sometimes things fall through the cracks. Both buyers and sellers should contact each other within three business days of the close of the auction. Sometimes winners contact sellers immediately, which can save you some trouble, but if you don't hear from the buyer within three business days of your initial contact, our first advice is *don't panic*.

People are busy; they travel, they get sick, computers crash, or sometimes your auction might simply slip the winner's mind. After a week of not hearing from the winner, you need to get into big-time *nudge-nudge mode* — as in, "Mr. X, remember me and your obligation to buy the Tiffany lamp you won on eBay last week?"

Send a friendly-but-firm e-mail letting Mr. X know that when he bid on and won your auction, he became obligated to pay and complete the transaction. If Mr. X doesn't intend to buy your item for any reason, he needs to let you know immediately.

Here's what to include in your nudge-nudge e-mail:

- ✔ A gentle rebuke, such as, "Perhaps this slipped your mind," or "You may have missed my e-mail to you," or "I'm sure you didn't mean to ignore my first e-mail."

- ✔ A reminder, also gentle, that eBay's policy is that every bid is a binding contract. You can even refer the buyer to eBay's rules and regulations if you want to.

- ✔ A statement that firmly (but gently) explains that, so far, you've held up your side of the deal and you'd appreciate it if he did the same.

- ✔ A date by which you expect to see payment. Gently explain that if the deadline isn't met, you'll have no other choice but to consider the deal invalid.

Technically, you can nullify the transaction if you don't hear from a buyer within three business days. However, eBay members are a forgiving bunch under the right circumstances. We think you should allow your buyer a two-week grace period after the auction ends to get in touch with you and set up a payment plan. If you don't see any real progress towards a closing of the deal at the end of the grace period, say goodnight, Gracie. Consider the deal kaput and go directly to "Auction Going Badly? Cut Your Losses" (later in this chapter) to find out what recourse you have.

Under very unusual conditions, eBay lets a bidder squirm out of a deal. To find out more about the circumstances under which eBay allows a buyer out of a deal, check out Chapter 7.

Don't threaten your buyer. The last thing you want to do is add insult to injury in case the buyer's facing a real problem. Besides, if the high bidder goes to sleep with the fishes, you'll *never* see your money.

Be sure you're not the one who erred. Did you spell the name right in your e-mail address?

Be a secret agent, man

We won't say history repeats itself, because that would be a cliché. (All right, so you caught us, but clichés are memorable because they're so often true.) After you send your polite and gentle nudge-nudge e-mail, but before you decide that the auction is a lost cause, take a look at the bidder's feedback history. Figure 11-1 shows you the Feedback Profile of a typical eBay user.

Figure 11-1:
If you find a lot of negative feedback in a buyer's Feedback Profile, you can get an indication of whether the buyer will complete the sale.

> eBay View User Feedback for marsha_c - Microsoft Internet Explorer provided by Americ...
>
> File   Edit   View   Favorites   Tools   Help   Links »
>
> Back   Forward   Stop   Refresh   Home   Search   Favorites   History   Mail   Print
>
> Address http://cgi2.ebay.com/aw-cgi/eBayISAPI.dll?ViewFeedback&userid=marsha_c   Go
>
> **Overall profile makeup**
>
> **638** positives. **599** are from unique users and count toward the final rating.
>
> **15** neutrals. **14** are from users no longer registered.
>
> **1** negatives. **1** are from unique users and count toward the final rating.
>
> **ebY ID card**   marsha_c (598)
>   me
>
> **Summary of Most Recent Comments**
>
> | | Past 7 days | Past month | Past 6 mo. |
> |----------|-------------|------------|------------|
> | Positive | 5 | 18 | 91 |
> | Neutral | 0 | 0 | 3 |
> | Negative | 0 | 0 | 0 |
> | **Total**| **5** | **18** | **94** |
>
> Auctions by marsha_c
>
> **Note:** There are 14 comments that were converted to neutral because the commenting users are no longer registered.
>
> You can leave feedback for this user. Visit the Feedback Forum for more info on feedback profiles.
>
> If you are marsha_c (598) , you can respond to comments in this Feedback Profile.
>
>   Internet

To check the feedback of a bidder starting at your auction item page:

1. **Click on the number in parentheses next to your winner's User ID.**

   This takes you to the Feedback Profile page of the member.

2. **Scroll down the Feedback Profile page and read the comments.**

Check to see if the bidder has gotten negative feedback from previous sellers. Make a note of it in case you need some support and background information.

3. **Conduct a Bidder search.**

Click on Search on the main navigation bar and do a Bidder search to see the buyer's conduct in previous auctions. How many has the buyer won? Click on the item number to see the history of the auction. For more info on Bidder searches, check out Chapter 5.

When all else fails, you might want to double-check with some of the bidder's previous sellers. It's okay to e-mail previous sellers who've dealt with the bidder. They're often happy to give you details on how well (or badly) the transaction went.

Be sure to ask (politely):

- ✔ Did Mr. X pay on time?
- ✔ Did his check clear?
- ✔ Did he communicate well?

If there's any indication that the buyer has gone AWOL in the past, start thinking about getting out of the transaction before too much time passes. If the buyer looks to be on the level, continue to give him or her the benefit of the doubt.

When e-mailing a third party about any negative feedback left, choose your words carefully. There is no guarantee that if you trash the bidder, the third party will keep your e-mail private. Make sure you stick to the facts. Writing false or malicious statements could put you in danger of being sued.

Step up your nudge a notch

If you don't hear from the winner after a week, your next course of action is to contact the winner by phone. To get the contact information of an eBay member for transaction purposes only:

1. **Click on the Search link on the navigation bar at the top of most eBay pages.**

   You see a subdirectory appear below the navigation bar.

2. **Click on the Find Members link and scroll down the page to the Contact Info box.**

3. **Enter the User ID of the person you're trying to contact.**

4. **Enter your User ID (or e-mail address) and your Password.**

5. Click on the Submit button.

eBay e-mails you the contact information of the person with whom you want to be in touch and also sends your contact information to that person.

Wait a day before calling the person. Because eBay automatically sends your request and your information to the bidder, that might be enough of a nudge to get some action.

If you do get the person on the phone, keep the conversation like your e-mail — friendly but businesslike. Explain who you are, when the auction closed, and ask if there are any circumstances that have delayed the bidder's reply. Often the bidder will be so shocked to hear from you that either you'll get the check immediately or you'll know this person is a complete deadbeat.

Try a last-ditch emergency effort

If e-mails and phoning don't work, and you really want to give the buyer one last chance to complete the transaction, check out eBay's Emergency Contact Board. This is where members who are having trouble contacting buyers and sellers leave word. Figure 11-2 shows you what the Emergency Contact Board looks like.

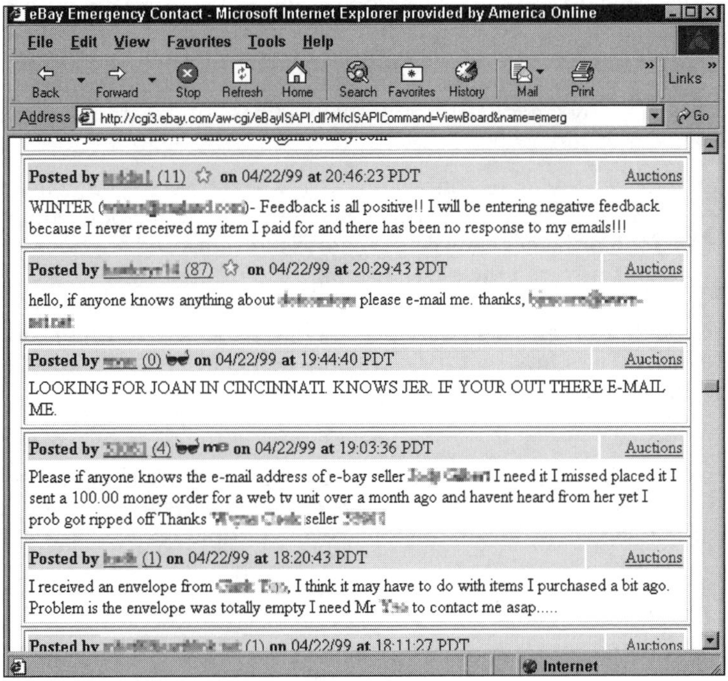

Figure 11-2:
Make one
last attempt
to contact
your buyer
on the
Emergency
Contact
Board.

To post a message on the Emergency Contact Board:

1. **Click on the Community link on the main navigation bar at the top of most eBay pages.**

   A submenu with additional links appears.

2. **Click on the Chat link on the submenu.**

   You're taken to the main Chat page, which lists all of eBay's chat boards.

3. **Scroll down the Chat page and click on the Emergency Contact link.**

   You're taken to the Emergency User Contact Board.

   Before you leave a posting, scroll down to the postings and look for postings from your AWOL buyer. Maybe he or she has been trying to get in touch with you, too.

4. **Type your User ID, Password, and message in the appropriate boxes.**

5. **Check your message for errors and then click on the Click here button.**

   Your message is instantly posted.

Not sure what to post on the Emergency Contact Board? Start off by sticking to the facts of the transaction and say what you want your buyer to do. Have the item number and the buyer's User ID handy before you start your posting.

You can send messages to specific users or post a general cry for help. Here are two examples of short-but-sweet postings that get your message across.

   ✔ Dear Mr. X, I've been trying to reach you via e-mail and phone for two weeks about Item number XXXXX and have had no response. Please contact me by (leave date) or I will invalidate the auction and leave negative feedback.

   ✔ I've been trying to contact Mr. X (mrx@completelybogusbidder.com) for two weeks now regarding an auction. Does anybody know this person or have a new e-mail address for him? Did anybody get burned by this buyer in the past? Thanks.

Your postings aren't very useful if you don't check back often and read other eBay users' postings on the Emergency Contact Board. See whether someone has responded to your message.

Even though you may be feeling like the transaction's a lost cause when you get to the point of posting a message on the Emergency Contact Board, keep your message neutral and don't make accusations.

Keep your eyes open as you scroll through the board. Although we suggest you don't trash anyone on this board, many people use the emergency board to issue an all-points bulletin about bad eBay members.

And Some Other Auction Problems

We're not quite sure why, but where money's involved, sometimes people act kind of weird. Buyers may suddenly decide that they can't purchase an item after they've made a commitment, or there may be payment problems, or shipping problems. Whatever the problem may be, look no farther than here to find out how to make things better.

The buyer backs out of the transaction

Every time an eBay member places a bid, he or she has made a commitment to purchase the item in question. In theory, anyway. In the real world, people have second thoughts, despite the rules. You have every right to be mad that you're losing money and your time's been wasted. Remind the buyer that making a bid is a binding contract. But, unfortunately, if the winner won't pay up, you can't do much except make the winner pay with negative feedback. Jump to Chapter 6 to find out more about buyer's remorse.

Leaving feedback after an imperfect auction experience

If the buyer never materializes, backs out, bounces a check, or moves slower than a glacier to send payment (but wants the item sent overnight from Boston to Khartoum at your expense), you need to think about how you want to word your feedback. You're well within your rights to leave negative feedback, but that doesn't mean you can go off the deep end. Remember to stick to the facts and don't get personal.

Here are a few feedback tips. For more information, check out Chapters 4 and 6:

✔ If the transaction was shaky but everything turned out all right in the end, go ahead and leave neutral feedback.

✔ If a blizzard stopped planes out of Chicago for three days and that's why it took a long time to get your check, take a deep breath, blame the fates, and leave positive feedback.

✔ If the buyer was a living nightmare, take a long break before leaving negative feedback — and have someone you love and trust read it before you send something into the virtual world that you can't take back.

Keep your cool

By all means, if the winner of one of your auctions tells you that the transaction can't be completed, no matter what the reason — remain professional, despite your anger. For one thing, at least such a would-be buyer has the heart to break the news to you instead of ignoring your e-mail and phone calls.

When Plan A fails, try Plan B, or even C

There are several options if the winner backs out. You can offer the item to the next highest bidder or relist the item and hope it sells again. In addition, you can request a full or partial Final Value Fee credit. (We give you more information on requesting a Final Value Fee credit, selling your item to the next highest bidder, and relisting your item later in this chapter.) Who knows? This bidder may actually *earn* you money in the long run.

Houston, we have a payment problem

A lot of things can go wrong where money's concerned. Maybe you never receive the money, or perhaps the check bounces. If the check bounces, contact the seller immediately. Honest winners will be completely embarrassed and make good while unscrupulous winners will offer lame excuses. Either way, insist on a more secure form of payment, like a money order.

If the buyer's paying by check, hang on to the check until it clears, and *then* ship the item.

The item you send is busted — and so are you

Uh-oh! Could it be true? Could you have sent the wrong item? Or is it possible that the crystal vase you thought you packed so well is a sad pile of shards at the bottom of a torn box? If so, go back and read Chapter 10 as soon as you take care of this catastrophe so you can get some hints on packing and insurance.

Time to do some serious problem-solving. If the buyer met his or her end of the deal, you need to do your best to fix the problem. Your communication skills are your number one asset in this situation, so get to work.

Picking up the pieces

No matter how carefully you pack an item, sometimes it arrives on the buyer's doorstep mangled, broken, or squashed. News of this unfortunate event travels back to you fast. The buyer will let you know in about 30 seconds how unhappy he or she is in an e-mail. Tell the buyer to locate the insurance stamp or paper tag that is attached to the package as proof of insurance and then take the whole mangled shebang back to his or her post office.

Here's what happens at the post office:

- ✔ If the item is insured for less than $50, the buyer immediately gets a postal service money order for the value of the item.

- ✔ If the item is insured for over $50, the buyer fills out a claim form, and you're contacted to fill out additional forms. You need to show the good people at the post office your insurance receipt. You have to wait 60 to 90 days for the paperwork to be processed before you actually get paid.

- ✔ Of course, the post office won't refund the postage. Hey, they delivered the item, didn't they?

If a package is lost — you can tell because the delivery confirmation never comes through or the buyer tells you the package is a no-show — you need to go the post office from which you sent the item in order to file for insurance. Then the postal service checks around. If your item isn't located in 30 days, it's declared lost, and there's another round of paperwork and processing before you get your money. And no, you don't get a return on the postage either.

Boxed out of a claim

In our experience, neither UPS nor the United States Postal Service will pay on an insurance claim if they feel you did a lousy job of packing. So, don't be surprised if your claim is declined. Always use good products, pack carefully, and get ready to plead your case.

Every shipping company has its own procedure for complaints. What they all seem to have in common is that none is hassle-free. Call your shipper as soon as there's a problem.

And the runner-up is . . . ?

If your winning bidder turns out to be a non-paying bidder — commonly known as a deadbeat — you can try and salvage an auction that's gone belly-up by contacting and offering the second-highest bidder the chance to buy the item. You can find the list of users who bid on your item on the auction item page. Figure 11-3 shows you the bid history of an item.

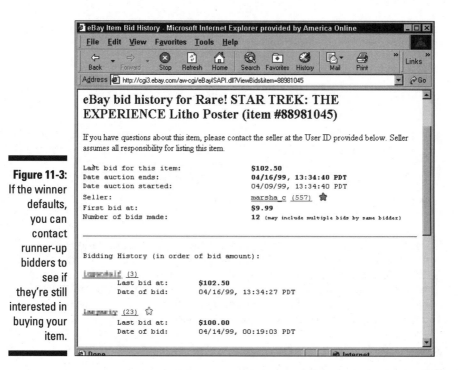

Figure 11-3:
If the winner
defaults,
you can
contact
runner-up
bidders to
see if
they're still
interested in
buying your
item.

You're not required to sell your item to runners-up, and although runners-up are sometimes willing to pay their highest bid price, they have no obligation to do so.

If you do sell to a backup bidder, expect to get less than the high bidder's bid. Just how much less depends on how good at negotiating the second-highest bidder is.

If you want to give the runner-up a chance to buy, send an e-mail explaining that the winning bidder defaulted on the auction. Offer to sell the item for that bidder's price (the runner-up may offer less now that he or she knows you've been left without a sale).

To e-mail the runner-up bidder, start on the main auction page of the item:

1. **Click on the Bid History link.**

   This takes you to the eBay Bid History page for your item.

2. **Scroll down the page to the Bidding History (in order of bid amount) heading and click on the User ID that's just below the name of the winning high bidder.**

3. **E-mail the bidder and make an offer.**

If you ran a private auction, you won't see any bidder User IDs listed here, and you won't be able to e-mail any of the other bidders for this auction.

If you don't want to take a loss by selling to the second-highest bidder, eBay gives you a second chance — you can relist the item. We explain how to do this in the section, "Déjà vu — relisting your item" section in this chapter.

You have regrets — seller's remorse

You've undoubtedly heard about buyer's remorse. Here's a new one for you — *seller's remorse*. If you were selling your velvet Elvis footstool because your spouse said, "It's me or that footstool!" and in the end you realize your spouse should have known how much you emulated the King when you went to Graceland on your honeymoon, you can end the auction. Read "Try canceling bids first" and "If all else fails, end your auction early," later in this chapter.

Auction Going Badly? Cut Your Losses

So your auction is cruising along just fine for a couple of days when you notice that same eBay user who didn't pay up on a previous auction is your current high bidder. You don't want to get burned again, do you? Of course not; *cancel* this deadbeat's bid before it's too late. While canceling bids — or, for that matter, entire auctions — isn't easy (you have a heap of 'splainin' to do, pardner), eBay does allow it.

If you feel you have to wash your hands of an auction that's given you nothing but grief, it doesn't mean you have to lose money on the deal. Read on to find out the protocol for dumping untrustworthy bidders or (as a last resort) laying a bad auction to rest and beginning anew.

Try canceling bids first

Face the facts: This auction is fast becoming a big-time loser. You did your very best, and things didn't work out. Before you kill an auction completely, see whether you can improve it by canceling bids first.

You might have a million reasons for thinking your auction is a bust — but eBay says your explanation had better be good. Here are some eBay-approved reasons for canceling a bid (or even an entire auction):

✔ The high bidder informs you that he or she is retracting the bid.

✔ Despite your best efforts to determine who your high bidder is, you can't find out — and you get no response to your e-mails or phone calls .

✔ The bidder makes a dollar-amount mistake in the bid.

✔ You decide mid-auction that you don't want to sell your item.

We can't drive this point home hard enough: *Say why, and your explanation had better be good.* You can cancel any bid for any reason you want, but if you can't give a good explanation why you did it, you will be sorry. Citing past transaction problems with the current high bidder is okay; canceling a bidder who lives in Japan because you don't feel like shipping overseas after you said you'd ship internationally could give your feedback history the aroma of week-old sushi.

Here's how to cancel bids, starting from most eBay pages, as shown in Figure 11-4:

1. **Click on the Services link on the navigation bar at the top of most eBay pages.**

   A submenu with additional links appears.

2. **Click on the Buying & Selling link of the submenu.**

   You're taken to the Buying and Selling Tools page, where you see the Manage Your Items for Sale heading.

3. **Under the Manage Your Items for Sale heading, click on the Cancel Bids on My Item link.**

   You're taken to the Canceling Bids Placed in Your Auction page.

4. **First, read all of the fine print, and then type in your User ID, Password, Item Number, and an explanation of why you're canceling bids, as well as the User ID of the person whose bid you're canceling.**

5. **Click on the Cancel Bid button.**

Be sure you really want to cancel a bid before you click on that button. Canceled bids can never be reinstated.

eBay says that you can't receive negative feedback on a transaction that wasn't completed. So if something in your gut says not to deal with a particular bidder, then don't. However, don't be surprised if you receive some pretty negative neutral feedback. Hey, this may be the price you have to pay for peace of mind.

Canceling bids means you removed an individual bidder (or several bidders) from your auction, but the auction itself continues running. If you want to end the auction completely, read on.

Figure 11-4:
If you want
to remove a
bid from an
auction
you're
currently
running, use
the Cancel
Bid form.

eBay Bid Cancellation - Microsoft Internet Explorer provided by America Online

File   Edit   View   Favorites   Tools   Help   Links »

Back   Forward   Stop   Refresh   Home   Search   Favorites   History   Mail   Print

Address http://pages.ebay.com/services/buyandsell/seller-cancel-bid.html   Go

Cancelling Bids Placed in Your Auction

You should only cancel bids if you have a good reason to. Also, please remember that bids cannot be reinstated once they've been canceled. Here are a few **examples of a legitimate cancellation**:

- Bidder contacts you to back out of the bid.
- You cannot verify the identity of the bidder, after trying all reasonable means of contact.
- You want to end your auction early because you no longer want to sell your item. **In this case you must cancel all bids on your auction before ending the auction.**

Because your cancellation will be put in the bidding history for this auction, bidders may ask you to explain your cancellation. So, **please include a one-line explanation of your cancellation for the official record.**

To avoid mistakes, please verify your password in order to cancel a bid. If you haven't selected a personal password, or if you've forgotten your password, please request a new temporary password before proceeding.

Your registered User ID

Your password

Internet

If all else fails, end your auction early

If you put your auction up for a week and the next day your boss says you have to go to China for a month or your landlord says you have to move out immediately so he can fumigate for a week, you can end your auction early. But, ending an auction early isn't a decision to be taken lightly. You'll miss all the last-minute bidding action.

eBay makes it clear that ending your auction early does not relieve you of the obligation to sell this item to the highest bidder. To relieve your obligation, you must first cancel all the bids and then end the auction. Of course, if there are no bidders, you have nothing to worry about.

When you cancel an auction, you have to write a short explanation (no more than 80 characters) that appears on the bidding history section of your auction page. Anyone who bid on the item may e-mail you for a written explanation. If bidders think your explanation doesn't hold water, you could get some negative feedback.

To end an auction early, start at the top of nearly any eBay page and follow these steps:

1. **Click on the Services link on the navigation bar.**

   A submenu with additional links appears.

2. **Click on the Buying & Selling link of the submenu.**

   You're taken to the Buying and Selling Tools page, where you see the Manage Your Items for Sale heading.

3. **Under the Manage Your Items for Sale heading, click on the End Your Auction Early link.**

   You're taken to the Ending Your Auction form.

4. **First type in your User ID, Password and the Item Number, and then click on the End Auction button.**

   A Verifying Ending Auction page appears.

5. **Click on the End Auction link.**

   An Ended Auction page appears.

   eBay sends an End of Auction Confirmation e-mail to you and to the highest bidder.

If you know when you list the item that you'll be away when an auction ends, let potential bidders know when you plan to contact them in your item description. Bidders who are willing to wait will still be willing to bid. Alerting them to your absence can save you from losing money if you have to cut your auction short.

Bidding on your own item is against the rules. Once upon a time, you could cancel an auction by outbidding everyone on your own item and then ending the auction. This privilege was abused by some eBay users who bid on their own items merely to boost the sales price. Shame on them.

Extending your auction (not!)

Is your auction red hot? Bids coming in fast and furious? Wish you could have more time. Well, the answer is no. eBay won't extend auctions under normal conditions.

However, eBay on occasion experiences *hard outages*. That's when the system goes offline and no one can place bids. (Of course, Murphy's Law would put the next hard outage right in the thick of a furious bidding war in the final minutes of *your* auction. Or so it seems.) Outages can last anywhere from 5 minutes to several hours or even a day. Because so many bidders wait until the last minute to bid, this can be a disaster. To make nice, eBay extends auctions by 24 hours if any of these three things happen:

✔ The outage is unscheduled and lasts 2 hours or more.

✔ The auction was scheduled to end during the outage.

✔ The auction was scheduled to end one hour after the outage.

eBay also refunds all your auction fees for any hard outage that lasts more than 2 hours. That means the Insertion Fee, Final Value Fee, and any optional fees. You don't have to apply for anything; all refunds are done automatically by eBay.

If your auction was set to end Thursday at 20:10:09 (remember, eBay uses military time, based on the Pacific Time Zone — which would make it 8:10 p.m.), the new ending time is Friday at 20:10:09. Same Bat-time, same Bat-channel, different day.

You can read about any hard outages on eBay's Announcements Board. See Figure 11-5 for an eBay outage report. To get to the outage report, start at the navigation bar (at the top of most eBay pages) and follow these steps:

1. **Click on Community on the main navigation bar.**

   That takes you to the Community Overview page.

2. **Click on News in the subnavigation bar.**

3. **Click on the Announcements link.**

4. **Scroll through the eBay announcements.**

Figure 11-5:
Compare your auction time to eBay's outage report to see if you're eligible for a refund.

```
User:  aw@ebay.com       *** UPDATE ***
Date:  08/08/99
Time:  21:59:16 PDT      We are working to bring the system back up. When we do,
                         Title Search and the Gallery will initially be unavailable.

                         Auctions that were originally scheduled to end between
                         19:47 PDT, Sunday, August 8, and 05:00 PDT, Monday, August
                         9, will be extended by 24 hours.

                         Should you wish to end your auctions early, information can
                         be found at:

                         http://pages.ebay.com/services/buyandsell/end-auction.html

                         Thank you for your patience.

                         Regards,
                         eBay
```

We make it standard operating procedure to check the Announcements Board every time we log into eBay. Sort of like checking the obituary in the morning to make sure you're not listed. More on the Announcements Board in Chapter 15.

Filing for a Final Value Fee credit

Hard outages are not the only time you can collect a refund. If closing a successful auction is the thrill of victory, then finding out your buyer is a non-paying bidder or deadbeat is the agony of defeat. Adding insult to injury, eBay still charges you a Final Value Fee even if the high bidder never sends you a cent. But you can do something about it. You can file for a Final Value Fee credit.

To qualify for a Final Value Fee credit you must prove to eBay one of the following:

- ✔ The winning bidder never responded after numerous e-mail contacts.
- ✔ The winning bidder backed out of the sale.
- ✔ The winning bidder's payment did not clear or was never received.
- ✔ The winning bidder returned the item to you, and you refunded the payment.

So what happens if the sale goes through but for some reason you collect less than the actual listed final sale price? eBay has you covered there, too. But first you may ask, "Wait a second, how can that happen?" Let us count the ways. Here are a few of them:

- ✔ Your high bidder turns out to be a deadbeat, and you sell to the next-highest bidder for a lower price.
- ✔ eBay miscalculates the final price (doesn't happen often, but always check).
- ✔ You renegotiate a lower final sale price with the winning bidder, and eBay still charges you on the basis of the posted high bid.
- ✔ Bidder(s) in your Dutch auction back out.

To apply for a full or partial credit:

1. **First click on the Services link on the navigation bar at the top of most eBay pages, and then click on the Buying & Selling link that appears just below it.**

   You're taken to the Buying and Selling Tools page.

2. **Under the Seller Accounts heading, click on the Request final value fee credit link.**

   You're taken to the Final Value Fee Credit Request page.

3. **Read the guidelines for applying for a Final Value Fee credit and click on the Final Value Fee Credit Request Form link.**

   You're taken to the Final Value Fee Credit Request Form page.

4. **First type your User ID, Password, and the /Item Number of the auction in question, and then click on the Submit button.**

   You're taken to a *second* Final Value Fee Credit Request Form page, which displays the date the auction ended and the final bid price.

5. **Answer the following questions:**

   • **Did you receive any money from the bidder?** If you answer yes, type the amount in the box; use numerals and a decimal point.

   • **Reason for refund.** eBay gives you a pull-down menu of choices. Click on the small down arrow on the right of the box, and all your options magically appear.

   • **Bidder's e-mail address.** Type in the e-mail address of the person who was the high bidder on your auction.

6. **Click on the Submit button on the bottom of the page.**

   You're taken to the Credit Request Process Completed page, which confirms that your refund is being processed by eBay.

You need to wait seven days before you can apply for a Final Value Fee credit. We think it's jumping the gun even at seven days; give it two weeks unless the bidder sends you a message about backing out (or you have good cause to believe you've got a deadbeat on your hands). Once your credit request is filed, eBay takes three to five business days to process it.

When your auction ends, you have up to 60 days after the auction closes to request a full or partial credit. Over 60 days, kiss your refund good-bye; eBay won't process it.

The instant you file for a Final Value Fee credit, eBay shoots off an e-mail to the winner of your auction and warns the eBay user of the non-paying bidder (deadbeat) status. After four non-payment warnings, eBay can boot a deadbeat from the site.

Anyone caught applying for either a full or partial refund on a successful item transaction can be suspended or something worse — after all, this is a pretty clear-cut case of fraud.

Always print out a copy of any refund and credit requests you make. This paper-trail can help bail you out later if eBay asks you for documentation.

If you want to verify eBay's accounting, grab your calculator and use Table 11-1 to check the math. (Why couldn't we have had one of those in high-school algebra class?)

Table 11-1	Determining Your Final Value Fee
Closing Bid	*To Find Your Final Value Fee*
$.01-$25	Multiply the final sale price by .05
$25.01-$1,000	Multiply the final sale price by .025 and then add $1.25 ($1.25 is the maximum final value fee for a $25 sale)
$1,000.01 and over	Multiply the final sale price by .025 and then add $25.63 ($25.63 is the maximum final value fee for a $1,000 sale)

Déjà vu — relisting your item

Despite all your best efforts, sometimes your auction ends with no bids or bids that are not even close to your reserve price. Or maybe a buyer won your auction, but the transaction didn't go through. eBay takes pity on you and offers you the chance to pick yourself up, dust yourself off, and start all over again.

But is she a natural blonde?

Here's an example of an item that would have made the seller a bundle if she'd done a little more strategizing up front:

Platinum Mackie Barbie: Beautiful Platinum Bob Mackie Barbie. MIB (removed from box once only to scan.) The doll comes with shoes, stand, booklet, and Mackie drawing. The original plastic protects her hair and earrings. Buyer adds $10 for shipping and insurance. Payment must be made within 10 days of auction by MO or cashier's check only. The starting price was $9.99, and even though the bidding went to $256, the seller's reserve price was not met, and the item didn't sell.

When relisting this item, the seller should lower the reserve price and add more description about the importance of the doll. (Unless, of course, $256 was far below what she wanted to make on the doll.)

The best way to improve your chances of selling a relisted item is by making changes to the auction. eBay says the majority of all the items put up for auction sell. If you sell your item the second time around, eBay rewards you with a refund of your Insertion Fee. You receive your refund after at least one billing cycle. Accept this refund as a reward for learning the ropes.

To be eligible for a refund of your Insertion Fee, here's the scoop:

✔ You must relist no more than 30 days after closing the original auction.

✔ You can get credit only if you got no bids in your original auction or if the bids you got did not equal the reserve in your reserve-price auction.

✔ You can change anything about your auction item description, price, duration, and minimum price, but you can't sell a different item.

✔ If you set a reserve price in your original auction, you must set the same reserve, lower it, or cancel the reserve altogether. If you set a higher reserve, you are not eligible for a relisting credit.

eBay's generosity has exceptions. They don't offer refunds for any listing options you paid for, such as **bold lettering** or use of the Featured in Category. Also, Dutch auctions aren't covered by this offer. And if you have a deadbeat on your hands, you can relist, but you don't get a return of your Insertion Fee. More bad news: If you don't sell the second time around, you're stuck paying *two* Insertion Fees. So give it your best shot!

To get your second shot at selling from the Items I'm Selling section of your My eBay page:

1. **Click on the auction item listing that you want to relist.**

   You're taken to the main auction page of the item.

2. **Click on the link that tells you that you can relist Now That the Auction has ended.**

   You see a brand new auction page to fill out, following the same directions offered in this chapter (so you're already good at it).

Here's a list of ideas if you want to improve your auction's odds for success:

✔ **Change the item category.** See if the item has sold better in another category. See Chapter 3.

✔ **Add a picture.** If two identical items are up for auction at the same time, the item with a photo gets more and higher bids. Zoom in on Chapter 12.

✔ **Jazz up the title and description.** Make it enticing, and grab those search engines. Breeze on over to Chapter 9.

✔ **Set a lower minimum bid.** The first bidders will think they're getting a bargain, and others will want a hot item. Mosey on over to Chapter 9.

No dancing around eBay penalties

eBay takes the issue of money (and who doesn't?) very seriously. If you use eBay's selling services and you're slow in paying — or don't pay at all — you have to face the music. You can't tap dance around what you owe. eBay bills you the first day of the month, and you have until the last day of the month to pay up. If not, here are eBay's penalties:

✔ A $15 service charge for bouncing a check

✔ 1.5 percent finance charge for late payments

✔ Suspension for very late payment

✔ $5 reactivation fee

✔ **Set a lower reserve price or cancel the reserve.** A reserve price often scares away bidders who fear it's too high. See (yup) Chapter 9.

✔ **Change the duration of the auction.** Maybe you need some more time. Go to (you guessed it) Chapter 9.

Long-time eBay veterans say that reducing or canceling your reserve price makes your auction very attractive to buyers.

Being as specific as possible with your item title improves your odds of being profitable. If you're selling an old Monopoly game, don't just title it **board game,** call it **1959 Monopoly Game Complete.**

Show me the money: Refunds

Rarely, but some folks rack up enough credits to want a refund. eBay will refund the amount in your account for anything over a buck. To get to the refund form that you have to fax to eBay, click on Services on the main navigation bar, click on Buying and Selling on the subnavigation bar, and then click on Cash out your credit balance. Fill out the form and send it in.

Chapter 12

Using Pictures and Strategies to Increase Your Profits

• •

In This Chapter:

▶ Attaching pictures to your auction

▶ Playing the links (golf cleats optional)

▶ Finding out all About Me

▶ Spotting trends and sharpening your marketing savvy

▶ Acquiring inventory to sell for bigger money

• •

*Y*ou may be enjoying most of what eBay has to offer, and you're probably having some good buying adventures. If you're selling, you're experiencing the excitement of making money. But there's more. Welcome to eBay, the advanced class.

In this chapter we take you to the head of the class by sharing some insider tips on how to jazz up the selling power of your auctions with images and spiffy text. Successful eBay vendors know that pictures (also called images) really help sell items. We show you everything you need to know in order to create images and give you advice on linking them to your auctions so buyers around the world can take a gander at them. Look no further if you want to know more about spotting trends and acquiring products to sell on eBay.

Using Images in Your Auctions

Would you buy an item you couldn't see? Most people wouldn't, especially if they're interested in purchasing collectible items that they want to display. Without a picture, you can't tell whether a seller's idea of "good quality" is anything like yours.

Welcome to the cyberworld of *imaging,* where pictures aren't called pictures, but *images.* ("Excuse me, could you pass the Grey Poupon while I examine my images?") Mass-market digital technology — including cameras and scanners is hardly a decade old but has revolutionized the way we capture, process, and view images. With a digital camera or a scanner, you can manipulate your images — crop, color-correct, and add special effects — so they grab viewers by the lapels. Even cooler: When you're happy with your creation, you can add it to your eBay auction.

Sellers, take heed, and read these other reasons why you should use well-made digital images in your auction pages:

- ✔ If you don't have a picture, potential bidders may wonder whether you're deliberately hiding the item from view because you know something's wrong with it. (Paranoid? Maybe. Practical? You bet.)

- ✔ Fickle bidders don't even bother reading an item description if they can't see the item. (Maybe they were traumatized in English class.)

- ✔ Everyone's doing it. We hate to put the additional burden of peer pressure on you, but digital images are the norm on eBay, so if you're not using them, you're not reaching the widest possible number of people who would bid on your item if only they could see it. From that point of view, you're not doing the most you can to serve your potential customers' needs. (Hey, fads are _driven_ by conformity. Might as well use them to your advantage.)

So which is better for capturing images — digital cameras or digital scanners? As for all gadgets, here's the classic answer: It depends. For our money, beating a digital camera is hard to do. But before you go snag one, decide what kind of investment (and how big) you plan to make in your eBay auctions. If you're already comfortable with 35mm camera equipment, don't scrap it — scan! The scoop on both these alternatives is coming right up.

 Whether you buy new or used digital equipment on eBay, make sure it comes with a warranty. If you _don't_ get a warranty, Murphy's Law practically ensures that your digital equipment will break the second time you use it.

Choosing a digital camera

If price isn't a factor, buy the highest-quality digital camera you can afford, especially if you plan to use images with a lot of your eBay auctions, and the items you plan to sell vary in size and shape.

Both Olympus and Epson make good basic cameras, starting at around $500 (we told you they can be pricey). Middle-of-the-road digital cameras sell for between $150 and $250. Compare prices at computer stores and in catalogs.

Another great place to buy digital cameras is (surprise!) eBay. Just do a search of some popular manufacturers like Olympus, Fujifilm, Sony, and Nikon, and you will find pages of listings — both new and used digital cameras — that you can bid on and (if you win) buy.

Look for the following features:

- **Resolution:** Look for a camera that has a resolution of at least 640 x 480 *pixels.* A pixel is a tiny dot of information that when grouped together with other pixels forms an image. The more pixels an image has, the clearer and sharper the image is — the more memory the image scarfs up, the slower it shows up on-screen. A 640 x 480-pixel resolution may seem paltry next to the 1.5-million-pixel punch of a high-end digital camera, but trust us: No one bidding on your auctions will nit-pick over the difference.

- **Storage type:** The instructions with your camera explain how to transfer images to your computer. (No instructions? Write the manufacturer.)

- **Extra features:** Make sure the camera is capable of taking close-up images; you need to be close to an item you photograph for an auction — from 3 inches to a foot away. A flash also comes in handy.

  If you plan to sell small or detailed items that require extreme close-ups (such as stamps, currency, coins, or Tibetan beads), look for a digital camera that lets you change lenses. Many newer, higher-end digital cameras have optional lenses for special uses, just as traditional photographers have for 35mm cameras. They cost more, but if you need extreme close-ups to sell your items, this is the way to go.

Choosing a digital scanner

Like digital cameras, digital scanners create images electronically with pixels. Your computer stores and reads these pixels (with software supplied with the scanner) and turns them into an image that you can e-mail, print out, or send to your eBay auction.

If you plan to sell flat items like autographs, stamps, books, or documents — or if you need a good piece of business equipment that can double as a photocopier — then consider getting a digital scanner. You can pick one up, brand new, for a little over $100; you can also find them on eBay.

Here's what you need to look for when you buy a scanner:

- **Resolution:** As with printers and photocopiers, the resolution of digital scanning equipment is measured in *dpi* (dots per inch). The more dpi, the greater the resolution.

  Some scanners on the market today can provide resolutions as high as 12,800 dpi, which looks awesome when you print the image — but to dress up your eBay auctions, all you need is (are you ready?) *72 dpi!* That's it. Your images will look great and won't take up a lot of storage space on your computer's hard drive. Basic scanners can scan images up to 1,200 dpi, so even they are more powerful than you need for your eBay images.

✔ **Flatbed:** If you're planning to use your scanner to scan picture of documents (or even items in boxes), a flatbed scanner is your best bet. Just lay your item or box on the glass (it's like a copier) and scan away.

✔ **Software and extras:** In addition to free photo-editing software, scanner manufacturers often include some great utilities. For instance, your scanner may come with copier software so that you can make photo copies. You can also get many scanners to act like word processors, fax machines, or copiers with just the touch of a button.

If you're using a scanner and need to create an image of an oversize item (say, that '59 Caddy limo with the huge fins) — or your flat item's just not practical to scan, even in sections (that original *Star Wars* marquee poster, for example), your film camera comes in handy. Use it to take a few good photos, get them processed on glossy paper, and then scan the best one. The end result is often as good as if the image came from a digital camera.

If you've got the money, we like digital cameras over scanners because you can instantly see the photo and redo it immediately if you don't like the way it looks. With a film camera, you won't know how the item looks until you pay for the prints and get them back. (Of course, if you're a pretty reasonable photographer, then scanning your photos and posting them on eBay gets the job done.)

Making Your Picture a Thing of Beauty

The idea of using images in your auctions is to attract a whole lot of potential buyers. With that goal in mind, create the best-looking image possible, no matter what kind of technology you're using to capture it.

Don't forget your camcorder!

The majority of eBay users use either a digital camera or scanner to dress up their auctions with images, but some just use what they already own — their handy-dandy camcorders! Yup, after videotaping your day at the beach, point your lens at that Victorian doll and shoot. With the help of a video-capturing device, you can create a digital image right from the camera.

Though several companies offer video-capturing devices, we're most impressed with the Snappy, made by Play Incorporated. It sells for around $100 and includes everything you need to transfer and save pictures from your camcorder (or VCR) to your computer. Go to the Snappy Web site at www.play.com for more details about how it works.

Even if you're not an expert photographer, don't be deterred if your snapshots of family reunions sometimes lop off miscellaneous limbs. These days, plenty of terrific software programs can help make your images of auctionables look great.

Still, don't forget the old computer acronym GIGO — *garbage in, garbage out.* Even the best software program can't do much if the source image of your item looks overexposed and blurry. Help is on the way, next.

Get it on camera!

Point-and-shoot may be okay for a group shot at the historical monument, but illustrating your auction is a whole different idea. Whether you're using a traditional film camera (so you can scan your developed photographs later) or a digital camera to capture your item, some basic photographic guidelines can give you better results.

For more on using 35mm cameras and scanners, zoom ahead in this chapter to "Use traditional photos? Yes, I scan." Then c'mon back to these Do's and Don'ts to ensure that your digital image is a genuine enhancement to your auction:

- ✔ **Do** take the picture of your item outside, in daylight, whenever possible. That way the camera can catch all possible details and color.

- ✔ **Do** forget about fancy backgrounds; they distract viewers from your item. Put small items on a neutral-colored, nonreflective towel or cloth; put larger items in front of a neutral-colored wall or curtain. You'll be cutting out almost all of the background later on, when you prepare the picture in your computer. (We explain how to do this later in this chapter.)

- ✔ **Do** use a flash, even when you're taking the picture outside. The flash acts as a *fill* — it adds more light to the item, filling in some of the shadowed spots.

- ✔ **Don't** get so close to the item that the flash washes out (overexposes) the entire image. The clearest way to figure out the best distance is by trial and error. Start close and keep moving farther away until you get the results you want. This method can get pricey if you're using film, but here's where digital cameras really shine: You can see the picture seconds after you shoot it, keep it and modify it, erase it, and start again.

- ✔ **Do** take two or three acceptable versions of your image; you can pick the best one later in your computer.

- ✒ If your item relies on detail (for example, an engraved signature or detailed gold trim), **do** take a wide shot of the entire item, and then take a close-up or two of detailed areas you want buyers to see.

- ✒ **Do** make sure you focus the camera; nothing's worse than a blurry picture. If your camera is a fixed-focus model (it can't be adjusted), get only as close as the manufacturer recommends. If you go beyond that distance, the item appears out of focus. Automatic-focus cameras measure the distance and change the lens setting as needed.

Some eBay creeps, whether out of laziness or deceit, steal images from other eBay members. (They simply make a digital copy of the image and use it in their own auctions — uncool because the copied image doesn't really represent their actual item.) This pilfering has happened to us on several occasions. To prevent picture-snatching, we add our User IDs to all of our photos. We just print out our names on a piece of paper and put it next to the item we're photographing so it shows up in the image. The next time somebody lifts one of our pictures, it has our name on it.

Use traditional photos? Yes, I scan

If you're using a scanner and 35mm camera to create images for your eBay auction, you've come to the right place in the chapter. (Also check out the tips in "Get it on camera!") Here goes:

- ✒ If you are scanning already-processed photographs of your items (taken with a 35mm camera, for example), make sure they're printed on glossy paper; it scans best.

- ✒ Avoid using incandescent or fluorescent lighting to light up the photos you plan to scan. Incandescent lighting tends to make your item look yellowish, and fluorescent lends a bluish tone to your photo.

- ✒ When you take traditional photos for scanning, get as close to your item as your camera will allow. Enlarging photos in the scanner will only result in blurry (or, worse, jagged) images.

- ✒ Scan the box the item came in.

- ✒ If you're scanning a three-dimensional item (such as a doll, jewelry, or a box) and you can't close the scanner lid, put a black or white tee-shirt over the item so you will get a clean background and good light reflection from the scanner.

- ✒ If you want to scan an item that's too big to put on your scanner all at once, scan the item in sections and assemble the digital pieces with your image-editing software. The instructions that come with your software should explain how to do this.

Software that adds the artist's touch

After you've taken the picture (or scanned it) and transferred it into your computer according to the manufacturer's instructions, the next step is to edit the picture. Much like a book or magazine editor, you get to cut, fix, resize and reshape your picture until you think it's good enough to be seen by the public. If you're a non-techie type, don't get nervous. Many of the programs have one-button magical corrections that make your pictures look great.

The software program that comes with your digital camera or scanner puts at your disposal an arsenal of editing tools that help you turn a basic image of your item into something special. Although each program has its own collection of features, a few basic tools and techniques are common to all:

- **Image Quality:** Enables you to enhance or correct colors, sharpen images, remove dust spots, and increase or reduce brightness or contrast.

- **Size:** Reduce or increase the size or shape of the image.

- **Orientation:** Rotate the image left or right; flip it horizontally or vertically.

- **Create an Image Format:** When the image is edited you can save it as a specific format, such as .JPG, .GIF, or others. The format most preferred on eBay (and the one we strongly recommend) is .JPG (pronounced *JAY-peg*).

Every image-editing software program has its own system requirements and capabilities. Read the instructions that came with your camera or scanner. If you feel the program is too complicated (or doesn't give you the editing tools you need), investigate some of the other popular programs. Here's a quick list of programs we use and recommend, along with their Web addresses so you can get more information online:

- **Adobe PhotoDeluxe Home Edition** is a popular program included with many digital cameras (or you can purchase it separately). It lets you do quite a range of special photo effects. More importantly, however, it allows you to make your photos Internet-ready, reducing the dpi through the "send to Web page" function. You can get updates or a free trial version at this site:

  ```
  www.adobe.com
  ```

- **Microsoft Picture It!** comes with some new computers and is available separately for purchase. Picture It! 99 has a full kit of features, allowing you to fix contrast, sharpen, and make your photos Web-ready — automatically. More information is available at

  ```
  www.microsoft.com/pictureit/default.htm
  ```

✔ **Lview** is a free, easy-to-use graphics program that allows you to do basic image editing and even includes some special effects. Find free copies of Lview at the following Web sites:

```
www.orenews.com/download/software/LView
www.udel.edu/ps/sw/lview.htm
```

Making your Images Web-friendly

Because digital images are made up of pixels, and every pixel has a set of instructions that have to be stored someplace, you've got two difficulties facing you right after you take the picture:

✔ Because they contain more computer instructions, bigger pictures take up more memory.

✔ Those big honkers take longer to *build* (to appear) on the buyer's screen — and time can be precious in an auction. To get around both these problems, think small.

Here's a checklist of tried-and-true techniques we've come up with for preparing your elegantly slender, fast-loading images to display on eBay:

✔ Whether you've scanned your item or taken a picture of it with a digital camera, set your image resolution at 72 dots per inch. You can do this with the software that comes with your camera or scanner. Although 72 dpi may seem a low resolution, it nibbles computer memory (instead of chomping), shows up fast on a buyer's screen, and looks great on eBay.

✔ When you're sizing your picture, make it no larger than 4 inches square, even if it's a snapshot of a classic 4 x 4 monster truck. These dimensions are big enough for people to see without squinting, and the details of your item show up nicely.

✔ Crop out any unnecessary areas of the photo. You just need to show your item; everything else is a waste.

✔ Use your software, darken, or change the contrast of the photo. When the image looks good on your computer screen, the image looks good on your eBay auction page.

✔ When you're done editing your picture, save it as a JPG image. Follow the instructions that come with your software on how to do this. JPG is the best format for eBay; it compresses information into a small file that builds fast and reproduces nicely on the Internet.

✔ After you save the image, check its total size. If the size is hovering around 40KB (kilobytes) or smaller, eBay users won't have a hard time seeing the image in a reasonable amount of time.

✔ If your image is larger than 40KB, go back into the image and reduce its size. Small is fast, efficient, and beautiful. Big is slow, sluggish, and dangerous. Impatient eBay users will move on to the next listing if they don't want to wait to see your image.

The Image Is Perfect — What Now?

Now that your masterpiece is done, you want to emblazon it on your auction for all the world to see, right? Whoa, Rembrandt. You still need to make a couple of final preparations. Yes, this arty stuff _is_ a lot of work, but we assure you the results are well worth it. (Buyers generally pick an auction _with a picture_ over a comparable auction item without one.)

When most people first get the urge to dazzle prospective buyers with a picture, they poke around the eBay site looking for a place to put it. Trade secret: You're not actually putting pictures on eBay at all; you're telling eBay where to _find_ your picture so that, like a good hunting dog, your auction _points_ the buyers' browsers to the exact corner of the virtual universe where your picture is. That's why the picture has to load fast — it's coming in from a different location. (Yeah, it confused us in the beginning too, but now it makes perfect sense. Uh-huh. Sure.)

You've heard this refrain before: _Pictures take up a lot of computer memory._ If eBay had to process and store two million pictures every week, you'd see a steady stream of smoke rising out of Silicon Valley as all the huge mainframe computers overheated and screeched to a grinding, silicon-melting halt. Hey, if it happens, it won't be because of _our_ pictures!

To help eBay find your image, all you have to do is type its address into the Picture URL box (shown in Figure 12-1) of the Sell Your Item form, so don't forget to write down the Web address (URL) of your image.

Snap it up — not!

Kodak Book: _New Joy of Photography,_ a classic guide to the tools and techniques of better photography. Published by the editors of Eastman Kodak Co., copyrighted in 1985 and containing 302 colorful pages of beautiful photographs. This is the completely updated and revised edition. In softback and in excellent condition. Buyer pays $3.20 shipping. This book's starting bid was $5, but it did not sell.

(Of course, maybe in another 20 years it'll be "antique" . . .)

You can highlight your image's URL with your cursor, right-click your mouse, and copy it to your computer's clipboard. Then, go to the auction page you're filling out on eBay, put your cursor in the Picture URL window, and paste the address into the box.

A typical address (from somebody using AOL) looks like this:

```
members.aol.com/~ebay4dummy/images/rolexwatch.jpg
```

If your image needs an address, that means you have to find it a good home online. You have several options:

- ✔ Your ISP (Internet Service Provider). All the big ISPs — such as AOL, Netcom, and Earthlink — give you space to store your Internet stuff. You're already paying for an ISP, so you can park pictures here at no extra charge.

- ✔ An image-hosting Web site. Web sites that specialize in hosting pictures are popping up all over the Internet. Some charge a small fee; others are free. The upside here is that they're very easy to use.

- ✔ If you have your own server (those of you who do know who you are), you can store those images right in your own home.

Figure 12-1:
To add an image of your item to your eBay auction, type in the image's URL or Web address here.

Picture URL optional	http:// [ ]
	It's easy! Learn the basics in the tutorial, and enter your URL here.

Using an ISP to store your images

Every ISP has its own set of rules and procedures. Go to the help area of your specific ISP for directions on how to *access your personal area* and how to *upload your images*. (And those are authentic computerese phrases!)

Once your images are uploaded to your ISP, get the Web address of your item's location and type it into the Picture URL box of eBay's Sell Your Item page. Now whenever someone views your auction page, the picture appears under the item description. Figure 12-2 shows you an auction page with a picture.

Figure 12-2:
Including
pictures
in your
auction
takes
practice, but
the results
are well
worth it.

NEW - LIMITED
Exclusive Harley Davidson
Bean Bag collectible!

This Harley exclusive sold out immediately in our area! Rocky is dressed in a black faux leather vest and slacks. The vest features the classic orange & white Harley Davidson emblem and "Harley Davidson USA" on the back. The slacks have "Harley" on one leg and "Davidson" on the other. His tail is black & white striped. The attached authentic Harley Davidson tag is in mint condition.

Bid with confidence and bid whatever you feel this great Harley collectible is worth to you as it is selling with NO RESERVE! *(Feel free to check my feedback!)* Winning bidder to pay shipping & handling of $4.55 (includes Post Office tracking number), and must submit payment within a week of winning the auction.
GOOD LUCK, HAPPY BIDDING!

Click below to...
View my other auctions

Here's a step-by-step guide on how to use your personal patch of online real estate, called My Place (available on America Online, version 4.0), to store your auction pictures.

Start at AOL's opening Home page, and then follow these steps:

1. **Using the main navigation bar, choose Internet⇨Go to FTP.**

   You're taken to AOL's My Place Main page.

2. **Select FTPspace, then click Members, and then click Go to FTP.**

   A window appears, listing FTP Favorite Sites. (FTP stands for *File Transfer Protocal,* which, translated into English, means that this is how one computer transfers files to another computer over the Internet.)

3. **Select Members.aol.com, and then click on Connect.**

   An informational screen appears that tells you how much disk space you're allowed to use with your files.

4. **Click on OK.**

   You're connected to your Members.aol.com page, which lists the folders you can create to hold your images. By default, AOL has a README folder that contains *Frequently Asked Questions* (FAQs) about My Place. There's also a folder labeled Private.

You also see the seven buttons you can use:

- **Open** opens the files you've saved in My FTPspace.

- **Download Now** downloads files from My FTPspace.

- **Utilities** offers links to more options for deleting or renaming your files.

- **Upload** transfers files from your computer to your My FTPSpace.

- **Create Directory** creates and personalizes files in My FTPspace.

- **Help** answers all your questions about My FTPspace.

- **More** allows you to view all your files.

5. **Click on the Upload Now button to put images you want to include in your eBay auctions in your My Place file.**

   A dialog box pops up, asking you to type in a remote filename.

   The *remote filename* is the exact name you gave your image when you saved it to your computer's hard drive.

6. **Type the remote filename and make sure that you've selected the circle next to Binary (programs and graphics). Then click on the Continue button.**

   Unless you're uploading a text file, you should always choose the Binary option.

   Don't forget to add the image file's three-letter extension. A filename for a JPG image of a Rolex, for example, would be **rolexwatch.jpg**.

   An Upload File box appears on your screen offering two options, Send and Select File.

7. **Click on the Select File button.**

   Another dialog box appears, containing a list of files from your computer's hard drive.

8. **Locate the file you want to upload, highlight it by clicking on it once, and then click on the Open button.**

   The Upload File dialog box appears again, displaying the file's new Internet address in the File field.

9. **Click on the Send button.**

   AOL begins receiving the image file. When the file is completely uploaded from your computer, you hear the famous AOL voice cheerily announce, "File's done!" (Ever get the urge to reply? Politely, of course.)

   When you upload your image with AOL, your image's address looks like this:

   members.aol.com/*username*/filename.jpg

Click on the My FTP Place button to see a new listing of your files, including the one you just uploaded.

Don't create filenames (on AOL or any other ISP) with the following symbols: ? @ # $*&! / ~ , % or spaces. These interfere with your uploads, and your file can't successfully transfer to the ISP. (Even if you *could* use them, you wouldn't want total strangers to think you were cussing . . .)

Using image-hosting Web sites to store images

Okay, realistically, a *lot* of people are combing cyberspace looking for the next great thing. eBay's success has entrepreneurs all over the globe coming up with different kinds of auction-support businesses. As usual, a lot of junk pops up on the Internet in the wake of such trends — but one promising development caught our attention recently — *image-hosting* Web sites. Instead of uploading images to AOL or any other ISP, you contact one of these Web sites and they handle your image for free (or for a small charge).

We tested two image-hosting Web sites and were pleased enough with the results to recommend them as an alternative to using your own ISP:

✔ **pBay** (www.pbay.com)

Despite the similar name, pBay is not affiliated in any way with eBay.

✔ **AuctionWatch.com** (www.AuctionWatch.com)

pBay.com, the unrelated twin of eBay

pBay was launched in April 1999 by PictureWorks Technology (makers of imaging software for digital cameras and scanners — *somebody* there sure thunk). The site features an easy-to-use, three-step procedure for sending images. You can upload images in about five minutes, and you immediately get back the Web address (URL) for your image (which is highly useful if you actually expect eBay to *find* your pictures). pBay also parks your images for free — and even with the burgeoning popularity of digital images on the Internet, PictureWorks promises to keep the basic service free.

If you have a Macintosh computer, you must have Netscape (version 4.08 or higher) or Internet Explorer (4.0 or higher) to register on pBay. If you're using Windows 95, 98, or NT4.0 on your PC, you should have version 3.*x* (or higher) of either browser.

pBay keeps an image online for 30 days. After that, the image goes bye-bye, but you can always repost the image if you need it again.

Free parking with AuctionWatch

We like AuctionWatch (www.AuctionWatch.com) as a place to park your eBay images for two reasons: (1) It's free, and (2) You can actually start your eBay auctions right from the AuctionWatch Web site. AuctionWatch will even let you know whether your image's size is Web-friendly. All you need do is have your image files ready on your computer, register on AuctionWatch, upload your pictures, and start your eBay auction.

Putting on the hits

So you have your great-looking auction running on eBay, and you're just dying to know how many people are stopping by to take a look? There's an easy way to monitor the number of *hits* — times visitors stop in to look at the goods — if you use a free *public counter* program from an online source. A counter's a useful marketing tool; you can check (for example) the number of times people have looked at — but not bid on — your auctions. If you have lots more lookie-loos than bids, you may have a problem with your auction.

If your counter indicates you're not getting many hits, consider the following potential problems so that you can resurrect your auction:

✔ Does the picture take too long to load?

✔ Is the opening bid too high?

✔ Are those neon orange and lime-green bell-bottoms just too funky to sell?

One of the most popular counters found on eBay comes from a Web site run by Honesty Communications. You can pick the Honesty counter up free and add it to your auction in just a few easy steps. But before you can get a public counter from Honesty Communications, you need to register — just go to www.honesty.com. Honesty takes it from there. Honestly.

The AuctionWatch site also offers a service that counts how many times eBay members view your auction. The service has an "intelligent" counter that counts hits but knows whether somebody's continually reloading your auction page, and doesn't count the extras as hits. AuctionWatch can provide counters to appear on your auction or keep this information on its Web site.

Working with HTML, your hyper friend

People speak a wide variety of languages in the world, but on the World Wide Web only one language is spoken (written, actually) — *HyperText Markup Language* (*HTML* for short). Every Web site you see on the Internet is created using HTML; programmers build in links, buttons, and other handy features so you can get around the site easily. The good news: All you have to know is how to use links; you don't have to sling HTML like a pro before you can navigate the Web.

If you're interested in learning more about how HTML works, and how to create Web pages using it, we suggest picking up a copy of *HTML 4.0 For Dummies,* 2nd Edition, by Ed Tittel and Natanya Pitts (from our own friendly publisher, IDG Books Worldwide — sheer coincidence, of course).

Chances are that if you already have a Web page (and who doesn't these days?) you already know a little bit about HTML. Remember, you can link your Web site to your eBay auctions and add links to your Web sites from your auction page. See "Playing the links fore fun and profit," waiting on the next green.

The second you or any other eBay user connects to a link that isn't owned or maintained by eBay, you're not protected by the eBay rules and regulations anymore. eBay cancels any auctions that contain links to Web sites that offer to undersell an auction by touting the same item at a cheaper price — or offer to sell items forbidden on eBay.

Playing the links fore fun and profit

By linking your eBay auctions to your personal or business Web page, you can increase the number of people who see everything you're selling. To link your auctions to your Web page, start at the navigation bar found at the top of most eBay pages:

1. **Click on the Services link.**

   You're taken to the Services Overview page.

2. **Click on the Buying and Selling link on the subnavigation bar.**

   You're taken to the Buying and Selling tools page.

3. **Scroll down the page and click on the Promote your listings with link buttons link.**

   You can choose to link your item to the eBay Home page — but why would you? Everyone visiting your auction already knows how to get there! — or create a customized link that goes directly to a list of items you have for sale.

4. **Be bold; select the box that allows you to create a customized link.**

5. **First type your User ID and password into the information windows, and then type in the URL of the Web site to which you want to link your auction.**

6. **Read eBay's link agreement and then click on the I Agree button. (It's so much more civilized that way.)**

   Read the Instructions for Installing Buttons on your site page.

   eBay generates a piece of HTML code and displays it on your screen.

7. **Copy the handy HTML code that eBay has generated for you; use your computer's clipboard to paste it into your Web site or text editor.**

   An eBay icon link appears on your personal or business Web page. Anyone who clicks on this link will be plucked from the Web page and automatically transported to your auctions.

To add a link to your item description that takes eBay users to your Web site, type the following code at the end of your item description when you set it up:

```
Click below...<br>
<A HREF=http://www.bogusISP.com/~yourUserID/sale.htm>
Visit my web site</A>
```

Check your ISP to get the actual URL for your Web site.

It's All About Me

Want to know more about the people behind those User IDs? Thousands of eBay members have created their own personal Web pages on eBay, called About Me pages. About Me pages are easy to create and are as unique as each eBay member. The way to spot eBay users with an active About Me page is to look for a special icon next to a User ID.

Copying someone else's auction text or images without permission can constitute copyright infringement, which ends your auction and gets you suspended from eBay.

Taking the time to create your own About Me page can improve your sales because when people come across your auctions and check out your About Me page, they can get a sense of who you are and how serious you are about your eBay activities. They instantly see that you're no fly-by-night seller.

Before you create your own About Me page, we suggest that you take a look at what others have done. eBay members often include pictures, links to other Web sites (including their personal Home pages) as well as links to just about any Web location that reflects their personality, which is why they're so entertaining. If your purpose is to generate more business, we recommend that you keep the focus on your auction listings.

Although you can look at other Web sites for ideas, you should not copy someone else's auction text or images without their permission. Borrowing other images and texts could constitute copyright infringement and get your auction ended and get you suspended by eBay.

Sellers with many auctions running at once often add a message to their About Me pages that indicates that they're willing to reduce shipping charges if bidders also bid on their other auctions. Subtlety, schmuddlety. This direct tactic may lack nuance, but it also increases the number of people who look at (and bid on) your auctions.

Here's how to create your own About Me page:

1. **First click on the Services link on the main navigation bar, then click on the About Me link on the submenu.**

   You're taken to the About Me page.

2. **Type in your User ID and your password.**

3. **Click on the Create and edit your page button.**

   You're taken to the About Me layout page, where you're offered three layout options, which eBay is kind enough to show you on the About Me page:

   - a two-column layout
   - a newspaper layout
   - a centered layout

4. **Click on the button corresponding to the layout option you choose.**

   You're taken to a second About Me creation page.

5. **Enter the following information:**

   Page Title: Type in what you want to call your About Me page, (for example, **Larry Lunch**).

   Welcome Message: Type in a personal attention-grabbing headline, such as **Welcome to Larry Lunch's Lunchbox Place.**

   Text: Type in a short paragraph greeting your visitors (like, **Hey, I like lunchboxes a lot**, only more exciting).

   Another Paragraph: Type in another headline for the second paragraph of the page, such as **Vintage, Modern, and Ancient, I Collect All Kinds of Lunchboxes.**

   Text: Type in another paragraph about yourself or your collection (such as, **I used to stare at lunchboxes in the school cafeteria . . .** only more, you know, *normal*).

HTML-lite: Awesome auctions without the messy code

There's a bevy of third-party software programs that do all sorts of interesting eBay-related tasks like record-keeping, accounting, image-editing, and special-effects, and we list some of them in Chapter 19. So far, we haven't found one that can make a decent cup of coffee. (Yet. We're still looking.)

Picture: If you're adding a picture, type in a sentence describing it, for example: **This is my wife Loretta with our lunchbox collection.**

URL: Type in the Web site address (URL) where people can find your picture. See the section earlier in this chapter that shows you how to upload digital images.

Feedback: Select how many of your Feedback postings you want to appear on your About Me page. (You *can* opt not to show any feedback, but we think you should put in a few, especially if they're complimentary, as in, "Larry sent my lunchbox promptly, and it makes lunchtime a blast! Everybody stares at it . . .")

Items for Sale: Select how many of your current auctions you want to appear on your About Me page. If you don't have any auctions running at the moment, you can select the Show no items option.

Caption: Type in a caption to introduce your auctions, for example: **Lunchboxes I'm Currently Selling.**

Favorite Links: Type in the names and URLs of any Web links you want visitors to see, for example, a Web site that appraises lunchboxes ("it'd be in Excellent condition except for that petrified ham sandwich . . .").

Favorite eBay Items: Type in the item numbers and select a comment from the options displayed to point out eBay auction items you think visitors should check out.

6. **Click on the Preview your page button, or, if you don't like your current layout, click on the Choose new layout button to go back to Step 1.**

   You're now looking at your final About Me page.

7. **Scroll down to the bottom of the page and you see a group of buttons:**

   Edit some more: Takes you back to Step 2.

   Save my page: Saves your About Me page so you're one step closer to publishing it on eBay.

Edit using HTML: If you know HTML code, you can customize your About Me page.

Start over: Takes you to a link page where you can delete what you've created and begin again.

8. **When you're happy with your masterpiece, click on the Save my page button.**

Yup, you did it — anybody in the world with access to the Internet can now find your personal About Me page on eBay.

Figure 12-3 shows you three About Me page layouts.

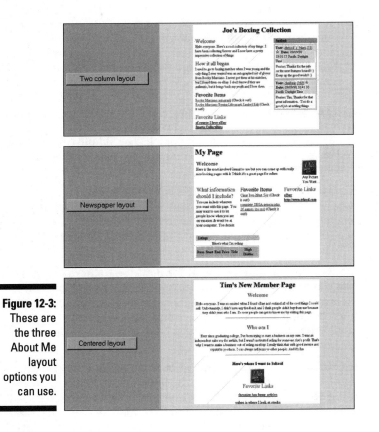

Figure 12-3: These are the three About Me layout options you can use.

Don't forget to update your About Me page often. A good About Me page makes bidders eager to know more about your auctions. An out-of-date About Me page turns off potential bidders. If you choose to update, you need to edit using HTML. If you don't use HTML, you have to re-create a whole new page.

Finding More Stuff to Sell

Once you pick clean everything not nailed down in your house, you may want to broaden your horizons. The key to being successful at selling is finding things people want to buy. (Wow, what an incredible observation.) We know it seems obvious, but having stuff to *sell* isn't always the same as having things people *want to buy*. Using this concept, you can teach yourself all kinds of effective marketing strategies. Knowing what people want — finding the item that may be "the next big thing" — takes lots of work, timing, and sometimes a dose of good luck.

Just as successful stockbrokers know about specific companies, they also need to know about the marketplace as a whole. If you want to sell big, don't stop with just knowing your merchandise. Sure, we know about the 300 Beanie Babies out there, and so does nearly everyone else. To get a leg up on your competition, you need to know the big picture as well. Here are some questions you should be asking yourself as you contemplate making serious scads of money (well, we can hope) by selling items on eBay:

✔ **What items are currently hot?** If you see everyone around you rushing to the store to buy a particular item, chances are good that the item will become more valuable as stocks of it diminish. The simple rule of supply and demand says that whoever has something everyone else wants stands to gain major profits.

✔ **Do I see a growing interest in a specific item that might make it a big seller?** If you're starting to hear talk about a particular item, or even an era ('70s nostalgia? Who knew?), listen carefully and think of what you already own (or can get your hands on) that can help you catch a piece of the trend's action.

✔ **Should I hold on to this item and wait for its value to increase, or should I sell now?** Knowing when to sell an item that you think people might want is a tricky business. Sometimes you may catch the trend too early and find out that you could have commanded a better price if you'd waited. Other times, you may catch a fad that's already passé and find that no one's interested anymore.

✔ **Is a company discontinuing an item I should stockpile now and sell later?** Could the manufacturer reissue the item later? Pay attention to items that are discontinued, especially toys and novelty items. If you find an item that a manufacturer has a limited supply of, you could make a tidy profit. If the manufacturer ends up reissuing the item, don't forget that the original run is still the most coveted — and valuable.

✔ **Was there a recall, an error, or a legal proceeding associated with my item?** If so, how will it affect the value of the item? For example, a toy recalled for safety reasons may no longer be appropriate for the kids, but it could be rare and collectible if intact. (Does that Cylon spaceship from *Battlestar Galactica* still have the pilot and the missiles that shoot? Cool. Just don't chew on them or put your eye out, okay?)

Some people like to go with their gut feelings about when and what to buy for resale on eBay. By all means, if instinct has worked for you in the past, factor instinct in here, too. If you've done some research that looks optimistic but your gut says, "I'm not sure," listen to it; don't assume you're just hearing that lunchtime taco talking. Try testing the waters by purchasing one of the prospective items for resale on eBay. If that sale doesn't work out, you won't have a lot invested, and you can credit your gut with saving you some bucks.

Catching Trends in the Media

Catching trends is all about listening and looking. You can find all kinds of inside information from newspapers, magazines, and on television, and of course, the Internet. Believe it or not, you can even find out what people are interested in these days by bribing a kid. Keep your eyes and ears open. When people say, "That Taco Bell Chihuahua is *everywhere* these days," instead of nodding your head vacantly, start getting ideas.

Not just any idea is workable. If you're tempted to deal in live creatures (like Chihuahuas — or the Dalmatians that were the rage after the updated Disney movie came out), don't. Live animals are off limits on eBay. Besides, posters and stuffed toys are a whole lot easier to ship.

In newspapers

Newspapers are bombarded by press releases and inside information from companies the world over. (Plus, they have great comics and crossword puzzles — some of which might refer to a trend that "everybody knows about.")

- ✔ Find out what's going on with retail companies and manufacturers in the business section, gauge your market, and start stockpiling!

- ✔ Scrutinize the entertainment section for more than just movie schedules — it can be a gold mine. If you're interested in selling celebrity-driven memorabilia (like the Dennis Rodman Wedding Dress doll, check for gossip on celebrities. If you see a movie's coming out and you have related memorabilia, now is the time to sell!

- ✔ Check the Lifestyles section of your newspaper to see if any old fads are making a resurgence. Check around your house and find things you wouldn't be caught dead in but you can sell as "retro chic."

Many newspapers (and magazines) also publish on the Internet. You probably don't see any reason to read newspapers online when you can have them delivered to your front door, but good online news sources provide links to the Web addresses of companies featured in their articles. You can jump to the company and read up on just about anything you want to know.

On television

No matter what you think of television, it has an enormous impact on which trends come and go and which ones stick. Why else would advertisers sink billions of dollars into TV commercials? And look at the impact of "Oprah's Book Club." Just one Oprah appearance for an author can turn a book into an overnight bestseller. Rosie O'Donnell also knows the power of her show. She's turning props and autographed items from guests into cash for charity (check out Chapter 16 for more on charity auctions).

Tune into morning news shows and afternoon talk shows. See what they're featuring. The producers of these shows are on top of pop culture and move fast to be the first to bring you the next big thing. Take what they feature and think up a marketing angle. If you don't, you can be sure somebody else will.

We call this the *Oprah* tip. If you get an idea for an item auction from something you see on an afternoon talk show, schedule your auction to end when viewers of the program are likely to log on to eBay — late afternoon, *after Oprah* goes off the air.

Catch up with "youth culture" . . .

. . . or at least keep good tabs on it. There is no catching up with it, just as there's no way to say this without sounding over-the-hill: If you remember cranking up the Beatles, James Brown, or the Partridge Family (say what?) till your parents screamed "Shut that awful noise off," then you may be at that awkward time of life when you hardly see the appeal of what young people are doing or listening to. But if you want tips for hot auction items, tolerate the awful noise and listen to the kids around you. Children, especially pre-teens and teens, may be the best trend-spotters on the planet. (Don't believe it? Ask a few Beanie Baby collectors how they got started.)

See what kind of marketing tips you get when you ask a kid:

- What's cool at the moment (or "rad" if you want to sound cool — whoops, that was '80s-speak, wasn't it)?

- What's totally uncool that was cool two months ago? (Their world moves at warp speed!)

- What music are you buying? (New Radicals, Barenaked Ladies, Sixpence None the Richer — yup, all hot bands with big hits — but maybe *ewww-that's-so-five-minutes-ago* by the time you read this.)

- What could I buy you at the moment that would make you really happy? (Hint: If the kid says, "a red BMW Z-3" or "liposuction," look for a younger kid.)

What a difference *Today* makes in sales

The *Today Show* ran a segment on a new version of a popular new children's book that included a CD produced by Steven Spielberg and chapters read by famous celebrities. An eBay veteran we know figures that whatever Spielberg touches turns to gold (or money), so she snapped up several copies of the book from an online vendor and sold them for a profit on eBay before anyone else thought of it.

Check out magazines

Magazines geared to the 18-to-34 age group (and sometimes to younger teens) can help you stay on top of what's hot. See what the big companies are pitching to this target audience (and whether they're succeeding). If a celebrity is suddenly visible in every other headline or magazine, keep a lookout for merchandise relating to that person. (Are we talking hysteria-plus-cash flow here, or just hysteria?) Here's a short list of youth-oriented magazines that can give you ideas for auctionable items:

- ✔ *YM*
- ✔ *Rolling Stone*
- ✔ *Teen People*
- ✔ *Vibe*
- ✔ *Vogue*
- ✔ *Seventeen*

You can also do some couch-potato research in front of television — take notes on MTV, VH-1, or (if you're really brave) Saturday morning cartoons.

The Hunt for eBay Inventory

If you're not sure what you want to sell for profit on eBay — but you're a shop-till-you-drop person by nature — then you've got an edge. Incorporate your advanced shopping techniques into your daily routine. If you find a bargain that interests you, chances are you have a knack for spotting stuff that other shoppers would love to get their hands on.

Collecting magazines

Though not quite a plethora, the number of magazines geared for collectors is definitely approaching a slew. While these won't help you catch a trend (by the time it gets into one of these, somebody's already caught it) they can give you great information on pricing, availability, and general collecting information. And you can follow the course of a trend for a real-life example of how it works.

Here's a list of collectors' magazines we like:

✔ White's Guide to Collecting Figures (www.whitesguide.com) has all the latest scoop on comics and sports collectibles, Beanie Babies, Barbie, Hallmark, die-cast

cars, and more. It boasts "The Hobby's Most Accurate Price Guide: 20,000+ items." That kind of says it all; we keep a copy next to our computer whenever we're eBay shopping.

✔ Collector's Mart, the leading magazine of advertising material in print. Check out their Web site at

www.worldcollectorsnet.com/
cmart

✔ Doll Magazine has info on everything doll-related. Go to www.dollmagazine.com.

The goods are out there

When you shop to sell on eBay, don't rule out any shopping venue. From the trendiest boutique to the smallest junk shop, garage sales to Bloomingdale's, keep your eye out for eBay inventory. The items people look for on eBay are out there; you just have to find them.

Keep these shopping locales in mind when you go on the eBay hunt:

✔ Upscale department stores, trendy boutiques, outlet stores, or flagship designer stores are good places to do some market research. Check out the newest items and then head to the clearance area and scrutinize the bargain racks.

✔ Do a tour of the discount stores in your area. Many of the items these places carry are *overruns* (too many of something that didn't sell), *small runs* (too little of something that the big guys weren't interested in stocking), or out-of-date fad items that need a good home on eBay. These places are hit-or-miss sources — they get all kinds of stuff in every day — and in fads (as in comedy), timing is everything.

✔ Garage sales, tag sales, and moving sales offer some of the biggest bargains you'll ever come across. The people running these sales are often motivated by one thought — *Everything must go!* — and aren't thinking about the value of what they have. Check for vintage kitchen pieces and old toys, and make 'em an offer they can't refuse.

✔ Go shopping online. eBay isn't the only place to snatch up Internet bargains. A growing number of discount Web sites advertise as wholesalers or liquidators (unlike eBay, they're not auctions; you pay a set price).

Online wholesalers or liquidators often sell in bulk, so if you're nervous about buying 450 swizzle sticks from the old Sands Hotel in Las Vegas, this may not be the best place for you to acquire your stock-in-trade.

✔ Thrift stores are great places to find inexpensive but well-made items. Feel good knowing that the money you spend in a nonprofit thrift shop is going to a good cause.

✔ Find going-out-of-business sales. You can pick up bargains if a shopkeeper just wants to empty the shelves so the store can close.

✔ Take advantage of any flea markets or swap meets in your area.

✔ Gift shops at museums, monuments, national parks, and theme parks can provide eBay inventory — but think about where to sell the items. Part of your selling success on eBay is *access*. People who can't get to Graceland may pay handsomely for an Elvis mini-guitar with the official logo on the box. Go, cat, go — and make profits too!

✔ Hang on to the freebies you get. If you receive handouts (lapel pins, pencils, pamphlets, books, interesting napkins, flashlights, towels, stuffed toys) from a sporting event, premiere, or historic event — or even a collectible freebie from a fast-food restaurant — they could be your ticket to some eBay sales.

Tips for the modest investor

If you're interested in making money in your eBay ventures but you're starting with limited cash, follow this list of eBay inventory Do's and Don'ts:

✔ **Don't** spend more than you can afford to lose. If you shop at boutiques and expensive department stores, buy things you like to wear yourself in case they don't sell.

✔ **Do** try to find something local that's unavailable in a wider area. For example, if you live in an out-of-the-way place that has a local specialty (like the cheddar cheese made in Grafton, Vermont), try selling that on eBay.

✔ **Don't** go overboard and buy something really cheap just because it's cheap. Figure out who would want the item first.

✔ **Do** stick to classic and traditional patterns, clothing, and furnishings. They're timeless and rarely go out of style. Laura Ashley and Ralph Lauren both became very successful selling traditional clothes and household items — take lessons from them.

✔ **Do** consider buying in quantity, especially if you know the item sells well on eBay or if the item is inexpensive. Chances are good that if you buy one and it sells well on eBay, by the time you try to buy more, the item's sold out. If an item is inexpensive (say 99¢), we always buy at least five of it. If no one bids on the item when you hold your auction, you're only out $5. (Anyone out there need any Bicentennial Commemorative coffee mugs?)

Part IV
Oy Vay, More eBay!: Special Features

The 5th Wave
By Rich Tennant

"What troubles me is that he spends all his time on eBay's Beanie Babies chat board."

In this part . . .

So you wanna protect yourself from bad apples, not just on eBay, but all over the Internet? We don't blame you. We want to keep safe as well, and that's why we wrote this part.

This is the place to come if you want to know just what eBay knows about you and is willing to share with other eBay users. We also introduce you to SafeHarbor, the next best thing to a super hero when it comes to protecting you from people who don't qualify for the "eBay User of the Year" Award.

eBay is a community, so we have to let you in on some of the ways you can commune with other collectors and get into the social scene. We also tell you about a lot of the special features that make eBay such a unique environment. Where else can you buy an item you really want and also help out a charity, all with the click of a mouse?

Chapter 13

Privacy: To Protect and Serve

● ●

In This Chapter

▶ Digging up what eBay knows about you

▶ Determining how safe your information is on eBay

▶ Finding out what eBay does with your info

▶ Protecting your privacy

● ●

*O*n the Internet, as in real life, you should never take your personal privacy for granted. Sure, you're ecstatic that you can shop and sell on eBay from the privacy of your own home, but remember: Just because your front door's locked doesn't mean your privacy's being protected. If you're new to the Internet, you may be surprised to find out what you're revealing about yourself to the world, no matter how many precautions you take. (Yes, we all know about that neon blue exfoliating mask you wear when you're bidding . . . just kidding . . . honest.)

In this chapter, we tell you how much eBay knows about you and who they're sharing your information with. We explain what you can do to protect your privacy and tell you some simple steps you can take to increase not only your privacy, but possibly your safety.

What (and How) eBay Knows about You

The irony of the Internet is that although you think you're sitting at home working anonymously, third parties such as advertisers and marketing companies are secretly getting to know you. (All together now: *Get-ting-to-know all a-bout youuu. . . .*)

While you're busy collecting World's Fair memorabilia and antique toasters, eBay is busy collecting nuggets of information about you. eBay gets some of this information from you, and some of it from your computer. All of the data eBay gets is stored in the eBay memory bank.

What you tell eBay

eBay gets much of what it knows about you *from* you. When you sign up, you voluntarily tell eBay important and personal information about yourself. Right off the bat, you give eBay these juicy tidbits:

- ✔ Name
- ✔ E-mail address
- ✔ Snail-mail address
- ✔ Phone number
- ✔ Password

"Okay, that's no big deal," you say, but if you're using your credit card to settle your eBay fees, you're also giving out personal financial information about yourself:

- ✔ Credit card number
- ✔ Expiration date
- ✔ Credit card billing address
- ✔ Credit card history

If you make a one-time payment with a personal check, you give eBay even more information about you. They instantly know your bank's name and your checking account number. The bottom line is that *every time* you pay by check, you're giving away personal info about yourself. eBay carefully locks up this information (in a hi-tech Alcatraz, of sorts), but other companies or individuals may not be as protective. Before you put the check in the mail, make sure you're comfortable with where it's going.

If you filled in the optional questions when you signed up, here's some other information eBay knows about you:

- ✔ Gender
- ✔ Interests
- ✔ Age range
- ✔ Schooling
- ✔ Income
- ✔ Employer

"Cookie? No, thanks, I'm trying to cut down."

All the cookies eBay uses are known as *session cookies,* which means that the second you log off the eBay site, any cookies you've picked up go away. *We* think these cookies are fine (and really useful, even if they aren't tasty). But if you still don't feel comfortable with them on your computer, you can put a lid on the cookie jar by setting your browser *not* to accept cookies, or you can set it to warn you and let you decide whether to accept a particular cookie.

What cookies gather

Web sites collect information about you by using *cookies.* No, they don't bribe you with chocolate-chip goodies. Cookies are nothing more than small files put on your hard drive by outside companies (such as eBay) that store data on your surfing habits.

Most Web site designers install cookies to help you navigate their sites — sometimes the cookie becomes sort of an "admission ticket" (so you don't need to register every time you log on).

eBay has a partnership with two advertising companies, Link Exchange and DoubleClick, which allows the two companies to display advertising banners on the site, whether you want to see the banners or not. If you click on a banner, a cookie from the particular advertiser goes onto your computer. Figure 13-1 shows you an advertising banner found on eBay.

Cookies have no fingers, sticky or otherwise; they can't steal information from other files on your computer. A cookie can access only the information that you've already provided to its Web site.

So how do you do all this? Well, you could make a big batch of your favorite technical guru's favorite cookies (the old-fashioned kind — tangible and yummy) and ask him or her to show you the ropes.

Figure 13-1:
Here's a typical advertising banner you may see on eBay.

DoubleClick says the company uses your information so it can limit the number of times you see the same advertisement. DoubleClick also measures the kinds of ads you respond to. There's no secret conspiracy at work here. The bottom line is that DoubleClick is just trying to sell you stuff with ads based on your personal interests. The upside is that you get to see stuff you might like.

You can learn lots more about cookies in general at `www.cookiecentral.com`.

What Web servers collect

Every time you log on to the Internet, you leave an electronic trail of information. eBay, like zillions of other Web sites, has *servers,* which are really immense programs that do nothing but collect and transfer bits (and bytes) of information day and night, night and day.

Web servers all over the Internet track some or all the following information:

- ✔ What Web site you came in from
- ✔ What ISP (Internet Service Provider) you use
- ✔ What auctions you are running
- ✔ What Web sites you linked your auctions to
- ✔ What Web sites are your favorites (if you link them to About Me pages)

The following information is collected by eBay for as long as you're on the eBay site. As soon as you log off, the server discards the data:

- ✔ What you do while logged on to a site
- ✔ What time you log on and when you leave

Like some incredible Internet archivist, eBay's server keeps a record of everything you bid on, win, and sell, which is great news if you have a problem with a transaction and need eBay to do an investigation. Also, eBay couldn't display feedback about you and other users if their server didn't store all the feedback you write and receive. Gosh, their computers must be *huge!* (And busy. Very busy.)

Did you send e-mail to eBay? eBay's server records it and keeps it in some murky recess of eBay's memory. Remember, we're living in the age of electronic commerce — more of it goes on all the time — and the people at eBay are running a serious business that depends on e-commerce. They have to keep everything in case they need to find it later.

BBBOnline and TRUSTe

If you feel a little apprehensive about all the information Web servers can collect about you while you innocently roam the Internet, we understand. But before you start looking for Big Brother watching over your shoulder, consider: On the Web, everybody's doing it.

Odds are excellent that all the information eBay knows about you is already in the hands of many other folks too — your bank, your grocer, the staff of any magazine you get by subscription, clubs you belong to, any airlines you have flown, any insurance agencies you use — in various combinations. That's life at the turn of the millennium. And if you're thinking, *Just because everybody knows all this stuff about me, that doesn't make it right,* all we can say is — you're right. But maybe you'll sleep a little better knowing that eBay is one place where folks take the privacy issue seriously. eBay also had a privacy policy for all their users to see before privacy policies were even vogue, and now eBay maintains the standards set forth by two pioneers in online safeguarding, the Better Business Bureau Online and TRUSTe, as shown in Figure 13-2.

Figure 13-2:
These icons indicate that eBay takes security seriously.

TRUSTe (www.truste.org) and the Better Business Bureau (www.bbbonline.org) set a list of standards that their member Web sites have to follow to earn a "seal of approval." The hundreds of Web sites that subscribe to one or both of these watchdog groups must adhere to their guidelines and set policies to protect privacy. eBay has been a member of both BBBOnline and TRUSTe since each privacy watchdog group was founded.

To look over the policy that has earned eBay the TRUSTe and BBBOnline seals of approval, first click on the Help link on the main navigation bar, and then click on the Community Standards link on the subnavigation bar. Then click on the Privacy Policy link on the Community Standards Overview page. Or click on the Privacy Policy link at the bottom of every eBay page.

The eBayla virus

In March 1999, eBay users detected a hacker who turned a covert grab for passwords into a somewhat baffling problem. On selected auctions, an unexpected window would pop up, prompting the bidder to type in his or her password. Smart eBay users knew better and dubbed this window the *eBayla virus* (a take-off on the deadly Ebola virus). These same members started spreading the word on message boards and in chat rooms. eBay solved the problem but, unfortunately, correcting it took over a month, and some eBay users were stung by this privacy invasion. This was a valuable lesson for eBay about hacking — and probably not the last time something like this will happen.

In addition to setting and displaying a privacy policy, eBay follows these guidelines as well:

- ✔ eBay must make the TRUSTe and BBBOnline links easily accessible to users. You can find either logo on eBay's Home page, click on one of 'em, and be taken to these sites for more information. Take advantage of this opportunity to find out how your privacy's being protected.

- ✔ eBay must disclose what personal information it collects and how it's using the info.

- ✔ Users must have an easy way to review the personal information eBay has on them.

- ✔ Users must have an option that lets them decline to share information. This is called *opting out* (and we explain it later in this chapter).

- ✔ eBay must follow industry standards to make its Web site and database secure so hackers and nonmembers have no access to the information. eBay uses SSL (Secure Socket Layers), which is an encryption program that scrambles data until it gets to eBay. Unfortunately, however, no Web site, including the CIA's Web site, is completely secure, so you still have to stay on your guard while online.

If you ever have any questions about security at eBay, send an e-mail to privacy@eBay.com or safeharbor@ebay.com.

So What Does eBay Do with Information about Me, Anyway?

While eBay does know a good chunk of information about you, it puts the information to good use — the fact that it knows so much about you actually helps you in the long run.

Do seals bite back?

Because eBay pays to display the TRUSTe Trustmark and the BBBOnline seal, some online critics say that the seals are nothing more than window-dressing. These critics wonder whether it would be in the Web watchdogs' best financial interest to bite the hand that feeds them all those display fees. They complain that the seals offer a false sense of security — and suggest that you view these seals as nothing more than a disclaimer to be careful in your Internet dealings.

Technically, TRUSTe and BBBOnline can pull their seals whenever a Web site becomes careless in its handling of privacy issues. However, the critics make a good point: *Always be careful in your Internet dealings,* no matter how much protection a site has.

Here's what eBay uses personal information for:

- ✔ **Upgrading eBay.** Like most e-commerce companies, eBay tracks members' use and habits to improve the Web site. For instance, if a particular item generates a lot of activity, eBay may add a category or a subcategory.

- ✔ **Clearing the way for transactions.** If eBay didn't collect information such as your e-mail address, your snail-mail address, and your phone number, then after an auction was over, you couldn't complete the transactions you started. Bummer.

- ✔ **Billing.** You think it's important to keep track of your merchandise and money, don't you? So does eBay. It uses your personal information to keep an eye on your account and on your paying habits. And on everybody else's. (Call it a gentle encouragement of honest trading habits.)

Grateful Dead cookie jar

This is one of the grooviest jars I have ever come across — a real find for the die-hard Grateful Dead fan or for the cookie jar collector who has it all. Made by Vandor. This Grateful Dead bus cookie jar looks like something the Dead *would* drive. Beautiful detailing on the peace signs; the roses are running lights. Painted windows. You have just got to see this piece. Only 10,000 made and I have only seen one other. Comes with box that has Grateful Dead logos on it. Buyer pays all shipping and insurance. The cookie jar started at $1 and sold on eBay for $102.50.

Oh wow, dude, that's some far-out cookie jar. (Cue the band: *Keep truck-in'.* . . .)

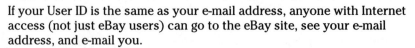

✔ **Policing the site.** Never forget that eBay tries to be tough on crime, and if you break the rules or regulations, they will hunt you down and boot you out. They use personal information to find eBay delinquents, and eBay makes it clear that they cooperate with law enforcement and with third parties whose merchandise you may be selling illegally. For more about this topic, read up on the VeRO program in Chapter 8.

Periodically, eBay runs surveys asking specific questions about your use of the site. Your answers are used to upgrade eBay. In addition, eBay asks whether they can forward your information to a marketing firm. eBay says that no information that could be used to personally identify you is forwarded, which means that any info you provide is given to third parties as raw data. However, if you are nervous about privacy, we suggest that you make clear that you don't want your comments to leave eBay if you decide to participate in eBay surveys. If you don't participate in the surveys, you won't have any hand in creating new eBay features, though, so you're not allowed to complain if you don't like how the site looks. Sometimes, however, eBay chooses to list the survey questions on its Home page.

What Do Other eBay Members Know about Me?

eBay functions under the premise that eBay's members are buying, selling, working, and playing in an honest and open way. That means that anyone surfing can immediately find out some limited information about you:

✔ Your User ID

✔ Your Feedback history

✔ All the auctions you're running

✔ Your current bids and any bids you've made within a given 30-day period

✔ Your e-mail address (Only registered eBay users can access it, but that still means that several million people can e-mail you.)

If your User ID is the same as your e-mail address, anyone with Internet access (not just eBay users) can go to the eBay site, see your e-mail address, and e-mail you.

eBay clearly states in its policies and guidelines that e-mail addresses are to be used for eBay business. If you abuse this policy, you can be suspended or even kicked off for good.

eBay provides limited eBay member registration information to its users. If another member wants to know the following facts, they're available:

✔ Your name

✔ The city, state, and ZIP code that you provide eBay

✔ The telephone number that you provide eBay

Following the auction, buyers and sellers exchange some real-world information. As we explain in Chapter 6 and Chapter 10, members initiate the exchange of merchandise and money by e-mail, providing personal addresses for both payments and shipments. Make sure that you're comfortable giving out your home address. (If you're not, we explain alternatives later in this chapter.)

Spam — Not Just a Taste Treat Anymore

Although you can find plenty of places to socialize and have fun on eBay, when it comes to business, eBay is — well, all business.

eBay's policy says that requests for e-mail addresses and registration information can be made only for eBay business. What constitutes "business" is subject to wide interpretation by both eBay (the company) and eBay members. We suggest that you communicate on eBay as you would in any professional place of business.

Here's a list of "business" reasons for e-mail communication, generally accepted by all on eBay:

✔ Responding to feedback you left

✔ Responding to feedback you received

✔ Communicating with sellers or buyers during and after transactions

✔ Suggesting to other eBay members items that buyers may be interested in

✔ Leaving chat-room comments

✔ Discussing common interests with other members, such as shared hometowns, interesting collections, and past or current auctions

Sending spam versus eating it

Sending e-mail to other members is a great way to do business and make friends. But don't cross the line into *spam*. Spam, originally a Hormel meat product (which we've given its own sidebar), now has an alternate identity. When you spell it with a small *s, spam* is unsolicited e-mail — most often, advertising — sent to multiple e-mail addresses gleaned from marketing lists. Eventually it fills up your inbox the way "Spam, Spam, Spam, and Spam" filled up the menu in an old *Monty Python* restaurant skit.

Think of it as the electronic version of the junk mail that you get in the real world. Spam may be okay for eating (if you're into that kind of thing) but sending it can get you banned from eBay.

Ninety-nine percent of the time, spam is completely annoying and mostly worthless. If you send it, it won't be opened or answered.

If you send e-mail advertising a product to people who you don't know, then you're guilty of spaming.

Trash your junk mail!

Don't open e-mail from anyone you don't know, especially if there's a file attached to it. Sometimes, if a spammer is really slick, it's hard to tell that you've received spam. If you receive an e-mail with no subject line, however — or if it has an addressee name that isn't yours, or is coming in from someone you never heard of — delete it. You never know; it could be just annoying spam — or worse, it could contain a computer virus as an attachment, just waiting for somebody to open it. (A virus you don't open won't infect your computer.)

If you receive spam that you believe is linked to eBay or is being generated by a member, alert eBay by e-mail at timesenstive@ebay.com and safe harbor@ebay.com.

Spam I am

Spam, the unwanted electronic junk mail, is named after Spam the meat product (Spam collectibles on eBay are another matter entirely). According to the Spam Web site (www. spam.com), more than five billion cans of Spam have been consumed worldwide. (By the way, Hawaiians eat more Spam than any other state in the union.) It is made from a secret recipe of pork shoulder, ham, and special spices. It was first produced in 1937 and got its name from the "SP" for spice and the "AM" from ham. It's widely believed that spam (the e-mail junk mail) got its name from the old *Monty Python* sketch because the refrain "Spam-Spam-Spam-Spam" drowned out all other conversation. Others say that it came from a bunch of computer geeks at USC who thought the junk e-mail was about as satisfying as a Spam sandwich. (Perhaps they've never enjoyed a Spam luau in Hawaii under the moonlight — aloha!)

Speaking of e-mail, if you're new to the technology, we recommend getting a good antivirus program that can scan e-mail attachments and rid your system of some annoying — and increasingly dangerous — computer bugs. Chapter 17 can steer you toward some good antivirus software.

For some interesting general anti-spam tips, drop in at `www.spam.abuse.net`. That Web site offers helpful advice for doing battle with spamsters.

I Vant to Be Alone — and Vat You Can Do to Stay That Vay

The Internet has a very long reach. Don't be surprised when you furnish your personal information freely on one Web site, and it turns up someplace totally different. If you don't mind people knowing things about you (your name, your hobbies, where you live, your phone number), then by all means share. But we think you should give only as much information as you need to do business.

Privacy is not secrecy. You shouldn't feel obligated to reveal anything about yourself that isn't absolutely necessary. (Some personal facts are in the same league as body weight — private, even if hardly a secret.)

Although you can't entirely prevent privacy leaks, you can take some precautions to protect yourself. Here are some tips we suggest to keep your online information as safe and secure as possible.

- ✔ **User ID:** When eBay first started, members used their e-mail addresses to buy and sell. Some still do. But your first line of defense against everyone who surfs through eBay is to choose a User ID that's different from your e-mail address. Non-members can't find out who you are, and members at least have to make the effort to get your e-mail address. Choose an ID that doesn't reveal too much about you. We offer pointers on how to choose your User ID in Chapter 2.

- ✔ **Passwords:** Guard your password as if it were the key to your home. Don't give any buyers or sellers your password. If a window pops up in an auction and requests your password, skip it — it's somebody who is up to no good. Use your password *only* on official eBay screens. (See Chapter 2 for more tips on choosing passwords.) If you're concerned that someone may have your password, change it. Click on Services on the main navigation bar. Scroll down to Change my password under the My eBay section. Click on it and follow the instructions. Your password will be immediately changed.

- ✔ **Credit card information:** Whenever you use your credit card on eBay, make sure you have clicked Yes for SSL, the Secure Socket Layer. This is an encryption program that scrambles the information so hackers have

Spam 50th anniversary metal bank

This bank is a replica of a can of spam. Slot on top to add coins. There is no opening to remove money. Top of bank says 50th anniversary of Spam. Good condition. Specks on the top are only dust. Buyer Pays S/H. Good Luck!! L@@K at our other items. The starting price for this can o' spam was $6.75, and it did not sell on eBay.

Maybe it was the non-removable dust?

almost no chance of getting your information. We explain how to use SSL in Chapter 2. When buying from an auction that accepts credit cards, check the seller's feedback and carefully weigh the risks of giving your credit card number to someone you don't know versus the added time of paying by money order or personal check.

✔ **Registration information:** When you first register, eBay requests a phone number and address for billing and contact purposes. We have never had a problem with anyone requesting our registration information and then misusing it. However, many people want an added measure of anonymity. You can give eBay the information it wants in several ways without compromising your privacy:

- Instead of your home phone number, provide eBay with a cell phone number, a work phone number, or the phone number hooked up to your computer. Screen your calls with an answering machine. You can also use your beeper number.

- Use a post office box instead of your home address.

- Start a bank account solely for eBay transactions. Make it a "TA" account — as in "Trade As" — so that you can use an alternate name. Your bank can help you with this.

✔ **Chat rooms:** eBay has more than two dozen chat rooms where members exchange information and sometimes heated arguments. We explain all about chat rooms in Chapter 15. But heed this advice: Be careful what you reveal about yourself in a chat room. Don't expect that "just between us" means that at all. Chat rooms can be viewed by anyone who visits the eBay site, not just eBay members.

Skim some of the category chat rooms, especially the board called Discuss eBay's Newest Features, for warnings about security problems on these boards — and how to avoid 'em.

✔ **Check feedback:** Yep, we sound like a broken record, but there it is again: *Check feedback.* eBay works because it's policed by its participants. The best way to learn about the folks you're dealing with is to see how others felt about the person or company.

Fighting back

Robbin was minding her own business, selling software on eBay, when she ran into one of the world's nastiest eBay outlaws. He was a one-stop-shopping outlet of rule-breaking behaviors. First, he ruined her auctions by bidding ridiculously high amounts and then retracting bids at the last minute. He e-mailed her bidders, offering the same item but cheaper. He contacted Robbin's winning bidders to say he was accepting her payments. Then he started leaving messages on her answering machine. When she finally had enough, she contacted SafeHarbor. They suspended him. But like a bad

lunch, he came back up with a new name. So Robbin fought back on her own. She got his registration information and sent him a letter. She also contacted Support at his ISP and told them what he was doing — and since he used his work e-mail address, she also contacted his boss. It must have done the trick. He finally slipped out of eBay and slithered out of her life. The lesson: Don't rely completely on eBay to pick up the pieces; if you're being abused, stand up for your rights and fight back through the proper channels!

Never give anyone your Social Security number online. It didn't start out as a "national ID number," but it sure works that way now. Guard it as if it were a bank account number.

Never say anything online that you wouldn't feel comfortable saying to the next person who passed you on the street. Basically, that's who you're talking to. You can find stories of romances blossoming on eBay — and we're happy for the happy couples, we swear — but come on, that doesn't mean you should lose your head. Don't give out any personal information to strangers; too often, that's asking for trouble. Have fun with eBay, but hang on to your common sense.

In the virtual world, as in the real world, cyberstalking is scary and illegal. If you think someone is using information from eBay to harass you, contact eBay immediately — as well as your local police.

Chapter 14

eBay's SafeHarbor Program

● ●

In This Chapter

▶ Keeping eBay members safe

▶ Staying away from eBay no-no's

▶ Filing complaints against eBay bad guys

▶ Docking with escrow companies

▶ Knowing your items through authentication

▶ Saving yourself: Where to go when eBay can't help

● ●

Millions of people enjoy smooth sailing on eBay. However, if you're new to the Internet, you may need a reality check. With two million items selling every week, the law of averages dictates that you're bound to run into some rough seas. If you do, know that you can dock in a SafeHarbor. (Because many of us have never set foot on a sailboat, we'll cut out the sea-faring metaphors for the moment. But don't let eBay's cute name fool you — SafeHarbor is the best place to go for help.)

In this chapter, we take you through all the facets of SafeHarbor — from reporting eBay abuses to resolving insurance issues. We explain how eBay enforces its rules and regulations, how you can use third-party escrow and mediation services, and even how to go outside of eBay if you run into some really big-time problems. There be treasure here, matey. Arrr. (Sorry.)

Keeping eBay Safe with SafeHarbor

SafeHarbor (shown in figure 14-1) is the area of eBay that focuses on protecting the Web site from members who aren't playing by the rules. It issues warnings and suspensions — and in some cases, it gives eBay bad guys the old heave-ho.

To get to SafeHarbor, click on the SafeHarbor link that you can find at the bottom of every eBay page. This link takes you to SafeHabor's Overview page. You can navigate throughout SafeHarbor right from this page.

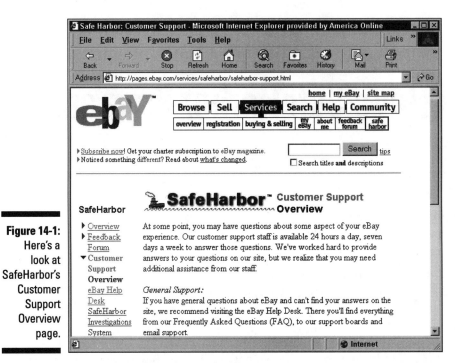

Figure 14-1:
Here's a
look at
SafeHarbor's
Customer
Support
Overview
page.

SafeHarbor is more than just a bunch of Web pages. It's also real, live people — a group of eBay staffers who handle complaints, field incoming tips about possible infractions, and dole out warnings and suspensions. The folks here investigate infractions and send out e-mails in response to tips. eBay staffers look at complaints on a case-by-case basis, in the order received. Most of the complaints they receive are about these problems:

- Shill bidders (see the section on selling abuses in this chapter)
- Feedback issues and abuses (see the section on feedback abuses in this chapter)

Keep in mind that eBay is a community of people, most of whom have never met each other. No matter what you buy or sell on eBay, don't expect eBay transactions to be any safer than buying or selling from a complete stranger. If you go in with this attitude, you can't be disappointed.

If you've been reading previous chapters in this book, you probably know about eBay's rules and regulations. For a closer online look at them, click on Help on the main navigation bar, click on Community Standards, and then click on The Link User Agreement. (The agreement is revised often, so check it often. We're waiting for the next User Agreement to be called *Revised User Agreement, Part 2: The eBay User Strikes Back, Again.*)

Gilligan, Ginger, and Marianne sold separately

Here's a classic example of an honest, accentuate-the-positive-but-point-out-the-negative auction description:

34-foot Sailboat, SEB Aloa — Fast & beautiful! This boat is sea-ready but needs some cosmetic work: retouching the fiberglass work, painting down below, covering the brand-new foam cushions, etc. Recently painted, brightwork in the process of being re-done. No engine, but if you have a VW or other small diesel, you can

drop its engine in; all engine electronics, gearing, etc., in great shape. I've lived aboard this boat for a few years, sailing her from the U.S. to the Caribbean during that time. This boat is fast, beautiful, seaworthy, and seakindly and will take you through any kind of weather. The starting price was $7,000; sold on eBay for $8,100.

The seller of this boat came clean and it paid off big-time.

Another helpful link is the FAQ for the User Agreement, which explains the legalese in clearer English. You can find that help by clicking on User Agreement Frequently Asked Questions and then clicking on User Agreement Revision Frequently Asked Questions. (Coming soon: *Son of . . . ?*) To get there quickly, click on the User Agreement link, located at the bottom of every eBay page.

Abuses You Should Report to SafeHarbor

Before you even consider blowing the whistle on the guy who (gasp!) gave you negative feedback by reporting him to SafeHarbor, make sure that what you're encountering *is* actually a misuse of eBay. Some behavior isn't nice (no argument there), but it *also* isn't a violation of eBay rules — in which case, eBay can't do much about it. The following sections list the primary reasons you may start SafeHarbor investigations.

Selling abuses

If you encounter any of these selling abuses, fire off an e-mail to SafeHarbor at SafeHarbor@ebay.com:

✔ **Shill bidding:** A seller uses multiple User IDs to bid or has accomplices place bids to boost the price of his or her auction items. eBay investigators look for six telltale signs, including a single bidder putting in a really high bid, or a bidder with really low feedback but a really high number of bids on items, or lots of bids between two users.

✔ **Auction interception:** An unscrupulous user, pretending to be the actual seller, contacts the winner to set up terms of payment and shipping in an effort to get the buyer's payment.

✔ **Fee avoidance:** A user reports a lower-than-actual final price and/or illegally submits a Final Value Fee credit. We explain how Final Value Fee credits work in Chapter 11.

✔ **Hot bid manipulation:** A user, with the help of accomplices, enters dozens of phony bids to reach the 30 bids needed to reach the Hot category. Let the experts at eBay decide on this one; but you may wonder if there are loads of bids in rapid succession, but the price has moved very little.

If a user is conducting auctions of prohibited, questionable, or infringing items, report the conduct to Community Watch: ctywatch@ebay.com. See Chapter 8 for more information.

Bidding abuses

If you want to know more about bidding in general, see Chapter 6. Here's a list of bidding abuses that eBay wants to know about:

✔ **Bid shielding:** Two users working in tandem: User A, with the help of accomplices, intentionally bids an unreasonably high amount and then retracts the bid in the closing moments of the auction — leaving a lower bid (placed by the offender or an accomplice) as the winning bid.

✔ **Bid siphoning:** Users send e-mail to bidders of a current auction to offer the same merchandise for a lower price elsewhere.

✔ **Auction interference:** Users warn other bidders through e-mail to stay clear of a seller *during a current auction,* presumably to decrease the number of bids and keep the prices low.

✔ **Bid manipulation:** A user bids a ridiculously high amount, raising the next highest bidder to maximum bid. The manipulator then retracts the bid and rebids *slightly* over the previous high bidder's maximum.

✔ **Non-paying bidder:** We call 'em deadbeats, and the bottom line is that these people win auctions but never pay up.

✔ **Unwelcome bidder:** A user bids on a specific seller's auction despite the seller's warning that he or she won't accept that user's bids. Impolite and obnoxious.

Feedback abuses

All you have on eBay is your reputation, and that reputation is made up of your Feedback history. eBay takes any violation of its Feedback system very seriously. Here's a checklist of feedback abuses that you should report to SafeHarbor:

- **Shill feedback:** A member uses secondary User IDs and/or accomplices to post unwarranted positive feedback.

- **Feedback bombing:** A member uses secondary User IDs and/or accomplices to post *negative* feedback, trying to ruin another member's feedback rating.

- **Feedback extortion:** A member threatens to post negative feedback if another eBay member doesn't follow through on some unwarranted demand.

- **Feedback solicitation:** A member offers to sell (or buy) feedback comments to boost his or her own feedback ratings.

- **– 4 Feedback:** Any user reaching a Net Feedback score of –4 or below is subject to suspension.

Identity abuses

Who you are on eBay is as important as what you sell (or buy). eBay monitors the identities of its members closely — and asks that you report any great pretenders in this area to SafeHarbor. Here's a checklist of identity abuses:

- **Identity misrepresentation:** A user claims to be an eBay staff member or another eBay user, or he or she registers under the name of another user.

- **False or missing contact information:** A user deliberately registers with false contact information or an invalid e-mail address.

- **Under age:** A user falsely claims to be over the age of 18. (You must be 18 to enter into a legally binding contract.)

- **Contact information:** One user publishes another user's contact information on the eBay site without the user's consent.

Operational abuses

If you see somebody trying to interfere with eBay's operation, eBay staffers want you to tell them about it. Here's two roguish operational abuses:

- **Hacking:** A user purposely interferes with eBay's computer operations (for example, by breaking into unauthorized files).

- **Spamming:** The user sends unsolicited e-mail to eBay users.

Miscellaneous abuses

The following are additional problems that you should alert eBay about:

- ✔ A user is threatening physical harm to another eBay member.
- ✔ A person uses racist, obscene, or harassing language in a public area of eBay.

For a complete list of offenses and how eBay runs each investigation, go to the following address:

```
pages.ebay.com/services/safeharbor/
        safeharbor-proc.html#feedback
```

Reporting Abuses to SafeHarbor

If you suspect someone of abusing eBay's rules and regulations, send an e-mail to SafeHarbor@ebay.com.

Make your message clear and concise by including everything that happened, but don't editorialize. (Calling someone a "lowdown mud-sucking cretin" doesn't tell SafeHarbor anything useful, and doesn't reflect well on you, either.) Keep it businesslike — just the facts, ma'am. Do include all pertinent documentation, such as e-mails, receipts, canceled checks, and of course the auction number.

Here's a checklist of what you should include in your SafeHarbor e-mail:

- ✔ Write only the facts as you know them.
- ✔ Attach all e-mails with complete headers (headers are all the information found at the top of an e-mail message). SafeHarbor uses the headers to verify how the e-mail was sent and to follow the trail back to the author.
- ✔ In the subject line of your e-mail message, be sure to name the violation and indicate whether the matter is time-sensitive. If the clock *is* running out on your case (for instance, if you suspect bidding offenses in a current auction), we suggest you send a copy of your e-mail to timesensitive@ebay.com.

After eBay receives your e-mail, you get an automatic response that your e-mail was received although, in practice, several days may go crawling by before eBay actually investigates your allegations. (They have to look at a *lot* of transactions.)

Depending on the outcome of the probe, eBay may contact you with the results. If your problem becomes a legal matter, eBay may possibly not let you know what's going on. The only indication you may have that some action was taken is that the eBay member you reported is suspended — or NARU (Not A Registered User).

If your complaint doesn't warrant an investigation by the folks at SafeHarbor, they pass it along to someone at the overworked Customer Support staff — who then contacts you (don't bawl the person out if the attention you get is tardy).

Unfortunately, NARU members can show up again on the eBay site — they just use a different name. In fact, this practice is fairly common, so beware! If you suspect that someone who broke the rules once is back under another User ID, alert SafeHarbor. If you're a seller, you can refuse to accept bids from that person. If they persist, alert Customer Support with e-mail.

As eBay has grown, so has the number of complaints about slow response from SafeHarbor and Customer Support. We don't doubt that eBay staffers are doing their best. But slow response can get frustrating. You can grin and bear it, or you can plunge ahead. Several eBay users report that the best way to get a reaction out of eBay is an e-mail blitzkrieg — sending e-mail over and over until they can't ignore you. Risky at best, inconsiderate at worst; hitting eBay with constant e-mails about the same issue slows down the process for everyone.

You can also call Customer Support. Phone 408-369-4830, but don't expect to hear the voice of a live human being — you hear a recording promising that someone will phone you back. Don't forget to leave your name and phone number.

If you're desperate for help, you can also post a message with your problem in one of the eBay chat rooms. eBay members participating in chat rooms often share the names of helpful staffers. Often, you can find some eBay members who faced the same problem (sometimes with the same member) and can offer advice — or at the very least, compassion and a virtual ear. (Jump to Chapter 15 for more info on bulletin boards and chat rooms.)

Be sure not to violate any eBay rules by sharing any member's contact information when you share your story in a chat room. In addition, be sure not to threaten or libel (saying untrue things or spreading rumors) the person in your posting.

Stuff eBay Won't Do Anything About

People are imperfect everywhere, even online (whoa, what a shock!). Chances are good you won't agree with some of the behavior (ranging from slightly annoying to just plain rotten) you run into on eBay. Although much of that conduct is detestable, it can (and will) go on as long as it doesn't break eBay rules.

In some cases, you may have to bite your tongue and chalk up someone's annoying behavior to ignorance of the unwritten rules of eBay etiquette. Just because people have computers and some things to sell or buy doesn't mean they have grown-up social skills. (But you knew that.)

Here's a gang of annoying issues that crop up pretty regularly but that *aren't* against eBay's rules and regulations:

- ✔ **You receive unwarranted or retaliatory feedback:** The biggest fear that haunts members who consider leaving negative feedback is that the recipient will retaliate with some more negative feedback. Remember that you can respond to negative feedback. Remember, however, that eBay will not remove a negative comment — no matter how unjustified you may think it is. The good news is that the comment becomes neutral if the writer is no longer a member of eBay.

  Often, people who leave retaliatory feedback are also breaking some heftier eBay rules and (sooner or later) disappear from the site, never to rant again.

- ✔ **A seller sets astronomical shipping costs:** eBay policy says that shipping costs must be reasonable. Basically, eBay is wagging its finger and saying, "Don't gouge your buyers." Some sellers are trying to avoid fees, or may be disappointed that a sale didn't make enough money, so they jack up shipping costs to increase their profit.

  Under its rules, eBay can't really stop someone from charging too much for shipping. Bidders should check shipping terms in the Auction Item description. Bidders have to decide whether to agree to those terms before they bid. The best way to protect yourself from being swindled is to agree with a seller on shipping costs and terms in writing — *before* you bid.

- ✔ **A seller or buyer refuses to meet the terms that you mutually set:** eBay has the power only to warn or suspend members. It can't *make* anyone do anything, even someone who's violating a policy. If *you* want to make someone fulfill a transaction, you're more or less on your own.

  We heard one story of a seller who refused to send a product after being paid. The seller said, "Come and get it." The buyer happened to be in town on business, and did just that!

  Often, reluctant eBay users just need a nudge from eBay in the form of a warning to comply. So go ahead and file a Final Value Fee Credit request (we explain how to do this in Chapter 11) and a fraud report (more on fraud reports later in this chapter).

- ✔ **E-mail spam:** An eBay bidder whose e-mail address and User ID are the same can receive unwanted e-mail from non-members who offer to sell similar items outside of eBay. eBay sees this as spam, but because these spamsters are not eBay members, eBay has no way to punish them. And although the items these spammers are selling may be perfectly good, eBay won't offer you any protection in these deals. We suggest that you either ignore these folks or report them to their ISP.

The best (and most obvious) solution to this problem is to choose a User ID that's distinctly different from your e-mail address. Doing so displays your creativity, helps insulate you from great slabs of spam, and helps block lazy unsavories from cramming your e-mail with reasons to send them money. (Without even looking up your address. The nerve.)

New eBay users are often the unwitting perpetrators of annoying behavior, but you're ahead of the pack now that you know what *not* to do. You can afford to cut the other newbies some slack and help them learn the ropes before you report them.

Launching a Fraud Report

The second you complain about a seller who's taken money but hasn't delivered the goods, a SafeHarbor investigation automatically starts.

If you have clearly been ripped off, use eBay's Fraud Reporting program to file a complaint. Here's how:

1. **Click on the Site Map on any eBay page.**

   You're taken to eBay's Site Map.

2. **Click on the SafeHarbor Investigations link.**

   You're taken to the SafeHarbor Customer Support Investigations page.

3. **Click on the Fraud Reporting System link at the bottom of the page.**

   Follow the form's directions for filing a new complaint.

4. **Click on either the File a new complaint or View a complaint in progress button.**

5. **Fill in your User ID and password on the next page, and then click on Continue.**

6. **Lodge your complaint.**

   When you're finished, review what you've written before confirming your report.

In order to file an insurance claim with eBay, you must register a fraud report within 30 days of the close of the auction. Be careful not to jump the gun and register a complaint too soon. We suggest waiting about two or three weeks to register your complaint; double check to make sure your e-mail is working, and that you have the correct address of the person you're having difficulties with — after all, neither eBay nor your ISP is infallible.

Even if your insurance claim isn't worth a nickel after 30 days, you can still register a fraud report and help the investigation of a lousy, terrible, *allegedly* fraudulent eBay user. That's payment enough, ain't it?

After you register a complaint, eBay informs the other party that a fraud claim is being made. eBay says that it will try to contact both parties and help reach a resolution. *Registering* the complaint is not the same thing as *filing* a complaint. Registering starts the process; filing comes after a month-long grace period if the situation isn't resolved by then.

If the accusation you are registering refers to a clear violation, eBay gives you information on the kind of third-party assistance you can get to help resolve the problem. If eBay deems the problem a violation of the law, it reports the crime to the proper law-enforcement agency.

Walking the Plank: Suspensions

Playing by eBay's rules keeps you off the SafeHarbor radar screen. If you start violating eBay policy, they're going to keep a close eye on you. Depending on the infraction, eBay may be all over you like jelly on peanut butter. Or you may be able to safely lurk in the fringes until your feedback rating is lower than the temperature in Nome in November.

Here's a docket of eBay no-no's that can get members flogged and keel-hauled, or at least *suspended*:

- Feedback rating of −4
- Four instances of deadbeat bidding
- Repeated warning for the same infraction
- Feedback extortion
- Feedback solicitation
- Bid shielding
- Unwelcome bidding after a warning from the seller
- Shill bidding
- Auction interception
- Fee avoidance
- Fraudulent selling
- Identity misrepresentation
- Under 18 years old
- Hacking
- Physical threats

Walk the plank, ye scurvy swab!

17 inch high sea pirate sword with leather sheath. 17 inches — wood and brass handle, stainless steel blade hand tooled custom leather sheath. Not for sale to anyone under the age of 18. Shipping is $5.99 CONT U.S. Cashiers Check/Money Order, same day shipping. Personal check, 2 week wait. THANKS FOR LOOKING AND HAPPY BIDDING!!! The starting price of this "high sea" sword was $9.99; it did not sell on eBay.

We're not sure, but we think the words "stainless steel" may have tipped some bidders off that this wasn't *really* a pirate's sword.

If you get a suspension but think you're innocent, respond directly to the person who suspended you to plead your case. Reversals do occur. Do not broadcast your suspicions on chat boards. If you're wrong, you'll regret it. Even if you're right, it's oh so gauche.

Be careful about accusing members of cheating. Unless you are involved in a transaction, you don't know all the facts. Perry Mason moments are great on television, but they're fictional for a reason. In real life, there's no sense in drawing yourself into a possible confrontation. Start the complaint process, keep it businesslike, and let eBay's staff figure out what's going on.

Toss 'Em a Life Saver: eBay Insurance

One thing's for sure in this world: Nothing is for sure. That's why insurance companies exist. Two types of insurance are available for eBay users:

- ✔ Insurance purchased by buyers to cover shipping (see Chapter 10).
- ✔ Insurance offered through eBay against fraud, which we discuss here.

To cover loss from fraud, eBay has a deal with the world-famous insurer, Lloyd's of London. The insurance covers money you paid for an item you never received (as a result of fraud, not shipping problems) or received but found to be materially different from the auction item description.

eBay insurance pays up to $175 (a maximum of $200 minus a $25 deductible). So if you file a $50 claim, you get $25. If you file a $5,000 claim, you still get only $175. Hey, it's better than nothing.

To qualify for an eBay insurance payment:

✔ The buyer and seller must be in good standing (no negative feedback ratings).

✔ The buyer must have proof that the item costs more than $25.

✔ The buyer must prove that the payment was sent.

✔ The buyer must prove that the seller didn't send the item.

> *OR*

✔ The buyer must prove that the item sent is substantially different from the auction description.

To be eligible for insurance, you must register a complaint with the Fraud Reporting System no more than 30 days after the auction closes. eBay then e-mails the seller that a complaint has been lodged. eBay hopes that by the time the 30 days are up, the differences have been resolved and you can withdraw your complaint.

Filing an insurance claim

To file an insurance claim on eBay, begin at the SafeHarbor Overview page. Get there by clicking on SafeHarbor at the bottom of every eBay page.

1. **On the SafeHarbor Overview page, click on the Insurance link.**

   You're now at the Insurance Overview page.

2. **Scroll down the page to the Fraud Reporting Process link and click on it.**

   You go to the Fraud Reporting Process page.

3. **Click on the File a New Complaint button and follow the step-by-step directions.**

4. **Click on either the File a new complaint button or the View a complaint in progress button.**

5. **Enter your User ID and then move to the next page.**

6. **Verify your name and address and contact info by clicking on Yes or No.**

7. **Click on the appropriate button (I was a bidder or I was a seller).**

8. **At this point, sellers should enter the item number and the buyer's User ID. Buyers should simply enter the auction number.**

9. **When you finish, print out the final page with your claim number.**

   Lloyd's promises to get back to you within six weeks to let you know the results of its investigation.

Lloyd's of London

Lloyd's of London is eBay's official insurer. The company is named for Edward Lloyd who opened a coffee shop in London in 1689. Lloyd never insured anything. But his wealthy clientele pooled their resources insuring local shippers. In the last 400 years or so, they've insured a list of items even more eclectic than eBay's auctions: the "car" that set the land speed record of 763 miles per hour, a 2000-year-old Chinese wine jar, Ringling Brothers Circus, Betty Grable's "million-dollar legs," Frank Sinatra, the Rolling Stones — and the world's longest cigar, which is 12½ feet long. (That cigar would take 339 days to smoke. It's still unlit; the owner's spouse is probably grateful.)

You can't file more than one claim a month.

Docking with escrow

Escrow is a relatively new concept for online trading. Escrow services act as the go-between between the seller and the buyer. We spell out all the details of using escrow in Chapter 6.

eBay has a direct link to i-Escrow (an online escrow service). From the SafeHarbor Overview page, click on the Escrow link. This takes you to the Escrow Overview page. On this page, click on the Begin Escrow link and follow the directions.

Rough Seas: Mediation

Even the best of friends sometimes have misunderstandings that can escalate to all-out war if problems aren't resolved early enough. If the going gets tough, it's time to call in the heavy artillery: a mediator. Just as pro boxing has its referees, a squabble over an auction needs a level head to intervene. eBay is readying a mediation service to be available on its Web site. As a third party with no axe to grind, often a mediator can hammer out an agreement or act as judge to resolve disputes. Expect to see links to mediation services on the SafeHarbor page soon — and if you don't, raise a ruckus (just kidding).

Trimming in the Sales: Authentication and Appraising

Despite eBay's attempts to keep the buying and selling community honest, some people just won't play nice. When the New York City Department of Consumer Affairs launched an investigation into counterfeit sports memorabilia sold on the Web site, errant eBay outlaws experienced some anxious moments. We can always hope they mend their ways, while at the same time advising *Don't bet on it*. Fortunately, eBay is offering a proactive approach to preventing such occurrences from happening again.

Topmost among the countermeasures is easy member access to several services that can authenticate specific types of merchandise. The good news here is that you know what kind of item you're getting; the bad news is that like everything else in life, it's going to cost you money.

Have a good working knowledge of what you are buying or selling. Before you bid, do some homework and get more information. Also (does this sound familiar?) *check the bidder's feedback*. See Chapters 5 and 8 for more information on research.

Before you spend the money to have your item appraised and authenticated, you should ask yourself a few practical questions (regardless of whether you're buying or selling):

- ✔ **Is this quality merchandise?** Am I selling/buying merchandise whose condition is subjective but important to its value — as in, *Is it really well-loved or just busted?* Is this item graded by some professionally accepted standard that I need to know?

- ✔ **Is this item the real thing?** Am I sure that I am selling/buying a genuine item? Do I need an expert to tell me whether it's the real McCoy?

- ✔ **Do I know the value of the merchandise?** Do I have a good understanding of what this item is worth in the marketplace at this time, considering its condition?

- ✔ **Is the merchandise worth the price?** Is the risk of selling/buying a counterfeit, a fake, or an item I don't completely understand worth the cost of an appraisal?

If you answered "yes" to any of these questions, consider calling in a professional appraiser.

In the case of *selling* a counterfeit item — otherwise known as a knock-off, phony, or five-finger discount item, that's a no-brainer: No way. Don't do it.

If you need items appraised, eBay offers links to various appraising agencies:

- ✔ **The ISA** (International Society of Appraisers). The ISA has a membership of hundreds of professional appraisers (they need to be top-notch to be part of ISA) to serve just about any category you collect in.

- ✔ **The PCGA** (Professional Coin Grading Service). serves coin collectors.

- ✔ **Real Beans.** Eight percent of all the millions of items sold on eBay are Beanie Babies. Real Beans ensures that you're getting the real McBean by acting as an escrow service. The seller sends the Beanie to Real Beans, Real Beans authenticates it, and it sends the Beanie Baby off to the buyer. We suggest using this service only for the high-priced and rare Beanie Babies.

- ✔ **PSA** (Professional Sports Authenticators). To help guard against counterfeiting and fraud with sports memorabilia and trading cards, eBay teamed up with PSA to grade and authenticate trading cards. PSA offers a 10 percent rebate to eBay members who use its service. The money is credited to your eBay account after the job is done.

To find links to these appraising agencies starting at the SafeHarbor Overview page:

1. **Click on the Authentication & Grading link.**

   You go to the Authentication & Grading overview page, where eBay offers good information about third-party appraisers.

2. **Click on the link that best suits your authentication purposes.**

   You're taken to a page that describes how the process works. You also see links to the Web site of the agency you've chosen.

3. **Complete the information you're asked for to find a professional appraiser in your area.**

Even if you use an appraiser or an authentication service, do some legwork yourself. Often, two experts can come up with wildly different opinions on the same item. The more you know, the better the questions you can ask.

If a seller isn't sure whether the item being auctioned is authentic, you may find an appropriate comment (such as *Cannot verify authenticity*) in the auction item description. Knowledgeable eBay gurus always like to share what they know, and we have no doubt that someone will supply you with scads of helpful information. But be careful — some blarney artist (there's one of *those* born every minute, too) may try to make a sucker out of you.

Verifying Your ID

During the later years of the Cold War, Ronald Reagan said, "Trust but verify." The President's advice made sense for dealing with the Soviet Union, and it makes good sense with your dealings on eBay too! (Even if you're not dealing in nuclear warheads.)

To show other eBay members that you're an honest type, you can buy a "trust but verify" option, called ID Verify, from eBay for five bucks. The giant credit verification service, Equifax, verifies your identity by asking for your *Wallet information,* including the following:

- ✔ name
- ✔ address
- ✔ phone number
- ✔ Social Security number
- ✔ driver's license information
- ✔ date of birth

Equifax matches the info you give to what it has in its database and presents you with a list of questions from your credit file that only you should know the answer to. For example, Equifax may ask you about any loans you have, what kinds of credit cards you own (and how many).

Equifax sends only the results of its Identity Test to eBay (whether you pass the test or not), and *not* the answers to the private financial questions it has asked you. Equifax doesn't modify or add the information you provide to any of its databases.

Equifax's questions are meant to protect you against anyone else who might come along and try to steal this information from you and assume your identity. The questions are not a credit check, and your credit worthiness is never called into question. This info simply verifies that you are who you say you are.

If you pass the test and Equifax can verify that you are who you say you are and not your evil twin (can you say "Mini Me"?), then you get a cool icon by your name for a year. If, after a year, you like the validation that comes from being verified, you can pay another fee and renew your seal.

While you can feel secure knowing that a user who has been verified is indeed who he or she claims to be, you still have no guarantee that he or she won't turn out to be a no-goodnik (or, for that matter, a well-meaning financial airhead) during auction transactions.

Even if an eBay member is verified, what makes this program so controversial is twofold:

- Many members object to giving out Social Security numbers. They see it as an unwarranted invasion of privacy.

- Some users also fear that this system creates a two-tiered eBay system, with verified users occupying a sort of upper class and anyone who is not verified stuck in the lower class. They're afraid that sellers will refuse to do business with *un*verified users.

You should consider all of eBay's current and future programs for protecting you from problematic transactions and people, but we think the "undisputed heavy weight champ" for finding out who someone *really is* and keeping you out of trouble is the first program eBay created. That's right, folks, feedback can show you other eBay members' track records and give you the best information on whether you want to do business with them or take a pass. Feedback is especially effective when you analyze it in conjunction with eBay's other protection programs. We suggest taking the time to read all about feedback in Chapter 4.

When It's Clearly Fraud

After filing either a fraud report or a Final Value Fee credit request, you can do more on your own. If the deal involved the post office in any way — if you mailed a check or the seller sent you merchandise that was completely wrong and won't make good — file a mail-fraud complaint with the postal inspector.

In the United States, you can call your local post office or dial 800-275-8777 for a form that you can fill out. After the form is completed, the USPS sends the eBay bad guy a notice that a fraud complaint has been filed. Perhaps that will get his or her attention.

If you're interested in learning about mail-fraud law, go to

```
www.usps.com/websites/depart/inspect/usc18
```

Along with the post office, you can turn to some other agencies for help:

- **The National Fraud Information Center.** NFIC has an online site devoted to combating fraud on the Internet. NFIC works closely with legal authorities. File a claim at `www.fraud.org/info/repoform.htm` or call them toll free at 800-876-7060.

- **Law enforcement agencies.** Contact the local District Attorney or State Attorney General's Office and local and state Consumer Affairs Department in the other person's state and city (look online for contact information or try your local agencies for contact numbers).

✔ **Federal Trade Commission.** The FTC accepts complaints and investigates repeated cases of fraud. File a claim at `www.ftc.gov/ftc/complaint.htm`.

✔ **Internet service provider.** Contact the member's ISP. You can get this bit of info from the person's e-mail address, just after the @ symbol. (See? This easy access to information does have its advantages.) Let the ISP know whom you have filed a complaint against, the nature of the problem, and the agencies you've contacted.

Any time you contact another agency for help, keep SafeHarbor up to date on your progress by e-mailing them at `safeharbor@ebay.com`. Also write them at eBay ATTN: Fraud Prevention, 2005 Hamilton Ave., Ste. 350, San Jose, CA 95125.

There's a very thin line between alerting other members to a particular person's poor behavior and breaking an eBay cardinal rule by interfering with an auction. Don't make unfounded and/or vitriolic accusations — especially if you were counting on them never to get back to the person they were about (or, for that matter, if you hoped they *would*). Trample the poison out of the gripes of wrath before you have your say. We recommend that you hunt for facts, but don't do any finger-pointing on public message boards or chat rooms. If it turns out that you're wrong, you can be sued for libel.

Communication and compromise are the keys to successful transactions. If you have a difference of opinion, write a polite e-mail outlining your expectations and offer to settle any dispute by phone. See Chapters 7, 10, and 11 for tips on communicating after the auction ends — and solving disputes *before* they turn wicked, aggressive, or unprintable.

Chapter 15

The eBay Community: Playing Nice with Other eBay Members

*e*Bay thinks of itself as more than just an Internet location for buying and selling great stuff. eBay makes clear that it has created (and works hard to maintain) a community. It's not a bad deal, actually — prime real estate in *this* community costs only pennies! As in real-life communities, you participate as much as works for you. You can get involved in all sorts of neighborhood activities, or you can just sit back, mind your own business, and watch the world go by. eBay works exactly the same way.

As you have probably heard by now, one of the main ways to participate in the eBay community is with feedback (which we explain in detail in Chapter 6). In this chapter, we show you some other ways you can be part of the community. You can socialize, learn from other members, leave messages, or just read what everybody is talking about through eBay's message boards, chat boards, and the corporate Announcements Board. We offer you tips on how to use all these places to your benefit, and then give you a change of scenery by surfing through some off-site message boards that can help you with your buying and selling.

Anyone who browses the eBay site can see your User ID and messages on any of the Community boards. Make sure your user ID is different from your e-mail address, and see Chapter 12 for more cyber safety tips.

News and Chat, This and That

It's not quite like *The New York Times* ("All the News That's Fit to Print"), but you can find all the news, chat boards, and message boards links from the Community Overview page. Figure 15-1 shows you what the page looks like.

Here's a list of all the main headings of the main Community page. Each heading offers you links to specific eBay areas:

- News
- *eBay Life* (covered in Chapter 16)
- Charity (also in Chapter 16)
- Suggestion Box
- Chat
- Library (covered in Chapter 5)
- eBay Store (covered in Chapter 16)
- About eBay

Figure 15-1: The main Community page has links to all the fun places to chat and post messages on eBay.

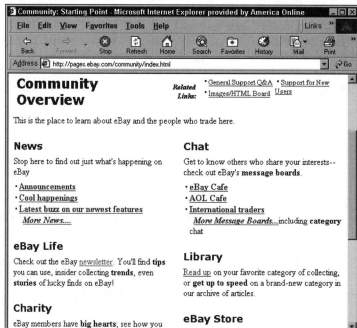

Hear Ye, Hear Ye! eBay's Announcements Board

If this were the 1700s, you'd see a strangely dressed guy in a funny hat ringing a bell and yelling, "Hear ye, hear ye!" every time you opened eBay's Announcements Board. (Then again, if this were the 1700s, there'd be no electricity, computers, fast food, or anything else we consider fun.) In any case, eBay's Announcements Board is the most important place to find out what's going on (direct from headquarters) on the Web site. And they don't even need to ring a bell.

This is the place where eBay reports outages and critical changes in policies and procedures. eBay also uses it to update users on glitches in the system and when those might be rectified. eBay also lists any new features and charity work auctions. Figure 15-2 shows you eBay's Announcements Board with information that could have an impact on your auctions.

Make stopping at the Announcements Board a vital part of your eBay routine.

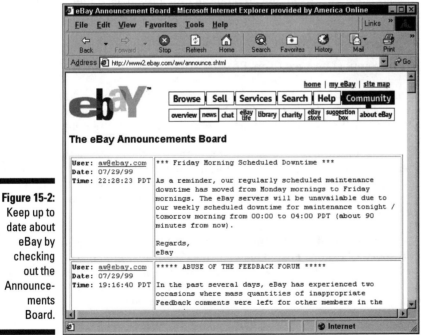

Figure 15-2:
Keep up to date about eBay by checking out the Announcements Board.

Keep your eye out for the outages listing in the Announcements Board to see if an outage may affect your auctions. Also on this board, you can discover any new procedures and rules that could impact what you're selling.

When new features are introduced, eBay sometimes offers explanations or links that appear in The Latest Buzz, which is below the Announcements link on the News.

eBay has several million members — a bigger population than in some cities — but it can still have that small-town feel through announcement boards, chat boards, and message boards. Start on the main Chat page by clicking on Community on the main navigation bar, and then click on Chat on the subnavigation bar. Now you've got access to three dozen chat boards, support sites, and message boards.

Help! I Need Somebody

If you ever have specific eBay questions to which you need answers, two eBay Customer Support–run message boards on the main Chat page can help you. These boards are located on the top of the page under Related Links:

- ✔ The General Support Q&A
- ✔ Live Support for New Users Board

eBay newbies often find that these boards are good places to add to their knowledge of eBay. As you scroll on by, read the Q & A postings from the past; your question may already be answered in an earlier posting.

To submit a question on a board, post it in the box at the top of the site. eBay staffers edit and post only some of the submitted questions. If your question is not urgent (or if you don't want it posted), click on the eBay Customer Support link. Questions that are not posted receive an e-mail response in about a business day.

Images/HTML Board: A third support board in this group is the critical *Images/ HTML Board.* Questions posted here are most often answered by other very knowledgeable eBay users who really know how to explain posting a picture (in a lot fewer words than a thousand). You can even ask someone on this board to look at your auction and provide an opinion on your picture.

Community Message Boards

Because eBay's Customer Service gets bombarded with a gazillion questions a day, they're sometimes frustratingly slow if you need an answer right away. You may get a faster answer by posting your question on one of the Community message boards.

Posted questions are generally answered by knowledgeable veteran eBay members as best as they can. The answers are the opinions of members and are certainly not eBay gospel. But you get a fast and honest answer; often you get more than one response. Most questions are answered in about 15 minutes. If not, re-post your question. Be sure to post your question on the appropriate board, because each board has a specific topic of discussion.

Members who post on these boards often share helpful tips and Web sites and alert other members to scams. Newbies may find it helpful to *lurk* (read without posting) on some of these boards to learn more about how eBay works. Occasionally, an eBay staffer shows up — which is kinda like inviting Bill Gates to a Windows 98 new users' meeting. eBay staff members are usually hounded with questions.

You can always tell an eBay staff member on a board because the top border line is in pink (not gray, as it is with regular users).

Rating the member help boards

You know you need help, but you don't know which help board is best for you. Here's our take on which boards are most helpful.

- ✔ **The eBay Q&A** — Good help for newbies from fellow members.

- ✔ **Images/HTML Board** — Good help from other eBay members for those with specific questions about using HTML.

- ✔ **Discuss eBay's Newest Features** (known as DNF) — Many of the folks on this board are devoted to protesting eBay's policies and new features. However, the regulars on this

board are extremely knowledgeable about eBay. Brace yourself a bit, though — conversation on this board can get nasty at times.

- ✔ **The New Board** — This is another good board for news and tips. Members here answer questions and swap gossip.

You can access The New Board from any other board. Scroll down to Select from This List. Click on the arrow, and a pull-down list appears. On it, you find The New Board.

If you like to keep your Chit-Chat in a box . . .

An old 12-terminal Chit-Chat box from the 1920s in pristine condition. This box was found along with many other items in the attic of an old upstate office building that was being gutted.

The wood has a beautiful finish and the brass a satisfying patina. Starting price was $29; sold on eBay for $92.

If a new policy or some sort of big change occurs, the boards are most likely going to be filled with discussion about it. However, on slow days, you may have to wade through personal messages and "chat" that has no connection to eBay. Many of the people who post on these boards are long-time members with histories (as well as feuds) that can rival any soap opera. On rare occasion, the postings can get rather abusive. Getting involved in personality clashes or verbal warfare gains nothing.

No matter how peeved the users of a chat room or message board may get — and no matter how foul or raunchy the language may get — no one on eBay will ever see it. eBay has a built-in "vulgarity checker" that deletes any (well, okay, *as many as possible*) words or phrases that eBay considers offensive or obscene.

One cardinal rule for eBay chat boards and message boards exists: no business. No advertising items for sale! Not now, not ever. eBay bans repeat offenders who break this rule from participating on these boards.

Remember that this is eBay and you're a member. This is not Speakers' Corner, that London park where protesters are free to stand on a soapbox and scream about the rats in government. If you feel the need to viciously complain about eBay — as the bar bouncers say, take it outside. See our suggestions later in this chapter. Better yet, click on the Suggestion link on the Community Home page!

Other Message Boards

There are about a dozen message boards on eBay specializing in everything from pure chat to charity work.

Stone egg fossils — no reserve

Fossil Egg with fossilized worms and crynoids. This egg will look special anywhere (. . . except maybe in a frying pan). Starting price was $5; sold on eBay for $11.01.

Café society

The eBay Café (eBay's first message board from back when they were just selling Pez candy dispensers) and AOL Café message boards are mostly regulars chatting about eBay gossip. Frequent postings include sharing personal milestones and whatever is on people's minds. Find useful information about eBay and warnings about potential scammers here.

Wanted Board

One of the coolest things about eBay is how many people actually find and buy that one whatchamacallit-thingamabob-doohickey they had as a kid. If a constant search of auction sites can't help you, post a "wanted" on the Wanted Board (but try to remember the item's real name!).

Giving Board

eBay isn't only about making money. On the Giving Board, it's also about making a difference. Members in need post their stories and requests for assistance. Other members with items to donate post offers for everything from school supplies to clothing on this board.

If you feel like doing a good deed, conduct a member benefit auction. You link your auction to the Giving Board so that the proceeds of that auction go to someone in need. For information on starting a member benefit auction, go to www.givingboard.com.

Emergency Contact Board

It's no *Rescue 911*, but if your computer crashes and you lose all your info, this is the place to put out an all-points bulletin for help. If your ISP goes on vacation, your phone line is on the fritz, or you've been abducted by aliens and can't connect to your buyers or sellers, post a message on the Emergency Contact Board.

If you're having trouble contacting another eBay member, posting for help from other members to track 'em down often gets the job done.

If you think you may be the victim of a rip-off, check the Emergency Contact Board. The buyer or seller may have left word about an e-mail problem. On the flip side, you may find out that you're not alone in trying to track down an eBay delinquent who seems to have skipped town. It's at least bad manners to post information about a potentially bad eBay guy on most boards. However, wrapped in the guise of emergency contact, other members can learn about a potential problem. Figure 15-3 shows some of the postings found on the Emergency Contact Board.

To get to the Emergency Contact Board:

1. **From the eBay Home page, click on the Community link.**

   A subnavigation bar appears.

2. **Click on the Chat link.**

   You're taken to the main Chat page.

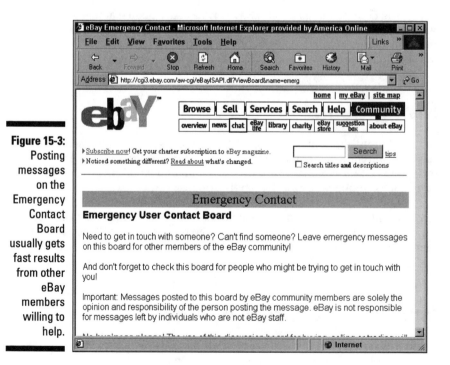

Figure 15-3:
Posting
messages
on the
Emergency
Contact
Board
usually gets
fast results
from other
eBay
members
willing to
help.

Coca-Cola soda jerk hat from the early '60s

Soda Jerk hat from the early 1960s. The hat is adjustable to fit any size head. The Coca-Cola theme during this era was "Things go better with Coke." This hat was never worn and condition is near mint. Buyer pays S&H. Starting price was $8; the item did not sell on eBay.

Maybe everybody already had logo sweatshirts from the cola wars.

3. Scroll down the Chat page and click on Emergency Contact.

You see a message board filled with all the desperate sellers and buyers trying to locate each other. It really is quite touching, isn't it?

eBay International Boards

People from all over the world enjoy eBay. If you're considering buying or selling globally, visit the International Boards. It's a great place to post questions about shipping and payments for overseas transactions. In addition to eBay chat, the International Boards turn up discussions about current events and international politics.

Got a seller in Italy? Spain? France? Translate your English messages into the appropriate language through

    babelfish.altavista.digital.com

Category-Specific Chat Boards

Want to talk about Elvis, Louis XV, Sammy Sosa, or Howard the Duck? Currently there are about two dozen category-specific chat boards where you can tell eBay members what's on your mind about merchandise and auctions. Reach these boards by clicking on Community on the main navigation bar and then click on Chat on the subnavigation bar.

Of course you can buy and sell without ever having been on a chat board, but you can certainly learn a lot from one. Discussions mainly focus on merchandise and the nuts and bolts of transactions. Category-specific chat boards are great for posting questions on items that you don't know much about.

Chatting outside of eBay

As you may have guessed, eBay is chock-full of information about, well, eBay. Sometimes it's helpful to go outside to get other views of the Web site (or online auctions in general). We suggest you visit a terrific Web site called AuctionWatch. One of the benefits of AuctionWatch is an image-hosting service, which we explain in Chapter 12.

AuctionWatch's message center is a terrific place to hear from eBay gadflies — the folks who love to use eBay but hate some of its policies. These folks feel freer to speak their minds because they are not on eBay's home turf. Folks who post here take eBay seriously. This is not the place for questions that are easily answered on eBay message boards. There are a few eBay cheerleaders, but you can find lots of solid information and even a few conspiracy theories.

AuctionWatch is a good place to double-check whether the eBay interface is working correctly. Members often post announcements here when eBay crashes.

On eBay, you get all kinds of responses from all kinds of people. Take some of the help you get with a grain of salt, because some of the folks who help you may be buyers or competitors.

These boards are also great for finding out where to go for more research and information on specific items. You can also find helpful sources for shipping information about items in that category (such as large furniture in the Antiques section or breakable items on the Glass chat board).

Don't be shy. As your second-grade teacher said, "There are no dumb questions." Most eBay members love to share their knowledge of items.

You can access AuctionWatch at www.auctionwatch.com. For specific information about eBay, scroll down to the Message Center, click on Stop by, and speak your mind! Then click on eBay outlook.

Another site that deals with eBay is Auctionpatrol. You can find this site at www.auctionpatrol.com. When you get there, click on The Station.

Chapter 16

Charities and Special Features

• •

In This Chapter

▶ Bidding for a good cause

▶ Using eBay's member specials

▶ Reading all about *eBay Life*

▶ Buying souvenirs at the eBay store

▶ Getting your own personal cyber-shopper

• •

*O*ver and over, eBay members show what big hearts they have. Yes, it's true that you can pocket some nice-sized profits from selling on the eBay Web site, but (just as in real life) people take the time to give a little back for worthy causes. But because this is eBay, giving back means getting something fabulous in return.

In this chapter, we not only tell you about the terrific charity auctions, we show you how eBay members can get great inside deals from manufacturers; we open the door of the eBay store where you can get stuff with the official logo on it; and we have news about *eBay Life*, which is an online newsletter that you should at least skim every month.

Truly Righteous Stuff for Charity

Most of us have donated to charity in one form or another. But here on eBay, charities really rock. Do you need a *Jurassic Park* helmet signed by Steven Spielberg to round out your collection (and deflect the odd dino tooth)? Post a bid on Rosie O'Donnell's charity site. How about a signed original photograph of Jerry Seinfeld from *People* magazine? Yup, you can get that, too. All these and more have turned up in charity auctions. In short, having a big heart for charities has gotten a whole lot easier — thanks to eBay.

Rosie's For All Kids Foundation

Rosie O'Donnell took TV by storm with her popular talk show, and now she's putting her high visibility to good use with her For All Kids Foundation. The foundation awards grants to help support disadvantaged kids throughout the country. In the past, Rosie has donated profits from books, a Rosie O'Donnell doll, and other projects to For All Kids. Now she's joined forces with eBay and is running auctions, with all proceeds going to her foundation.

To get to Rosie's For All Kids auctions, just click on Cool Happenings on the Home page, then click on the Rosie's For All Kids link. Bid as you would on regular auctions. (We explain bidding in detail in Chapter 6.)

Here's a sampling of some of the neat stuff Rosie put up for auction, along with their selling prices:

- *Ally McBeal* pilot script, signed by the cast ($6,100)
- Movie poster of *The Graduate,* signed by Dustin Hoffman ($1,150)
- A shirt signed by Rosie and Bill Cosby ($565)
- Princess Leia action figures signed by Carrie Fisher ($205)

You can catch up with current auctions by doing a Seller Search (see Chapter 5 for details on searches) using Rosie's User ID: **4allkids**.

Other charity auctions

New charities are popping up all the time on eBay. To see what temporary auctions they're running, go to the Cool Happenings page. To get there, start at eBay's Home page and click on the Cool Happenings link, or go to the Community page and click on the Cool Happenings link. Among some of the recent charity auctions held on eBay are:

- A March of Dimes auction of limited-edition, signed Mattel toys. We participated in this auction and won a few items for this wonderful cause.

- A *People* magazine auction that offered signed and limited-edition celebrity photographs. The proceeds of this auction went to the Until There's A Cure Foundation. The foundation's goal is to help raise millions of dollars to fund HIV/AIDS youth education programs, scientific research, and care services for those who have the disease.

  You can leaf through *People* magazine's latest auction by doing a Seller Search with the User ID: **peoplemag**.

- An auction from the folks at MTV, which, keeping with its irreverent tone, was called MTV Cool Crap. If the name implies silliness, the cause was dead serious. MTV donated all of the proceeds of the auction to

Take A Stand Against Violence — a charity whose mission is to educate the public about violence in our society. The Cool Crap auction featured all kinds of fun stuff, from supermodels' bathing suits (one size fits none), to all kinds of sports and music memorabilia.

✔ Athlete Direct is a company that runs eBay auctions of major sports stars memorabilia, such as game-worn uniforms. Each athlete who puts an item up for auction donates the sum of the item's selling price to a charity of his or her choice. When we last checked in, Karl Malone, Dennis Rodman, and Chris Webber had all donated clothing and signed items. Click on Athlete Direct on the Cool Happenings page for more information on the company's current auctions.

TIP

If you go to the About Me pages of any of the charities listed above, you can find out exactly where the money that eBay users bid goes.

TIP

Charity isn't just for the big guys. Individual users can also run charity auctions. For rules and regulations, click on Community on the main navigation bar, then click on charity on the subnavigation bar. eBay doesn't authorize or verify individual charities; however, 80 percent of the final selling price of an item in a charity auction *must* go to charity.

And Now for Our Feature Presentation

As an eBay member, you're entitled to some features offered on the Web site. The perks aren't quite as high-end as you might receive with, say, a country club membership, but hey — your membership dues are a lot less! With about two million registered users, eBay can get outside companies and manufacturers to listen up to what it has to say. You know the old saying, "There's power in numbers?" On eBay, you find "savings in numbers" on items or services you can buy outside the Web site.

The following sections explain some of the savings and other services you can find on eBay.

Member specials

As eBay gains popularity, more and more outside companies are offering special deals exclusively for members. These are not auctions, these are conventional "pay the price and get the item or services" transactions.

To find the member specials, start at eBay's Home page and click on the Cool Happenings link. Find the Member Specials link, and you're there.

These special deals change all the time, but here's a small sampling of things available to you:

- ✔ **Compaq computers:** Compaq offers exclusive computer packages for eBay members. They come with extra software, Internet access, and other goodies that are not usually included with its computers.

- ✔ **Authentication services:** Get a special discount (usually 10 percent) when you authenticate coins through Professional Coin Grading Service (PCGS) or trading cards through Professional Sports Authenticator (PSA). Have a Beanie Baby you need looked at? Real Beans can authenticate it for you. See Chapter 14 for tips on authenticating your items.

Read all about it in eBay Life

Every community needs a newspaper; eBay has one too. The online version is called *eBay Life*. You won't find any fast-breaking news stories here, just interesting articles, tips, and information about eBay and its members. See Figure 16-1 for a copy of *eBay Life*.

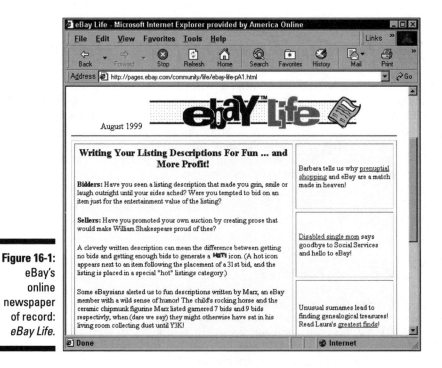

Figure 16-1: eBay's online newspaper of record: *eBay Life*.

eBay Life isn't delivered to your doorstep. You find eBay's newspaper online starting at eBay's Home page. Click on the Cool Happenings link, scroll down the page, and then click on the *eBay Life* link. You can also click on Community in the navigation bar and then click on eBay Life in the subnavigation bar.

Missed an issue? eBay archives past editions. Just click on the Archived Issues link (the month and year) of the *eBay Life* you want to see. The links are located at the bottom of the page.

Who's minding the eBay store?

eBay is minding the eBay store, of course (and freshening up its window-dressing from time to time). If you can't find the perfect item for your favorite eBay member with over two million auctions running at any given time, go browse around the eBay store. You won't find any auctions here, just eBay logo items, such as shirts, bags, coffee mugs, and even an eBay clock (we don't know if it'll help you be a better sniper!).

To get to eBay's online store, start at the Home page. Scroll down to the very bottom and click on the eBay Store link.

Just pick and choose what you like, add it to your shopping cart, and then check out when you're done. They ask you for specific billing information, so have your credit card handy.

Personal Shopper

If you're too busy to explore the nooks and crannies of eBay on your own (or you're the type who wants to cut to the chase), then sign up for eBay's Personal Shopper.

We think this is one of eBay's better ideas. Personal Shopper lets you find what you're looking for *and* have a life because it sifts through the new listings for you, 24 hours a day, looking for the items that meet your personalized description. Sniffs 'em out like a bloodhound. Then Personal Shopper sends you an e-mail with a list of items you might want to bid on, complete with links that take you right to them. Hey, best of all, it's free!

To register for the Personal Shopper, begin on the navigation bar at the top of most eBay pages.

1. **Click on Search on the navigation bar.**

   The subnavigation bar appears.

2. **Click on the Personal Shopper link.**

   You're taken to the Personal Shopper page.

3. **Type in your User ID and password and click on the Submit button.**

   You're now at the Personal Shopper Existing Searches page.

4. **Click on the Add a New Search button.**

   This takes you to the Add a New Search information page.

5. **Complete the following information:**

   - **Search:** Type in the item title you're interested in and select the Search Item Title and Description option.

     Searching item descriptions adds to the possibility of finding exactly what you are looking for.

   - **Price Range:** Enter the dollar amount (range) you're willing to spend.

     If you leave this blank, Personal Shopper searches all price ranges.

   - **e-mail Frequency:** Select how often you wish to be notified about new items that Personal Shopper finds for you.

   - **e-mail Duration:** Select how long you want Personal Shopper to search for this specific item. The longer you choose, the better your chances of coming across the item you're looking for.

6. **After completing the page, click on one of the following buttons:**

   - **Preview:** You see a description of your actual search, along with current search results, based on the criteria you've specified. If you're happy with the results, click on the Save button, and your Personal Shopper begins hunting for your item.

   - **Undo:** Deletes the information you entered in the search description line.

   - **View:** You see an itemized list of searches that are currently active for your Personal Shopper search.

The sincerest form of flattery

They say imitation is the greatest form of flattery, or maybe this is just really good e-commerce sense, but even before eBay launched its Personal Shopper, another company unveiled its own version, now called iTrack.

In addition to searching eBay, iTrack also searches other auction sites, Yahoo! Auctions, Auction Universe and Amazon Auctions, and iTrack will conduct your first three searches for free. An annual fee of $25 gives you up to eight search *patterns* or item searches, updated once or twice daily. You can receive 20 patterns per year for $50. You can register for iTrack at www.itrack.com.

Part V
The Part of Tens

The 5th Wave — By Rich Tennant

"Oh sure, it'll float alright, but I want to check your feedback rating before you place a bid."

In this part . . .

*I*n keeping with a long tradition, we give you the short version in this part. Check here for the golden rules every eBay user needs to know, whether you buy or sell (or, like most eBay users, both).

We also give you information on some of the best third-party software programs available. These programs can make creating a catchy auction item page easy and fun. And, of course, they can help you snipe a final bid in an auction while you sleep, walk the dog, wash your hair, or otherwise go on with your life. The best thing about some of these programs is that the price is just right — you can get started for free.

Hey, we told you community is what makes eBay work, which is why the Appendix of this book gives you your first course in eBay chat-speak. With a little help from this glossary and a little practice, you'll be talkin' the eBay talk and walkin' the eBay walk in no time.

Chapter 17

Ten (or So) Golden Rules for eBay Buyers

In This Chapter

▶ Sizing up item descriptions and sellers

▶ Accepting terms and methods of payment

▶ Researching items and prices

▶ Bidding wisely

▶ Utilizing feedback

▶ Protecting your privacy and your money

No matter how much experience an airplane pilot may have, there's always a checklist to go over. The same is true on eBay (although the only crashing you have to worry about is on your computer!). No matter how many times you buy, the advice in this chapter can help you survive and thrive on eBay.

Carefully Read Item Descriptions

In the excitement of finding just what you want, you may develop a tendency to leap before you look. Even if the item is closing soon, carefully read the item description. Does the item have any flaws? Can you live with them? Is there something missing from the description that should be there? Did you read the terms of payment and shipping?

Check the Seller's Feedback

Never bid without checking the seller's feedback. It's important to trust the person you're buying from. It also can't hurt to check some of the seller's other auctions, past and present, to get an idea of the seller's history. As badly as you may want something, it's risky business sending money to someone who has a high feedback rating but recently got a bunch of negatives.

Ask the Seller Questions

Don't be shy or embarrassed. If you have any questions, send an e-mail! It's better to cover your bases before you place a bid than it is to have to retract a bid or be disappointed after making a purchase. Make sure parts are original and check for a warranty or return policy. Clarify everything up-front. If the seller doesn't answer back, you've got an early warning that dealing with this person may be a mistake!

Make Sure You're Comfortable with Post-Auction Charges

Before you bid on an item, make sure that you and the seller agree on shipping, insurance, and escrow. It's a bummer to buy a $10 item and find out that shipping and handling are going to cost more than your closing bid. You can figure out shipping costs yourself with online rate calculators. Don't forget to ask about any "handling charges." Many sellers don't want the added hassle of an escrow service; make sure that they're agreeable if you want to use that option.

Make Sure You're Willing to Accept the Method of Payment

Make sure that you and the seller can agree on the form of payment before the deal closes. Is the seller willing to accept a personal check? Are you willing to wait until it clears? Is credit card payment available? Is the seller using a secure method of accepting credit cards?

Research How Much an Item Is Worth

Before you bid, make sure you have some knowledge of the item, even if you limit your search to completed auctions to get an idea of how much the item went for in the past. If it sounds too good to be true, it could well be.

We love eBay! But not for every single thing we buy. Be sure you can't get the item cheaper at the store or from an online seller.

Bid Wisely and Seriously

Getting caught up in the frenzy of last-minute bidding is an easy thing to do. Whether you choose proxy bidding or sniping, decide how much you're willing to pay before bidding. If you set a limit, you won't be overcome with the urge to spend more than an item's worth — or worse — more than you have in your bank account.

Although eBay is lots of fun, it's also serious business. Bidding is a legal and binding contract. Don't get a bad reputation by retracting bids or becoming a deadbeat.

Make Good Use of Feedback

Always leave feedback after you put the finishing touches on a transaction. It's your responsibility to leave feedback and help other members.

What if you get negative feedback? Don't freak out! Don't retaliate. Do, however, post a response to the feedback by using the Respond to feedback link on your My eBay page. Potential buyers or sellers who read your feedback will be able to see past a single disgruntled message.

Promptly Send Money after Winning an Auction

Just because you are transacting through the computer doesn't mean you have to lose your manners. Live by the golden rule: Do unto others as you would have others do unto you. Contact the buyer within three business days. And keep all your correspondence polite.

Help me, eBay

Do you smell trouble? If a seller hasn't sent your merchandise but has cashed your check, try contacting the seller through e-mail and then by phone. After two to three weeks have passed, it's time to contact SafeHarbor and begin the process of formally complaining and trying to get your money back.

Protect Your Privacy

Remember, just because you're conducting transactions from the privacy of your own home doesn't mean you're doing everything you can to protect your privacy. Legitimate buyers and sellers never need to know your password or Social Security number. If anyone does ask, contact eBay's SafeHarbor to report the person. You can also post your concerns on one of the eBay chat boards.

To fight back against computer viruses — which can be spread through e-mail attachments and ruin your day, your auction, and maybe your computer — purchase a good antivirus software program and update it often. McAfee VirusScan (www.mcafee.com) and Symantec's Norton AntiVirus (www.nortonutilities.com) are both excellent antivirus programs, and Norton boasts international Web pages if you live outside the United States.

Chapter 18

Ten (or So) Golden Rules for eBay Sellers

*T*he eBay community thrives on honesty and trust — that's no lie. Heed the sage advice in this chapter to establish yourself as a reputable and trusted seller and, at the same time, max out your eBay enjoyment (and hopefully your profits!).

Know Your Product

Do some homework. Know the value of your item. At the very least, get an idea of your item's value by searching completed auctions of similar items. Knowing your product also means that you can accurately describe what you have and not pass it off as a fake. Make sure that your item is not prohibited, questionable, or infringing.

Establish the Terms You're Willing to Accept

Before posting your auction, you should

- ✔ Establish what kinds of payment you will accept.
- ✔ Set your check holding policy (usually seven to ten days).
- ✔ Spell out your shipping and handling charges.

Add each of the preceding pieces of info to your item's description to avoid any unnecessary disputes later on.

Create an Attention-Grabbing Title

Make sure that your title is descriptive enough to catch the eye of someone browsing a category and detailed enough to be identified by eBay's search engine. Don't just write *1960s Board Game*. Instead, give some details: *Tiny Tim Vintage '60s Board Game MIB*. That'll get 'em tiptoeing to your auction.

Create Honest and Error-Free Item Descriptions

On eBay all you have is your reputation, so don't jeopardize it by lying about your item or your terms. Let buyers know about flaws. Give as complete a description as possible with all the facts you can include about the item.

Misspellings — in either your title or description — can cost you money on eBay when a search engine keeps skipping over your *Miky Mouce Cokie Jare*. Spelling counts — and pays. Double-check your work!

Make Sure Your Photo Helps Sell Your item

Double-check the photo of your item before you post it. Is the lighting OK? Does the photo paint a flattering image of the item? Would YOU buy this item?

Make sure your photo is actually posted on your auction page (did it get lost in cyberspace?) and doesn't take too long to download. And just because you added an image doesn't mean you can ignore a detailed item description.

Respond to Bidder Questions and Requests

Respond quickly and honestly to all questions and use the contact to establish a good relationship.

If a bidder makes a reasonable request about payment or shipping, it's worth it to make a sale. Remember, the customer is always right! (Well, some of the time, anyway.)

Be Honest About Shipping and Handling Costs

You won't make a fortune overcharging for shipping and handling. The buyer will see when the item arrives what it cost to ship. Unreasonable charges inevitably lead to bad feelings and negative feedback.

Don't Skimp on the Packing

Use good materials and sturdy boxes for your shipping to prevent disaster. Broken or damaged items can lead to reputation-damaging, negative feedback. Pack like someone's out to destroy your package! Your buyers will appreciate it.

Send the Merchandise Promptly

Ship the goods as soon as you can (in accordance with the shipping terms you outlined in the item description, of course). An e-mail stating that the item is on its way is always a nice touch, too. That way, buyers can eagerly anticipate the arrival of their goods.

Keep Your Registration Information Current

You'd be surprised at the number of users who get suspended even though they have automatic credit card payment. Or they move. Or they change Internet service providers. If you don't update the contact and credit card information and eBay and other users can't get to you, you can be suspended. As soon as you know your new credit card number, your mailing address, e-mail address, or contact phone number, click Services on the main navigation bar. Scroll down to My eBay and update the appropriate information. Leaving outdated information can lead to a suspension.

Make Good Use of Feedback

As we state in our golden rules for buyers in Chapter 17, don't underestimate the power of positive feedback. Your reputation is at stake. Always dole out feedback — whether positive or negative — when you complete a transaction. Your buyers will appreciate it and should, in turn, return the favor.

If you get slammed with negative feedback, don't retaliate. *Do*, however, add a response to your own feedback, explaining your side of the story.

Stash Away All Transaction Correspondence

Keep all e-mail until a transaction is completed. Also keep a copy of the final auction page. Being a bit of a pack rat can help you if disputes arise.

Chapter 19

Ten (or So) Programs to Ease Your Way on eBay

In This Chapter

▶ Keeping track of your auctions with management programs

▶ Doing something else while your computer does your bidding automatically

▶ Crafting an auction look that'll kill the competition

▶ Moving your pictures around eBay the easy way

▶ Posting auctions while sleeping or away from your computer

▶ Joining eBay's Power Sellers club

*R*eady to take your auctions to the next level? Are you looking for cool text or fancy layouts to make your auctions scream out "Buy me!"? Need to slip in a bid in the middle of the night without losing sleep? If so, here's a list of ten software programs and services to make your bidding life easy and help put your auctions ahead of the pack.

As online auctions grow in popularity, software developers are constantly upgrading auction software to meet eBay's changes. Many of these programs even look for new versions of themselves — and update themselves when you start them. (Aladdin never had it so good.)

Virtual Auction Ad Pro

Virtual Auction Ad Pro takes you through an easy-to-use, step-by-step process that helps spruce up your eBay auctions with great-looking auction descriptions. We like Virtual Auction Ad Pro's simple approach, and it's easy for beginners. Virtual Auction Ad Pro lets you

✔ Design auction descriptions in four different fonts with seven different sizes in millions of colors.

✔ Create auction titles and subtitles in your description in three different sizes.

✔ Create descriptions in a snap with six templates (layout designs).

✔ Easily add up to two photos along with your description.

Download Virtual Auction Ad Pro for under $10 at the following Web site:

```
virtualnotions.com/vadpro/index.htm
```

It is also available as part of a larger package, Auction Aid, also available at virtualnotions.com, which includes a ton of great graphics and auction utilities.

The Oracle

The all-knowing Oracle manages your eBay auction activity. Oracle does all the work, so you don't have to be constantly checking eBay. Oracle gives you the bidder's edge by placing pre-programmed sniping bids for you. Oracle also

✔ Keeps track of your bids and sales on eBay, updates the bidding progress at regular intervals, gives you items' numbers, current bids, bidder names, seller names, closing times, and how long until auctions end. It also sounds an audible alarm to let you know when you've been outbid.

✔ Provides a highly accurate, pre-programmed, automatic sniping feature that allows you to get your bid into eBay's system at the very last second, whether you're asleep, out to lunch or even surfing another Web site.

✔ Gives you the Sales Tracker and Purchase Tracker features, enabling you to easily keep your eye on payments, and contact and shipping info.

✔ Synchronizes your computer's clock with eBay's.

✔ Enables you to search eBay directly from The Oracle.

You can get a free, limited trial version of The Oracle (or the full version for $19.99) from the following Web site:

```
www.the-oracle.com
```

Blackthorne Software AuctionAssistant 2

AuctionAssistant 2 helps you design your auction item pages, upload your images, fill in forms automatically, place your auctions, and track them on eBay. Its management forms keep you up to date on the progress of your transactions with the help of its Auto Fetch feature, downloading auction info directly from eBay. Here are some of its other talents:

- ✔ The Ad Studio allows you to design your own auction with interesting typefaces, sizes, and colors. You can use the pre-designed themes to customize the look of your auctions with decorative graphics, animation, backgrounds, and music files! (So easy!)

- ✔ An internal FTP (File Transfer Protocol) program to get your images onto your server.

- ✔ After the auction, the program creates custom e-mails to send to winners.

- ✔ When you're done with your transactions, you can place feedback at the click of a button.

Download a free trial version of AuctionAssistant 2 (which is fully operational, minus a few features) at

```
www.blackthornesw.com
```

The full version is available online for $59.95.

A new program, AuctionAssistant Pro, will be coming out soon and will incorporate the best of Auction Assistant and will add important management, reporting, and accounting features. Keep checking the Web site for more information.

CuteFTP

As you become more proficient with eBay and want to run more auctions, you may need to expedite the uploading of your images to your Web server. Images must be uploaded with File Transfer Protocol (FTP) software for viewing in your eBay auctions. CuteFTP does the transfers so quickly and perkily, you'll think it's almost *too* cute. But wait! CuteFTP also

- ✔ Provides a very complete (and free) manual for eBay users on its Web site.

- ✔ Comes with free CuteHTML, a very handy HTML editor for adding snappy-looking text in your auction descriptions.

Download it free for 30 days, and then buy the code number for $34.94 to keep the software fully functional after the trial period lapses. Go to

```
www.globalscape.com
```

EasyAuction

EasyAuction is an auction management utility for both buyer and seller. It includes a dual-time-zone clock, a utility for posting and tracking auctions, a contact manager, an e-mail and feedback manager, and even accounting features. With EasyAuction, you can

- ✔ Produce reports that show the days since an auction ended, list your transactions and auctions in progress, and plunk a top-100 auction profit report on your screen.
- ✔ Save auctions for later reposting.
- ✔ Create automated (boilerplate) e-mail, which reads and uses the e-mail addresses imported from auctions.

You can download a 14-day trial version (which only supports 10 auctions and does not support AOL) — as well as the full-fledged version for $34.99. The software is being continually updated; a new version with many more features should be available soon. You can also find a collection of EasyAuction-oriented links and utilities at this Web site:

```
www.auctiontools.net
```

eBay Auto Submit

Want to start an auction when you can't get to a computer? Then let eBay Auto Submit do your listings for you. With eBay Auto Submit, you can

- ✔ Prepare your auction listings at your convenience and then post your auctions whenever you designate.
- ✔ Build a database of item descriptions and keep them in an Auto Submit directory; you can use them over and over again.

You can get a free, 30-day downloadable demo of the software. The demo comes with three additional eBay automation programs that are available online. If you decide you like eBay Auto Submit, you can unlock your demo to a fully functioning version for $35. For more information, go to

```
www.every-era.com
```

AuctionPoster98

Enter your profile information once, and you're on your way to simplify posting eBay auctions. AuctionPoster98 enables you to

- ✔ Automatically create your HTML for your auction description, check your spelling, insert your photo, fill in the default information on eBay's forms, and with one click, preview and post your auctions.
- ✔ Put a free counter in your ad without cutting and pasting code.
- ✔ Save auctions, so you can post them again at any time.
- ✔ Store your photos (for a per-photo fee) if you don't have an FTP site.

The program includes a one-week posting pass and 20 tokens for future postings or photo-hosting. Longer service options range from $6.95 for one month to $29.95 for a year. The program (and upgrades) can be downloaded for free at

```
www.auctionposter.com
```

eBay Quickmailer

This straightforward piece of software automates the sending of e-mail at the end of auctions. It was designed for (and is especially useful for) Dutch auctions, which often require many e-mails to be sent at once. Quickmailer enables you to

- ✔ Save the End of Auction e-mail that comes to you from eBay as a text file, import the winners' names, e-mail addresses, and winning bid amounts, and insert the whole shebang automatically into a pre-written winner's letter.
- ✔ Automatically add the shipping charges into a total with the winning bid.

A 10-day *free* demo version includes a help file and tutorial. After 10 days, registration is $10. You can find both versions at the following site:

```
www.flyingzebra.com/ebay/quickmailer/download.htm
```

eBay Power Sellers Service

eBay has an elite club for Power Sellers who have fulfilled the following requirements:

✔ Maintain a 98 percent positive feedback average with 100 or more feed-back comments.

✔ Guarantee buyers that items are exactly as described.

✔ Maintain minimum monthly gross sales of $2,000 (Bronze level).

✔ Have an account in good standing.

No, you don't have to wear an ugly tie. Power Sellers get a special icon next to their User IDs on the eBay site, thereby giving potential bidders the assurance that they are dealing with a seller of good reputation who will stand behind each sale. Power Sellers also get access to a special squad of eBay staff experts for e-mail support, 24 hours a day, 7 days a week. Serious business!

✔ At the Bronze level and above, you get a physical display sign for your place of business or for trade shows, identifying you as an eBay Power Seller.

✔ $10,000 in monthly gross sales (Silver level) gets you all the benefits of the Bronze level, plus you can opt to have phone support handled in real-time during eBay business hours, by a dedicated team of account specialists.

✔ $25,000 a month in gross sales (Gold level) means you get Bronze-level benefits, plus eBay gives you a dedicated account manager and a dedicated support hotline, 24 hours a day, 7 days a week!

You can't sign up for eBay's Power Sellers service — eBay knows who you are and notifies you when you reach the appropriate sales level to join.

KillTimer

If you use AOL, you may notice that your connection can be cut if you haven't had any online activity for a few minutes. This cutoff can happen while you're uploading or downloading files from the Internet or even when you're placing auctions on eBay using your browser. KillTimer sends a code that keeps your connection active so that AOL doesn't cut you off. Download it free at

```
members.tripod.com/~cbajgier
```

AuctionWatch Desktop

One of our favorite eBay software programs comes from the AuctionWatch Web site. AuctionWatch Desktop does just about anything you can think of. You can use AuctionWatch Desktop to

  ✔ Make unattended bids and out-snipe your competition.

  ✔ Automatically transfer items won or sold to a closed auction area.

  ✔ Track payments, shipping, and e-mail.

The best thing about AuctionWatch is that you can download it for free. Go to

```
www.bidstream.com/bn
```

AuctionWatch can also help you out if you're selling. Check out the section in Chapter 12 on adding images to your auctions.

Appendix

FWIW: Auction Chat Terms for the Digerati-Wannabe

@@: Just lurking — reading but not participating on a chat board

404: Somebody who hasn't got a clue; from the Internet error message
`404 Not Found`

ADDY: E-mail address

AKA: Also known as

AOL: America Online

ASAP: As soon as possible

ATM: At the moment

B&W: Black and white

BBC: Bottom of back cover

BBIAB: Be back in a bit

BC: Back cover

BRB: Be right back

BTW: By the way

CC: Cut corner or carbon copy

CIB: Cartridge instructions/box (as in computer equipment)

CONUS: Continental United States (which means Alaska and Hawaii are out)

CYE: Check your e-mail

Digerati: People who are fluent in the digital world; from *literati*

E-mail: Electronic mail sent from computer to computer through phone lines over the Internet

Emoticon: A specific group of characters used to form a facial expression in electronic communication; for example :) is a smiley face

FAQ: A list of Frequently Asked Questions and answers

FB: Feedback

Flame: An angry message or feedback, often resulting in a "flame war," a series of flames that escalates

FTP: Method for transferring files over the Internet

FVF: Final value fee

FWIW: For what it's worth

Gently Used: Item that has been used but shows little wear, accompanied by explanation of wear

HP: Home page

HTML: The language used to create Web pages; HyperText Markup Language

HTTP: The method used to transport HTML on the Web; HyperText Transfer Protocol

IE: Internet Explorer

IMAO: In my arrogant opinion

IMHO: In my humble opinion

IMO: In my opinion

INIT: Initials

ISP: A company that gives you access to the Internet; Internet Service Provider

JPG: Preferred file format for pictures on eBay (pronounced J-Peg)

Link: A photo or text on a Web page that, if clicked upon, takes you to another place on the Internet; also hyperlink

LMK: Let me know

LOL: Laughing out loud; see also ROFL

LTD: Limited edition

Mint: In perfect condition (a subjective term)

MIB: Mint in box

MIJ: Made in Japan

MIMB: Mint in mint box

MIMP: Mint in mint package

MIP: Mint in package

MNB: Mint no box

MOC: Mint on card

MOMC: Mint on mint card

MONMC: Mint on near mint card

MWBT: Mint with both tags

MWMT: Mint with mint tags

NARU: Not a registered user (suspended user)

NBW: Never been worn

NC: No cover

NM: Near mint

NRFB: Never removed from box

OEM: Original equipment manufacturer

OOP: Out of print

OTOH: On the other hand

Patina: The shine on the item

PM: Priority Mail

Rare: The most overused word on eBay auctions; use it only if you mean it

ROFL: Rolling on floor laughing; see also LOL

RSVP: Respond as soon as possible; French, *Respondez s'il vous plait*

S/O: Sold out

Sig: Signature

Snail Mail: United States Postal Service delivery

Spam: Unwanted or unrequested e-mail; on eBay, sending e-mail to bidders in another seller's auctions is illegal

SYSOP: System operator

TBB: Teenie Beanie Babies

TIA: Thanks in advance

TM: Trademark

TOS: *Star Trek* term, "The Original Series"

URL: The address that identifies a Web site; Uniform Resource Locator

USPS: United States Postal Service

VHTF: Very hard to find

WYSIWYG: What you see is what you get

Index

• *C* •

• *G* •

• S •

• *Y* •